Thom Yorke

RADIOHEAD & TRADING SOLO

Published in 2009 by
INDEPENDENT MUSIC PRESS
Independent Music Press is an imprint of I.M. P. Publishing Limited
This Work is Copyright © I. M. P. Publishing Ltd 2009

Thom Yorke – Radiohead & Trading Solo
by Trevor Baker

British Library Cataloguing-in-Publication Data.
A catalogue for this book is available from The British Library.
ISBN: 978-1-906191-09-2

Cover Design by Fresh Lemon.
Cover photograph by Ian Patrick/Retna

Printed in the UK.

Independent Music Press
P.O. Box 69,
Church Stretton, Shropshire
SY6 6WZ
Visit us on the web at: www.impbooks.com
and www.myspace.com/independentmusicpress
For a free catalogue, e-mail us at: info@impbooks.com
Fax: 01694 720049

Thom Yorke

Radiohead & Trading Solo

by Trevor Baker

Independent Music Press

ACKNOWLEDGEMENTS

The author would like to thank the following people for the original and exclusive interviews conducted for this book:

Martin Brooks (band-mate in the Headless Chickens)
Andy Bush (session musician on 'The National Anthem')
Mark Cope (a friend from the Oxford music scene)
Eileen Doran (University contemporary)
Laura Forrest-Hay (band-mate in the Headless Chickens)
Grant Gee (director, *Meeting People Is Easy* and 'No Surprises')
Dave Goodchild (boss of Headless Chickens' record label)
Richard Haines (engineer on early Radiohead demo)
Steve Hamilton (session musician on 'The National Anthem')
Stan Harrison (session musician on 'The National Anthem')
Ashley Keating (drummer in The Frank And Walters)
Paul Q Kolderie (co-producer of *Pablo Honey*)
John Matthias (band-mate in Headless Chickens)
Shaun McCrindle (Exeter University housemate)
Sophie Muller (director of 'I Might Be Wrong' video)
Nigel Powell (school friend, drummer and lighting man)
Sean Slade (co-producer on *Pablo Honey*)
Jamie Thraves (director of 'Just' video)
Chel White (director of 'Harrowdown Hill' video)

CONTENTS

INTRODUCTION

Many famous singers have a story about telling a teacher they were going to be a star, only to be told, politely or not, that they should think again. If it's true that the best way to make God laugh is to tell him your plans, then the same joke works even better with career advisers. For Thom Yorke, this moment first happened when he was only seven. He'd just heard Queen's Brian May playing the guitar and he confidently informed his music teacher that he was going to be a "rock star"

Predictably she snorted with laughter and said, "Of course you are, dear." She probably said the same thing to the kids who told her that they were going to be Batman or Superman. Still, Thom wasn't discouraged. He was angry and indignant that she didn't take him seriously. Eleven years later when he arrived at Exeter University, a shy teenager who could barely look anyone in the eye, he would still mutter, with his own steely inner confidence, that he was going to be a rock star.

A rock star. Not an artist. Not a musician. That's what everybody who met him at the time remembers. It's like finding out that JD Salinger wrote *Catcher In The Rye* because someone told him that it would make him famous and popular with girls.

Because, of all the great rock stars of the last thirty years, there are few who seem to have enjoyed it less (and lived to tell the tale) than Thom Yorke. He has greeted gigantic, life-changing success like somebody sneezing in his face.

The problem might have been that success arrived with a song, 'Creep', that cast him as a kind of pantomime loser. It turned him into a weird, hall-of-mirrors caricature of his own personality. The worst thing was that he knew he should be grateful to 'Creep'. The song gave him everything he wanted – it made it possible for his stuttering, spluttering band to carry on when their other singles flopped and their very existence was threatened.

From then on, Radiohead leapt forwards and sideways, leaving many of their fans and most of the press to catch up months after each album release. Not since The Beatles had a major band been so determined to reinvent themselves with every album. With *OK Computer* they became the most critically acclaimed band in the world and seemed to have positioned themselves on the launching pad to become the biggest band in the world. It was a complete vindication of everything that Thom had believed.

"Being in a band is about wreaking revenge on the world," he said to *The Times* early in his career. "It's like when you get chucked by your first girlfriend. You just say to yourself: *I'm going to be famous one day, and she'll regret that ...*"

She might have regretted it when Radiohead became the most celebrated act in the world, but clearly not as much as he did. Thom had been offered the opportunity that he'd desperately wanted when he was sixteen: to be a huge, acclaimed Rock Star in capital letters. To be the new Bono.

He turned it down. He turned his back on 'rock' as a genre, an attitude and even a sound. He suffered emotionally crippling writer's block and the side-effects of 'Rock Stardom' became even harder to take. Recordings did not get any easier. Thom had other ideas. He had the absurd task of telling a band with no fewer than three guitarists that he didn't really like the sound of the guitar anymore. Even more ridiculously, the gamble – *Kid A* – debuted at Number 1 in the USA and made them even bigger.

Since then, Radiohead have done what seemed impossible and reinvented what being a rock band means. Most bands, whether or not they actually wear leather jackets, seem to have leather jackets under their skin. Radiohead's whole career has been a battle against Thom's original concept of rock stardom, or at least a battle to save the original essence of rock stardom and cut all the chaff away.

In the eighteen-year history of the full-time band, it's as if Thom tried, with every album, to rethink every part of the rock process. Most recently this has meant trying to find a new way to get the music from the studio to the fans without having to go through an emotionally, creatively and almost literally bankrupt music industry. The reason Radiohead have managed this is because the bond formed in the years before they became successful has proved stronger than the obstacles they've encountered since.

But only just.

This book starts with a pre-school Thom Yorke struggling to deal with a series of operations on his eye, and nothing he's achieved since has come without a huge struggle. The result has been a band who have, since the disappointment of their first album, never settled for second best because Thom, beneath manifest uncertainties, has always remained certain of one thing. Absolutely nothing but the best would ever be enough.

1

THE ALL-SEEING EYE

Sometimes it seems like Thom Yorke's story begins with his eye. The 'lazy' one that, according to music magazine folklore, snaps to attention whenever he's feeling particularly riled or passionate about something. It's been used as the symbol of his strangeness, his 'creepiness' even at one point, but also, maybe, of his ability to see things differently to other people.

Thom is not the first such example. It's why so many villains and anti-heroes, from Shakespeare to Dickens, have some form of visible affliction; however, it's striking that this prejudice is still so powerful today. It's perhaps led some people to think that Thom Yorke is 'weird'. It's also meant that he's been battling against, or sometimes revelling in, a perception of his own weirdness for most of his life.

When he was born in Wellingborough, Northamptonshire on October 7, 1968, his left eye was completely paralysed. Initially, doctors told his parents that he'd never be able to see out of it. However, surgical techniques were moving on quickly and they took him to a specialist who suggested he could graft a whole new muscle on to the eyelid.

It was a highly complicated procedure and so in between his second birthday and the age of six, Thom underwent five separate operations. When he had the first one he'd just learned to talk and, as he came round from the anaesthetic, he doubled over and started crying. On later occasions he would lie there in his hospital bed hearing old men in the geriatric ward next door talking to themselves or, on one occasion, somebody vomiting violently outside. "Hospitals are fucking horrifying places," he said later.

At first, the operations were relatively successful. They managed to open the eye and save his sight but the last operation went wrong and he was left half-blind. The doctors told him that his eye had simply grown lazy from lack of use. Their solution was that he should wear a patch. A patch on his good eye.

"The most annoying bit was bumping into things really, because it didn't work," Thom told *Hot Press*. "They had this theory in the late 1970s, that if you had a lazy eye, they put a patch over the other one to make this one work harder, which was actually complete bullshit as they later found out. You have a kid bumping into things for a year, being miserable."

It didn't help that Thom's father had a job as a salesman and, in a six-month period after Thom started wearing the patch, the family moved twice. Each time Thom was forced to explain again to a new set of curious children just why it was he always came to school looking like a pirate. One child nicknamed him "salamander" and the thin-skinned Thom ended up getting into a fight with him. But the taunts didn't stop.

"If you think about it, if I had a kid and he had to wear a patch on his eye for a year, I'd be worried about what he'd be like at the end of that year. You know what I mean?" Thom continued.

Despite this, he wasn't some kind of emotional wreck. He had a girlfriend. He had his first kiss at the age of seven. Typically he still remembered the girl's name, years later, Kate Ganson. More surprisingly, considering his later views on drivers, he also remembered that her dad had, "a great Lotus car."

His mum described him later as a quiet, happy child who would spend all his time in a corner making things with Lego. She was the creative one in the family while his dad was an energetic hard worker and amateur boxer who tried, mostly unsuccessfully, to teach his older son to box, too.

"One of the first things he ever bought me was a pair of boxing gloves," Thom said to *Rolling Stone's* Jon Wiederhorn. "He used to try to teach me ... but whenever he hit me, I'd fall flat on my ass."

He picked up a guitar for the first time when he was four years old but, when he cut his fingers on the sharp strings, he threw it against the wall and broke it. The first, but not the last guitar to die that way. By the time he was seven, this indiscretion had obviously been forgotten because he was given a Spanish guitar as a present and promptly decided that he was going to be just like his new hero – Brian May of Queen. Instead, his guitar teacher had him plucking away, learning to play 'Kumbaya'. Nevertheless he stuck with it and, when he was ten-years-old, he formed his first band. They were a duo. Thom played the guitar and his co-writer would make as much noise as possible, on one occasion by rewiring a TV so that it exploded. This went well with the subject matter of their songs. The first one was called 'Mushroom Cloud' and, Thom said later, "it was more about how they looked than how terrible they were."

But things went downhill when the family moved again, this time to Oxfordshire. Thom's brother Andy once said of their hometown of Abingdon that it was, "quite horrible ... Abingdon swims around in this sea of cultural emptiness."

And the public school of the same name was even worse. Although it had a highly musical ethos, which in many ways was great for Thom, it was also deeply conservative and old-fashioned. And the fact that Thom went to a fee-paying school meant that he'd decisively stepped over an invisible line in Britain's class divide. His new schoolmates didn't think much of him and his old friends rejected him, too.

"They blanked me out," he said in an interview with *Blender* magazine. "I used to cycle around, and one of them once got his older brother to kick the shit out of me and throw me in the river, just because I'd gone to that school."

By then he'd become the kind of person who constantly feels the glare of the world's attention and finds it frightening but also gratifying. His nascent feeling that everybody was watching him was, at that point, probably justified, or else it was a self-fulfilling prophecy. He stood out. Not just because of his eye but because of his manner. When everybody else was desperate to fit in with the crowd, he seemingly did everything he could to assert his individuality. After Queen, his next musical obsession was with the band Japan and, in homage he wore make-up like singer David Sylvian, grew his hair long and dyed it blonde. Later on he dressed like an old man in long overcoats or bought the sharpest suits he could find in Oxford's charity shops. "In terms of school stereotypes," Abingdon contemporary, Nigel Powell, told this author, "Thom was the guy who wore long coats and scowled. That was the way he wanted to present himself."

By then he'd found a new identity for himself as a fan of outsider bands like Magazine and Joy Division. In 1983, this wasn't considered cool at Abingdon. Even the kids who hung around the musical department preferred classic rock, or singer-songwriters like Simon And Garfunkel. Thom found himself the subject of bullies.

"He was very noticeable at school because of the way he looked," another Abingdon pupil Alex Keyser told me, "and he used to be picked on by the older boys. He used to get picked on really badly and have his bag thrown away and stones kicked at him and stuff."

The one place he could escape was the soundproof booths at the back of the music room. He found an ally there in the music teacher, Terence Gilmore-James. "I was a sort of leper at the time, and he was the only one who was nice to me," Thom told writer Alex Ross in the *New Yorker*. "School was bearable for me because the music department was separate from the rest of the school. It had pianos in tiny booths, and I used to spend a lot of time hanging around there after school, waiting for my dad to come home from work."

In interviews since, Thom has been highly disparaging of Abingdon. He saw it as a kind of hothouse where ambitious parents sent their children to be force-fed an unhealthy desire for material success. He once said that the dominant ethos of British public schools was that "achievement is everything and if anybody gets in the way you just want to kill." This attitude was summed up more positively by then Abingdon Head Teacher Michael St John Parker's mission statement for the school: "Competition is promoted, achievement is applauded, and individual dynamism is encouraged."

Nevertheless Thom's experiences there played a massive part in forming his world-view. On the one hand, he was one of the privileged seven percent of British children who get to attend the kind of school that has pianos in soundproofed booths but, in the highly stratified social scale of the British public school system, he didn't feel in any way 'posh'. For pupils at minor public schools like Abingdon, there's always the consciousness of a whole other layer of 'posh' above them, at schools like Eton and Harrow. And even at Abingdon, Thom regarded himself as a townie. His dad was a salesman. If it's true that England's classes are generally in a state of cold war, enlivened by occasional skirmishes, Thom was, to quote Magazine, "shot by both sides."

Holidays provided a kind of respite, particularly one summer when he attended the National Youth Music Camp near Milton Keynes in Buckinghamshire. It was run by a woman called Avril Dankworth. She was the sister of famous jazz musician Johnny Dankworth and an inspirational educationalist in her own right, with a philosophy called "allmusic". Thom would be there for a week having intensive lessons on the guitar, trying out other instruments and regularly performing with other kids.

Sarah Shrimpton was a tutor then and is now artistic director of the camps. She told me that "schools were very classical music orientated at the time. So people came to get their fix of other sorts of music. There was no genre bias. They rubbed shoulders from musicians of all genres. It's incredible what they achieve in a week. They have their 'A' session, which is on their principal instrument that they play and then 'B' and 'C' sessions, which is something they haven't done before or [perhaps if they] want to participate in a group, like a rock band or folk group. Then they put on a production."

The kids at the camp weren't like the kids at school and, although Thom still didn't exactly fit in, his ability to perform gave him a unique identity that, suddenly, wasn't wholly a disadvantage.

One of the other campers, Martin Brooks, told this author that he stood out even then. "He wore very different clothes to everybody else," Martin says. "Everybody else was in jeans and T-shirts and he was quite deliberate in the way he wore waistcoats. He clearly wanted to dress differently. It was kind of farmer chic, tweeds and neck-ties and stuff like that. A bit Kevin Rowland. He had a very clear un-ironic focus about who he was and that he wanted to get up onstage and perform. Even at that age he was not self-obsessed, but very deliberate about 'This is who I am.' He had a very strong concept of who he was and what he wanted to do."

What Thom wanted to do was play and at the end of the week he got his chance, cranking out ("painfully", Martin says) a version of The Police's 'Roxanne'. Although he might not have been very good technically (yet), he already had a confidence onstage that was missing in his normal life.

"It was the first time that I found something that I really loved and I suppose I just loved the attention," Thom said later of his first experiences with playing live. "I wanted to be famous, I wanted the attention. What's wrong with that?" (Typically he answered his own question: "There is also something really seriously fucking unhealthy about it.")

At the time it wasn't unhealthy at all. He made new friends, albeit only for a week, and he learned that there were people in the world who were as passionate about music as him. Being a fan of Joy

Division, or even Sting, didn't necessarily mean he had to sit in his bedroom, alone with his guitar.

"It was a great way of trying new things, getting into new things and meeting lots of other kids," Martin says. "When you go on a week's camp, you kind of make friends with everyone and get to know them quite well. We weren't close friends but there were about 70 kids and you remember one or two of them standing out, either for the way they look or the way they perform and stuff, and one of them was Thom. He was a very self-assured performer onstage but offstage he wasn't self-assured at all."

"Sometime children arrive with an attitude that they've obviously got in everyday life," says tutor Mike Oliver, who taught at the camp in the 1980s, "and in the camp people find a different outlook on life. Sometimes the attitude they've had disappears and they find they can mix in much better."

When Thom got back to school that autumn, he was determined to take his music further. He started recording his songs but he was taken aback when a close friend listened to some of the songs he'd been working on. "Your lyrics are crap," she blurted. "They're too honest, too personal, too direct and there's nothing left to the imagination."

"She was right," Thom said to *Q* later. "When I first started, I wasn't really interested in writing lyrics. Which is strange in a way because if I didn't like the words on a record, if it wasn't saying anything, I would never bother with it again. But at 16 your own songs are half-formed and you don't really expect anyone to hear them, so you don't care what the words are."

At the time, Abingdon had one punk band, known as TNT. Their most talented member was the bass player, Colin Greenwood. Thom became the singer (because, as singers always say, "no one else would") and, united by the fact that neither of them fitted in at Abingdon, they became friends. Colin used to wear catsuits, dressing in a way calculated to wind up the more conservative elements of the school. Thom would wear frilly shirts and the suits he'd bought in Oxford's second-hand shops (altered by his mum). When Thom left TNT, bored of the rest of the band's lack of ambition and originality, Colin soon followed and they started plotting to form a new, better band. Although Thom liked the kind of bands cool, outsider kids were supposed to like – Magazine and Joy

Division for example – he was also a huge fan of U2 and had recently acquired a massive passion for the then relatively obscure REM. He wanted to do something like that. Something bigger and more emotional than punk. A month later he saw Ed O'Brien walking down the street carrying a guitar that he'd just been given for his sixteenth birthday.

"He thought I looked like Morrissey," Ed said in an interview with *The Plain Dealer* magazine. "I was a fan of Morrissey's band, The Smiths – and Thom said I should be in a band." "No one would let us be in their gang," Thom said later, "so we had to form our own."

In fact, Ed remembered Thom from a school performance of *A Midsummer Night's Dream*. Ed – tall, handsome and well-spoken – was one of the actors. Thom was crouched with his guitar way up at the top of a tower of scaffolding. He was supposed to be providing the musical accompaniment but, during the first dress rehearsal, the sounds he was making were becoming increasingly bizarre and inappropriate. He was playing what Ed described as "a kind of cod-jazz". Eventually the teacher had had enough. He shouted up to Thom to stop, trying to find out what was going on and Thom shouted down, "I don't know what the fuck we're supposed to be playing. And this," Ed remembered in an interview later, "was to a teacher."

To start with, the band was just the three of them and a drum machine, a Bon Tempe that they'd bought in a charity shop. They didn't know anybody of their own age who was cool enough to own a drum kit. That seemed fine until they had their first gig. It was in a village hall with most of their parents in attendance. Halfway through every song, the drum machine would either crash or get stuck in one of its bizarre, cheesy pre-set rhythms. Thom got more and more wound up until he totally lost it, screaming obscenities into the microphone as yet another song fell to pieces. There was only one option. They had to ask the only drummer they knew, Phil Selway whether he would join.

At that point, even talking to Phil was a daunting prospect. He was two years older than Thom and Colin and, at that age, two years seemed like a huge generation gap. "We were all scared of Phil," Colin said later. "He was in the class above us and he was in a band called Jungle Telegraph so we called him the 'Graf'.

Ed, the most self-assured of the band, was sent to ask him whether he would consider joining but even then he couldn't ask outright. "I was a bit scared going up to him," he told journalist Clare Kleinedler. "It was like a scene from *Grease*. I was like, 'Um, so how's it going?' And Phil was like, 'OK, how was your gig last night?' And I say, 'Yeah, cool, man. We had a bit of trouble with the drum machine.' Phil says, 'Yeah?' And I say 'We're rehearsing next week, wanna make it?'" He did want to make it. Phil turned up on the appointed day and was disconcerted when Thom listened to him play and then muttered, "Can't you play any fucking faster?"

"They had one of those Dr. Rhythm things," Phil told *Modern Drummer* magazine later, "which always stalls after around ten bars. Of course, you get a drummer and he stalls after eleven bars."

Thom might have been shy and reserved in some circumstances but where music was concerned he was never slow to speak his mind. Even then he was highly critical of everything they did and, although they took a narcissistic delight in listening to tapes of their songs, he was frustrated that he couldn't get them to sound how he wanted. He was intrigued when he heard the tape of another school band, Illiterate Hands. The recordings sounded much more professional than anything he'd managed. They'd been recorded by another pupil, Nigel Powell. At the time, Nigel was much more advanced in his musical knowledge than most of the kids at Abingdon. He'd gone there from London and had been in bands with his brother since he was eleven years old.

"Thom thought, 'That's really good' for some reason," says Nigel of the Illiterate Hands tape. "Listening back I don't know what he was thinking! He phoned me up and asked if I would do his band as well, which I did."

Nigel can probably claim to be Thom Yorke's first ever producer, although he wouldn't make any such claim himself. Essentially he was the one who knew where to put the microphones. He was also another source of advice and feedback on songs, something Thom always craved.

"There wasn't a lot of production going on because I was only 15!" Nigel admits. "One of the few things that I said that could be counted as production was that Thom should sing in an English accent. At the time he was a big fan of REM and he used to sing in a thick American accent. That's about the only creative input I would have had apart from setting microphones up, stuff like that."

THOM YORKE

Thom eventually poached Illiterate Hands' keyboard player, Colin's younger brother Jonny Greenwood, for his own band! Jonny had wanted to join his older brother's band since they'd started. He'd heard Thom's songs and genuinely thought that they were as good as the records by Elvis Costello and REM that he was listening to at the time. He was already highly talented for his age on a variety of different instruments; piano, viola, violin and guitar. He also played with the Thames Valley Youth Orchestra. This might not have seemed a natural fit with a rock band and, according to legend, he regularly turned up to rehearsals with different instruments in a vain attempt to be allowed to join in. Eventually Colin relented, so during one Sunday morning rehearsal he persuaded the rest of the band that it wouldn't hurt to let him play the harmonica every now and then.

The week after that he performed for the first time at the Jericho Tavern in Oxford. They'd taken the name On A Friday and started gigging locally. They'd still only played a handful of gigs and most of those were just in village halls or at the school. Sadly, before long, playing at the school was no longer an option. Another band had played a gig that turned – by the school's conservative standards – a little rowdy and the headmaster promptly banned 'pop music' of all kinds. Perhaps as a result, Thom has always painted a picture of the place that sounds like Lindsay Anderson's public school rebellion film *If*. He focused much of his teenage hatred on the headmaster, a man of stern morals and an old-fashioned outlook.

"We went to a school where you had to go to church every morning, which is quite weird looking back," said Jonny in a radio interview, "very weird." "The headmaster was definitely a man out of time," admits teacher, Andy Bush, who taught music once a week at Abingdon much later. "He was from a different era. It was incredibly British public school at that time, it's moved on since then, but it was absolutely the antithesis of everything that Radiohead stand for artistically and politically."

Thom hated the headmaster and the school itself and some of that hatred was focused in the lyrics he was now writing. By the time Jonny joined the band, Thom was working much harder on the words. They were the springboard for the melodies and dictated the kind of music he was writing, too. It varied enormously in style, from four-track demos that were just a Soul-II-Soul rhythm and some vocals, to attempts to emulate U2 and REM. They were continually experimenting, trying to find something that worked. They weren't a great band; initially Thom and Colin were some way ahead of the others in technical ability, but they worked far harder than most of their contemporaries.

"For a school band they were very good," says Nigel Powell. "But if you put a really good singer in any band they sound a hundred times better. They probably would have been a completely typical school band if it hadn't been for Thom and, honestly, listening back to those tapes, Colin was well ahead of the rest of them in terms of playing prowess as well. He was a really good bass player."

But it was Thom who stood out.

"Thom was already an amazing singer," says Nigel. "I remember saying to somebody at the time, while we were still at school, 'We're all trying to make it and get record deals but if Thom doesn't get one then there's no point in anybody trying.' He'd just got such an amazing voice and, even at the time, I recognised that it's the voice that's the most important thing about any band."

The five of them wouldn't have been friends if it wasn't for the band. Thom was in some ways a difficult person to get to know and there was something of the 'mad scientist' about the curious, creative Jonny but the other three were simply nice, normal blokes. Phil was the most mature and Ed and Colin were the most gregarious and outgoing, but they were all very different characters. Later they would hate having their picture taken as a band partly because they felt they looked so ridiculous together, particularly the towering Ed O'Brien at six-foot five and Thom at five-foot seven.

By the time he was sixteen, people already found it hard to work Thom out. He was obviously shy and yet took great delight in making a statement with the way he dressed. He wanted people to notice him and yet he wanted to be left alone. He had a great sense of social justice and worried constantly about the state of the world, his own health and that of his friends and yet at times he would throw himself into music to the exclusion of everything else.

His tendency towards nervousness and introspection was exacerbated when he got his first car at the age of 17. By this point his parents had moved further away from Oxford and he'd gone with them, so he was regularly driving back to go out with the rest of the band. One night he hadn't slept and that morning he was driving with his then girlfriend when he had a serious crash, almost killing himself and giving her severe whiplash. When he did eventually get another car, an old Morris Minor, he was scared to go above 50mph in it. He told *Addicted To Noise* magazine that, from then on, things got worse and worse.

"On the road that went from my house to Oxford, there was fucking maniacs all the time," he said, "people who would drive 100 miles an hour to work, and I was in the Morris Minor, and it was like standing in the middle of the road with no protection at all. So I just gradually became emotionally tied up in this whole thing."

This came out later in a whole series of songs – 'Stupid Car', 'Lucky' and 'Airbag' – about crashes and death. He hated saying goodbye to friends when they had to drive home and he frequently dwelt on the everyday insanity of driving.

He was also deeply affected by the events of August 19, 1987, when unemployed labourer Michael Ryan armed himself with two semi-automatic rifles and a handgun and walked out on to the streets of Hungerford. He shot sixteen people, including his mother, and then turned the gun on himself. Thom was sixteen at the time and he wrote the song 'Sulk' in response, which would later appear on Radiohead's second album *The Bends*. Although oblique, it was said to originally contain a line about shooting guns.

Still, his position as a sensitive outsider can be overstated. He had a girlfriend; he had a group of friends. At least part of his air of alienation and disillusionment was just the same pose that many people put on during their teenage years as a kind of protective barrier against the world. Everybody who knew him then and later said that once you got past that, he was a perfectly nice person and easy to talk to.

But with On A Friday he was already creating a kind of cocoon around his creativity. They weren't an ordinary group of friends. They respected his prodigious musical talent. They also gave him the security that he liked and the affirmation that the songs he was writing were genuinely good. Like many artistic people, he swung wildly between an absolute belief that he was destined to produce great work and a terrible feeling that perhaps what he was doing wasn't any good at all. Even in the early days, this made producing music a painful process. He probably thought at the time that the feelings of inadequacy would go away but the writing process was still exactly the same, if not worse, years later ...

In classic pop psychology, this should all be laid at the door of that dodgy eye, the difficult childhood, the car crash and the bullies. In reality he would probably have been the awkward, creative type even if both eyes had functioned perfectly. His younger brother, Andy, born four years after him in 1972, was very similar in some ways. He also formed a band (the fleetingly successful and acclaimed Unbelievable Truth) and he too struggled with the mutually contradictory urges to be a "rock star" as against a private person. Andy gave Thom the nickname "Dodo" and there was a distinct vulnerability to both of them, a sense that they were targets because of their refusal to blend in with the crowd. Nevertheless, long after he ceased to be a child, Thom still occasionally had to explain himself over again.

"When I was eighteen, I worked in a bar," he said to *Rolling Stone*, "and this mad woman came in and said, 'You have beautiful eyes but they're completely wrong.' Whenever I get paranoid, I just think about what she said."

2

ON A FRIDAY

In retrospect, it's lucky that Thom didn't become a star when he was eighteen. He was already talented enough that it was entirely possible. He had an enormous pile of songs, many of which would turn up in various forms years later. For example, a bass riff he came up with when he was just sixteen would later become the centrepiece of 'The National Anthem', a song that wouldn't be finished until 1999. But if On A Friday had made it as teenagers, history would have been very different. On A Friday was very much a 1980s band. They had a faintly embarrassing whiff of white funk about them which chafed disturbingly with influences from the likes of U2 and REM. It's not hard to imagine them becoming as big and important as, say, Fine Young Cannibals, if they'd had a break in 1987.

Their very different sound is partly explained by the fact that the five original members of On A Friday were conscious that they lacked something. Thom wasn't yet the charismatic front man that he became later and, onstage, they were just another bunch of five blokes playing music. The solution, suggested by Colin, was to bring in a brass section. He had three friends who could play the tenor sax.

"It's just the way things are at school when you're in a band," says Nigel Powell. "You bump into somebody and say 'Do you play anything?' and they say, 'Yes, I play glockenspiel' and you say, 'Hey! Join our band!' There happened to be three saxophonists who were relatively close in age to them, so they got them in the band. Two of them were good-looking sisters, which certainly helped."

The three other members of On A Friday, Rasmus Peterson, Liz Cotton and her sister Charlotte were also pretty talented. By 1987 the band, as a collective, was getting better and better. They could have played more often but Thom wasn't sure they were good enough. This might just have been the same lack of confidence that has dogged him throughout his career. They played a gig in 1987 at the Old Fire Station in Oxford (described by Thom as looking like "it was designed by the people who build Little Chefs. The stage is almost an afterthought, you feel like you're playing on a salad bar.") And Nigel was impressed by how much they'd improved.

"I'd just done a demo for them and it was the release party," he says. "They'd made lots of tapes and they were going to sell them to people. I particularly remember the horn section. They sounded really good that night. It was almost R&B."

This comes across in another demo recorded in 1988 at Woodworm Studios in a small village called Barford St. Michael in Oxfordshire. The studio had been set up by Dave Pegg, the bassist in folk rock band Fairport Convention. He was also the studio engineer and he did a good job of capturing their sound on three very different tracks. The first, 'Happy Song', has a jaunty calypso rhythm overlaid with jangly guitars like early REM. The second, 'To Be A Brilliant Light', has a sax opening that sounds like Duran Duran before it heads off, once again, in more of an REM direction and the third, 'Sinking Ship', sounds like a cross between The Wonder Stuff and Violent Femmes.

They weren't great songs by any means but for a teenage band that'd played only a handful of gigs they were pretty impressive. Most teen bands struggle to master one genre, yet Thom already had them hopping from one distinct style to another in every track. It was a sign of his talent but also an indication perhaps that he hadn't yet found his voice. For someone who loved performing so much, it is surprising that he didn't get the band to play more shows at this point, but then they were only kids, and the student dominated live music scene in Oxford must have been quite intimidating. Thom had lived there since he was eight-years-old but he had highly ambiguous feelings about the city. In an interview with *The Observer*, he once said that it made him feel like an outsider, one of the few places in England where the expensively educated members of Radiohead wouldn't feel middle-class.

"The middle-class thing has never been relevant,' he told journalist Andrew Smith. "In Oxford we're fucking lower-class. The place is full of the most obnoxious, self-indulgent, self-righteous oiks on the fucking planet, and for us to be called middle class ... well, no, actually. Be around on May Day when they all reel out of the pubs at five in the morning puking up and going, 'Haw haw haw' and try to hassle your girlfriend."

Nevertheless he also said, in his first interview with fanzine *Curfew*, that although it was a "weird place", it was "very important to my writing." He would often sit and just watch people, scribbling ideas for lyrics in his notebook. His main inspiration was purely negative. He learned to despise certain elements of the student population, a feeling that may have been bolstered by the fact that, in the poorer southern parts of the town, he would have been considered much more like a student than a townie. He was desperate to disassociate himself from some of the grating public school types who poured into the city each year.

"Seeing these fuckers walking around in their ball gowns, throwing up on the streets, being obnoxious to the population," he said to *Q*. "They don't know they're born and they're going to run the country. It's scary. Of all the towns in the country, it's one of the most obvious examples of a class divide."

At one point he even considered changing the name of the band from On A Friday to 'Jude' after the protagonist of Thomas Hardy's novel *Jude The Obscure*. It is, in part, the story of somebody desperately trying to get into Oxford University and being driven mad by their failure. By then Thom was already starting to get bored of repeatedly being told how awful the name On A Friday was, but for some reason they couldn't think of anything better. They considered calling themselves simply 'Music', which says something about how seriously they were taking things. But the name On A Friday stuck, even if no particular style of music did. They tried country, ska, funk, punk and rock. "We used to change musical styles every two months," Colin Greenwood once said.

If they'd wanted to get attention fast, the best thing would have been to take their inspiration from My Bloody Valentine's 1988 album *Isn't Anything*. At that point, a whole swathe of bands in Oxford and the surrounding area were about to do just that, inventing the so-called 'Shoegazing' scene. Bands like Ride would soon be the 'Big Thing' in the music press, with a sound that relied on a wall of guitars and dreamy, ethereal vocals. But Thom was always much too spiky and acerbic to be interested in anything purporting to be "blissful". Instead he leapt from one sound to another, constantly finding inspiration from new bands. His latest discovery was an American act called the Miracle Legion. He and his brother Andy were obsessed with them and their singer Mark

Mulcahy. Miracle Legion were similar to REM but with a darker, more intense sound. Thom wanted his own music to have the same emotional feel but he wasn't quite sure how to find it. The result was an incredibly prolific burst of songwriting that he'd still be drawing from years later.

"They just stuck with it," says Nigel Powell. "Everybody else was shooting about going, 'I'll try this, I'll try that, I'll do the other', whereas even though these extra people, like the saxophonists, came and went, the core of the band were just there plugging away going, 'Let's try new things'. Even when the band weren't playing very often, Jonny and Thom would borrow the school four-track and go and demo stuff in Jonny's bedroom, using drum loops and Soul II Soul [style] loops and throwing stuff over the top of them. They seemed to be able to forge ahead better than a lot of people."

Perhaps they could have made it then, in 1988 or 1989. Things could have been very different. But they weren't rock 'n' roll outlaws with no option but to play music or starve. They'd had expensive educations and there was a lot of pressure on them to make good use of that. They had a foretaste of what would happen when Phil disappeared off to Liverpool University to study English. The following year Colin, Thom and Ed also had to make a decision about what they were going to do next. Colin had a promising academic career ahead of him. He got top grades at A-Level and went to Cambridge University to study English, while Ed had gone to Liverpool to study politics. Thom was reluctant to follow them. He was starting to form an impressive songwriting partnership with Jonny (who was still at school). He also had a slightly tortuous and intense relationship that he didn't seem to be able to get out of. ("Have you ever seen *Who's Afraid of Virginia Wolf?* It was like that for a year and a half," he said to *Melody Maker*, "lots of fighting in public".)

He deferred his place at university and spent a gap year doing unrewarding jobs while continually writing songs and recording demos with Jonny. One of his jobs was at a clothes store selling suits. When his boss asked him why he hadn't managed to sell any he replied, "because they're crap and no one wants to buy them."

This kind of honesty wasn't going to get him anywhere in sales. His boss took over the role of his designated hate-figure, a replacement for Abingdon's much-loathed headmaster. The day he handed in his notice, after wrongly being accused of stealing some stock, was a great moment but Thom was uncharacteristically restrained. "I wish I'd told my boss to fuck off," he said later. "He had this twisted little mouth and you could tell that he was desperate to make everybody's life hell."

Still, it was a frustrating year. The band could only rehearse and play very occasionally. After leaving the shop, Thom – with characteristic perversity – got a job at a mental hospital as an orderly. He still hated hospitals as a result of his childhood memories and now his experiences dealing with people who had severe problems shocked him. He was particularly amazed when many of them were released.

"I used to work in a mental hospital around the time the Government was getting passionate about care in the community," he said in an interview with *The Times* in the late 1990s, "and everyone just knew what was going to happen. It was one of the scariest things that ever happened in this country, because a lot of them weren't harmless."

After another job working in a bar, Thom eventually headed off to Exeter University to study English Literature and Art. In some ways it was another perverse choice. He claimed to despise the spoiled rich kids he saw in Oxford but Exeter University, at that time, was known as the place where middle-class kids who weren't clever enough to get into Oxford or Cambridge went to create a similarly cloistered environment. It was a fairly long way from Oxford but socially it wasn't a giant leap. It was the same thing on a smaller, less intimidating scale.

Nevertheless, it had its advantages. At a place like Exeter it was much easier to be seen as 'alternative'. And when he got there Thom found that although there weren't many people who shared his tastes, those who did formed a much more solid bond than they might have done elsewhere. Also, when he arrived in 1988, being 'alternative' was suddenly about to become fashionable and much more mainstream.

Just like a young couple heading off to different universities, the rest of the band must have wondered whether their relationship would survive. What would happen, say, if one of them met somebody else?

3

HEADLESS CHICKENS

One of the first people Thom saw when he got to Exeter University was Martin Brooks, whom he'd first met at the National Youth Music Camp several years before. It was in the main hall during Freshers' Week, or 'Freshers' Squash' as they called it at Exeter. Martin was sitting at one of the stalls when he saw the unmistakable figure of Thom Yorke walking into the room.

"I used to run the University magazine," Martin explained to me. "And I was trying to get new people to write [for it]. I saw him over the other side of the room and remembered him and went, 'Thom!'"

Thom had a long blonde bob at the time. He was looking at the floor with his usual air of not wanting to talk to anybody and yet unmistakably wanting to be noticed. Nevertheless when he realised that there was somebody at university that he already knew, Thom was undoubtedly relieved. After his experiences at Abingdon, coming to another institution was an intimidating prospect.

"He was quite dweeby in that he'd walk into a room and be very shy about talking to anybody," says Martin. "He'd just look into his fringe and was generally quite shy but he had this self-concept about being a rock star. When you're at university everybody carries their guitar around all the time with that, 'I'm gonna be someone' thing. And often it was the ones who were like, 'No, I really am' who you knew absolutely never would. He wasn't quite a joke in the, 'I'm going to be a rock star', sense but you didn't need to ask him what his future was going to be because he was very clear."

But, beneath his self-conscious 'rock star' persona, Martin found that Thom was still the same person he'd been at camp. "My main recollections from that time," he says, "are that he was a very nice bloke, right from the start, very friendly and keen to be nice." Martin was in his second year. The previous year he'd been in a band with another student, an old school friend called Simon 'Shack' Shackleton. They'd played covers but were planning on starting a new group to play original songs. Shack would sing and play bass and Martin could play drums so they still needed a guitarist. Thom was the obvious choice. "I knew that he could play guitar and I knew he had some attitude and he looked good," Martin says.

At this point, the band had the ridiculously 'studenty' name of 'Git'. Despite this, Thom readily agreed to join. His university life couldn't have had a better start. It was far removed from his experiences at school, particularly in the art department where being moody and creative was the norm. Thom quickly made far more friends than he ever had at school. He was still self-consciously "different" but at university so were lots of other people. His desire to make a statement no longer seemed unusual.

"I love that sensation when you walk into a room and everyone looks at you twice," he admitted to Andrew Collins in *Select* magazine later. "That's great. Pure vanity, you're there for effect. When I went to art college it was the first time in my life that I'd ever been with people who did the same thing as me, they'd dress up for effect, get on the bus for effect."

Thom discovered that Exeter University had everything he loved and everything he hated. He couldn't stand the lazy complacency of so many of his fellow public school educated students but the art course offered him a huge amount of freedom. Initially it was almost too much freedom. They told him he could do whatever he wanted but, for most of the first year, nothing appealed. His sketchbooks were full of lyrics and designs for possible future record sleeves. He was heavily into Francis Bacon so, on the rare occasions he did touch a paint brush, the results were large, morbid pictures with heavy splashes of black and red. He once said the best painting he did in the first year was of "a man blowing his brains out".

In the first year, he lived in halls and found himself part of a large scene of people who didn't feel like they fitted into Exeter's dominant, 'Sloaney' ethos. The band quickly dumped the name Git, only to choose the almost-as-bad moniker Headless Chickens; nonetheless, it provided a ready-made social life. In the first year, as well as Thom, Shack and Martin, the band included two talented violinists, John Matthias and Laura Forrest-Hay. They felt like they were part of their own, very distinct arty clique. Although Thom never took Headless Chickens entirely seriously, he appreciated how it gave him a social standing at Exeter, as well as a ready-made group of friends.

"He had a kind of awkwardness about him, that somehow he didn't quite fit, so when people were nice to him he really appreciated it," says Martin. "I wouldn't say for a moment that I took him under my wing, but the fact that on the second or third day of university there was somebody who knew him and said, 'Do you want to join a band?' I think he appreciated it. And I used to pick him up and tell him where things were and he definitely appreciated it."

To their surprise, Headless Chickens quickly became very successful, albeit in the tiny world of Exeter student life. Thom might not have liked everything about the university, but the fact that it was so conservative made it even easier to stand out and make a statement.

"Because Exeter was such a Sloaney university, there was an awful side to it," Headless Chickens' violinist Laura told the author, "which was all these very rich, upper-middle-class kids who hadn't got into Oxbridge who'd been sent by their parents to Exeter and were definitely not clever enough to go to university. They had way too much money and lived out in farmhouses in the countryside and had gambling parties. But what that meant was, those of us coming to Exeter from less well-off backgrounds, or normal backgrounds, were a little minority and that brought us together. Anyone who wasn't Sloane-y and who was remotely interested in the arts formed this weird little gaggle of people who weren't into anything else. We all mixed together and it was quite intense. We went to Edinburgh, and we had these one-off Dada nights and [we had] Headless Chickens, anything not to be with the Sloanes.

"It was very easy to be alternative at Exeter because the norm was so conservative," she continues. "It was *so* conservative it was embarrassing. There were so many very comfortable people. If you were in Headless Chickens you were the pinnacle of the alternative scene! If you were a bit unsure of yourself and knew that you didn't fit in with the main crowd, it was great to have the kudos of being in this band."

Despite its reputation, that era of Exeter University produced a number of people who would later be highly successful. JK Rowling was there a couple of years before Thom, while Basement Jaxx's Felix Buxton was a contemporary, as was sculptor John Isaacs and presenter and documentary maker Toby Amies.

"Exeter was still quite a provincial place and everything had to stop at 1a.m. in most places," says the band's other violinist John Matthias. "But there was a lot going on. There were six or seven really good student bands and there were clubs set up by students. There were six or seven really dynamic people around and that's all it takes to make something happen in a small place like Exeter. The art college was full of lots of very talented people."

"Looking back," Laura says, "I think that generated an intense atmosphere of activity. We started up a magazine as well. It was supposed to be a little bit alternative and not about the things Exeter was supposed to be about, which was twin-set and pearls. I would say that atmosphere pushed anyone who was interested in anything alternative together. I lived with Martin, Toby Amies and John Isaacs. Felix used to come round, who was in Basement Jaxx later. There were two semi-detached houses and there was always somebody there planning something. There was always something happening."

In his first few months Thom also wrote for the university magazine, *3rd Degree*. Martin remembers he wrote an adulatory piece about U2's album of the previous year *The Joshua Tree*. "He adored Bono for years and years," says Martin. "I remember U2 was the number one, most important thing in his life. He was also a massive REM fan as well." But initially Headless Chickens were much rougher and rowdier than that. They were as much about making a visual statement as they were about the music. Thom wasn't even asked to audition. He looked right and then at their first rehearsal they all realised how talented he was.

"I remember thinking his voice was lovely even though he was doing backing vocals while I was in the band," Laura says. "His voice was so distinctive already."

"We were a noisy guitar band," says violinist John Matthias. "But Thom has always had a great pop sensibility and he can't help writing great tunes that work in a pop sense. The exciting music at the time was people like The Pixies and Fugazi. That was what we were playing in the clubs. Our band was kind of a bit like that but a bit more English and a bit more poppy."

At the time bands like The Wonder Stuff were very big in Britain and, with two violinists, there was an element of that sound in Headless Chickens. "I think they were into that but Shack was more into heavier stuff and quite experimental stuff," says Laura. "On one of our videos there's a whole ten minutes where Shack has gone over to the keyboards and is just freewheeling and Thom was putting stuff in with his guitar and nobody really knows what's happening. There was a nod at The Wonder Stuff but with lots of heavy guitar, thrashy with lots of pedals and effects. Bit odd. A bit of an odd mixture!"

It was basically Shack's band to start with. He was lead vocalist and Thom contributed backing vocals. Perhaps surprisingly, considering his talent, Thom made little effort to stamp his own personality on proceedings, at least at the start. He was just happy to have an outlet for his creativity while he was away from On A Friday. He made no effort to try and take over.

"It is bizarre that we didn't let him sing to start with," Martin says. "I used to do some of the singing, which is really bizarre, because I've got a crap voice and he's got quite a good voice! But he really loved performing live and really lived for it. You could tell that when he was onstage his slightly awkward, dweeby side would disappear and out would come a pretty crazed rock persona."

"He was never arrogant or cocky at gigs or rehearsals," says Laura. "He didn't try and take over musically, which I have subsequently come across in bands. Sometimes you meet somebody and there's an arrogance that comes out in the music. They seem perfectly nice and then you realise they've cranked their amp up to 11 and nobody can hear anybody but them. You wouldn't have got that with Thom. Certainly onstage he wasn't arrogant. One of the interesting things about him in hindsight was that he was able to sit in the background on something even though he was so talented. He didn't argue about doing the backing vocals and that's quite a testament to his character I'd say. But then he knew he was doing it with [On A Friday] and we were a bit of fun to keep him going while he was at university."

At that point, although he'd had a fairly serious relationship before he came to university, Thom was still shy around girls, something he often blamed on the fact that he went to an all-boys school. Laura Forrest-Hay wasn't quite sure of what to make of him.

"I wouldn't say he was moody but he was withdrawn," she says, "which I suppose was shyness but coupled with his confidence it sometimes seemed like arrogance. I think I misinterpreted his shyness at the time."

Martin thinks that Thom partly relished his reputation as an outsider and an outcast. "I think he kind of enjoyed it," he says.

"He certainly nurtured that. Rather than walking into a room and going, 'Hello everyone!' He would walk in and look at the floor and be slightly mysterious."

At the same time there was genuinely a shy and unassuming aspect to Thom's character. He wasn't a raconteur but at Exeter he made several close friends and, even more significantly, met his long-term girlfriend Rachel Owen. Rachel was also doing a joint course, in Fine Art and Italian.

"She really thought I was a freak," he said to *Melody Maker* later. "She thought I was impossible to talk to, really moody, difficult, unpleasant and idiotic. And I think I was. But she bashed a lot of that crap out of me."

Rachel was heavily into music, too, and another Exeter contemporary of Thom's, Shaun McCrindle remembers that it was Rachel who first got him into the Pixies. "The first impression he made on me was when he came into the Hall Of Residence we were staying in at the time singing 'Gigantic', the Pixies' song," he says. "Rachel had just introduced Thom to them."

If his initial attempts to woo her had been unsuccessful, then it must have helped that Headless Chickens were becoming increasingly successful, albeit in the tiny world of Exeter University's alternative scene. Very soon Thom had the disconcerting realisation that his 'fun' band at university was much more successful and popular than his 'real' band back in Oxford. Martin, who now runs a successful internet advertising company, worked hard at promoting them and the band were able to draw, at times, several hundred people to their gigs.

"We did start taking it more seriously," says Laura. "We started getting asked to play the stupid Balls they have every term at places like Exeter. We got to headline some of those gigs and they were quite big, they'd be maybe 500 people and we'd get paid for that so we'd practice properly and work out our set. Shack was very driven. He was very focused on his music and it was an outlet for that."

"When we were there, Exeter University was about 7,000 – 8,000 people and a lot of them were Sloane Rangers who'd just rent a big house in the country and fuck off," says Martin. "Which meant if you wanted to do something, you could get an audience because there wasn't that much going on. Through the network of maybe fifty of your mates, you could guarantee 150 people turning up to whatever you did. If we'd been at Manchester or London we'd never have got that. So it was a massive confidence booster to us as a band when, at our very first gig, a load of people came. We genuinely had a following who knew our songs and really liked a few of them."

The main thing that made Headless Chickens so popular in their own little world was the amount of effort they put into their performances. Unlike On A Friday, they were as much about the spectacle as they were about the music.

"Thom had that long blonde bob that he used to swish about onstage," says Martin. "Shack had very long hair and I was a Goth so I had dyed, back-combed hair. We looked quite good and had a lot of energy and attitude onstage. We used to shout at the audience. People would scream and shout. There'd be lots of banter. It was always a fun night rather than, 'there's a band up there taking themselves seriously'. This was the fun band where Thom could let his hair down."

"We did lots of stupid covers," Laura Forrest-Hay remembers. "Like a really heavy, thrash version of 'Postman Pat'. And we did Prince's 'Raspberry Beret' at four times the speed. Shack was quite into punk, as well, and anarchic music. Myself and John Matthias were bringing in more melodic stuff on top of it."

"We did a very hard, grungy cover of 'Funky Town', continues Martin. "Thom would prance up and down in a way that … although his onstage presence got quite professional, musically, he would definitely fuck about. We also used to get a lot of dancers in who'd strip off and paint themselves in funny coloured paint and all that. Part of it was that if you have a visual appeal and make it a party, people will come. I remember a couple of gigs where we had four to six dancers covered in DayGlo paint down to their underwear. We did a couple of gigs at farms in the middle of nowhere with properly decent light shows. There was definitely a buzz about it. I mean I didn't leave [the band] thinking, *Oh my God, I've just done a Pete Best*. I was never good enough as a drummer to have gone the distance. But it had enough of a buzz about it that a lot of people would have remembered those times, regardless of what Thom had gone on to do. It was a good enough band and stage show and a good enough thing that happened for people to say that, 'Yeah, there was a band called the Headless Chickens and they were really good and we had a lot of fun.' We were better than the average student band."

This was proved when they achieved something else that On A Friday had never come close to – their own record. Local promoter Dave Goodchild had a record label, Hometown Atrocities, and when he saw the small following that Headless Chickens were building up among the student population, he suggested that they record a song for an EP of Exeter bands. The Headless Chickens' song was called 'I Don't Want To Go To Woodstock' and Dave arranged for them to go to a studio in nearby Honiton to record it.

The other three bands on the record, Jackson Penis, Beaver Patrol and Dave's own band Mad At The Sun, had a completely different sound, much louder and heavier. Headless Chickens were unmistakably a student band.

"They were different from all the other punk bands in Exeter," Dave told this author. "The big influence in Exeter at the time was hardcore. We were into Emo bands like Fugazi, which is very different to what they call Emo now, but they'd branched off into more of an avant-garde thing. It had more of an indie appeal."

"Thom had done a bit of demo recording before but none of us had been involved in anything like that," says John. "It was great. It was a laugh. We went to a studio called Daylight Studios in Honiton. And it was just a day. I remember Thom over-dubbing lots and lots of very noisy guitar, very quickly. Then we over-dubbed the violin. I think we did the whole thing in about four hours and then took about an hour and a half to mix it and it was mastered the next day and that was it."

Despite the fact that it was a micro-budget recording, it was a fantastic moment for all of them when they heard the finished record. It was an anti-hippy piece beginning with Shack ranting, "with flowers in their hair/they say that they don't care" and ending, "don't let the hippies get me". The biggest influence seems to be the cussed humour of The Wonder Stuff's Miles Hunt. In the background you can just about make out Thom's backing vocals, a falsetto that would later become very familiar.

"It was brilliant, totally brilliant," says Martin. "As a drummer I'd never heard myself play in a band before. I'm sure it wasn't that polished at all but it did sound great. It was fantastic to hear, particularly Thom's vocal over the top of Shack, [it] sounded really good. It was a real buzz hearing it and I remember thinking it would be great fun to do more of that."

"Thom's very high backing vocals are probably the best thing in it, looking back!" says Laura. "I remember my string broke so I had to do it with three strings like Paganini because I didn't have a spare violin string. It was very fast."

The result was the kind of frantic indie rock that was designed to be played live to an audience of enthusiastic, and, ideally, drunk students. "It sounds like The Wonder Stuff or something," says John. "It's very of its time, 1989, poppy, grungey English pop music."

Dave Goodchild arranged for an impressive 1,000 copies of the EPs to be pressed at a plant in Czechoslovakia. When he collected them, though, hundreds were missing. "What happened was a box of them broke and got lost somewhere in between the Czech pressing plant and Exeter," he says, "so there's not many of them around. I think a load of sleeves went missing as well. There were 1,000 run and literally about 600 of them got lost."

It didn't cause the band too much concern. 1,000 records seem like rather a lot for an EP which would surely only ever be of interest within the small alternative scene of one small city. Plus the cost was spread between the four bands and Hometown Atrocities, so it wasn't as expensive as it might have been. It was just one of those things," says Dave. "It did end up costing us. One box arrived instead of five but because it was a collective, nobody really cared."

It also means that the EP is now worth a lot of money. There were two different sleeves and one is particularly rare. Above a picture of a fang-toothed female zombie it bears the legend: *Hometown Atrocities Present ... A Disgrace To The Corpse Of Kylie ... The Hometown Atrocities EP*.

It was an incongruously 'punk' image for a band who had much more in common with the indie scene but the EP, and particularly Headless Chickens' song, received an enthusiastic response in Exeter. In their own tiny world they were now almost pop stars and when it was sold in local shops their fan base expanded.

"After the EP we had a following, not just in the university but in the town as well," says Martin. "Dave Goodchild was a local rather than a university type and he bridged the gap. Quite a few people bought that EP and they'd love it when we played it and we'd always get encores and stuff."

As a band they were increasing in confidence. What had started out as a bit of fun was starting to become a little more serious.

THOM YORKE

At that point, Thom didn't particularly stand out from any of the other people in his clique in terms of his talent. They were all very talented. But he stood out with his attitude and his work ethic.

"He was quite a good guitarist in the way that the other people in the band were quite good as well," says Martin. "It was more in his attitude and his energy and his belief that he was conspicuous, rather than his actual ability at that point. Although he was an art student, there were no particular themes or passions or points that he was trying to make. It was kind of, 'I want to be different like everybody else'. He had this general thing of wanting to do stuff and be passionate but not quite being sure of what he wanted to let out. So, later on, probably catalysed by his friendships with the other guys in [On A Friday], those things started to come out. He worked fucking hard at being a musician. We'd do a song and then the next time you saw him he'd really polished it and worked on it and made an effort to make it as good as it could be. He'd always got loads of ideas. He was very good at collaborating. So although some people might think it was all about him, it wasn't. He was definitely passionate about the band and the music coming over well and everybody getting on. It's interesting in that he's gone full-circle in that his persona now is very much a shy bloke who doesn't like talking about it, who just wants to get up and do it and doesn't want to project himself as unusual or as a pop star or anything else. Whereas [back] then he was definitely all about his persona. He was an OK guitarist. He could kind of sing and looked alright onstage but it was almost the other way round."

As he started to feel more confident in Headless Chickens, Thom started contributing his own songs. One of them, in an odd throwback to his first, childhood song, 'Mushroom Cloud', was called 'Atom Bomb'. It was just "generic indie", says Martin, but it was a sign that Thom wasn't just along for the ride. Nevertheless, even as he became more confident and started bringing more to the band there were still moments when they were reminded that he wasn't a rock star, yet.

"In the first year in halls, everybody was a little bit green," says Laura. "I've got this video of our gig and everybody's desperately trying to be so cool and Thom's there in these cut-off shorts like your man out of AC/DC and we're all onstage and he suddenly shouts into the microphone, 'This one's for everyone in Moberly', which was one of the Halls Of Residence. Which was so uncool! The rest of us were going, 'Would you shut up! You've just completely ruined our street-cred!'"

4

SUPERSTAR DJ

In the second year, Thom moved out of halls and into a shared house. There were only 12 people on his course and so they decided to split into two groups of six. He lived in the basement of a big, three-storey house on Longbrook Street in the centre of Exeter. Unsurprisingly it was a very arty environment. Perhaps slightly too arty at times. One housemate, Shaun, was an amateur film-maker and he remembers that, although on occasion they worked together, there was some friction between them, too.

"There were some funny things going on in that house," Shaun recalled in an interview for this book. "I used to do a lot of my film stuff there. We'd perplex each other with our idiosyncrasies! I'd say me and him were quite similar but I'm a bit more easy-going. I would do weird things. I was doing films and things would come spilling out of my room. He just thought I was mad. And I think a lot of people thought Thom must be mad because of his music! But there was a conventional side to his character as well."

Nevertheless, Thom was happy to collaborate with his housemates on their projects. On one occasion Thom and Shaun went to nearby Dawlish-by-the-Sea to work on another film for their art class, almost getting trapped by the rising tide. Another time Thom sang '10 Green Bottles' for one of Shaun's films. "It's nice that he was happy to get involved with something like that," says Shaun. "It's not the stereotype of the intense, depressed person.

The rest of the house would regularly hear Thom working on songs downstairs and, on one occasion, Shaun and Thom wrote a song together. Thom was still experimenting and didn't have a clear idea of what kind of music he wanted to make. Shaun says that the result was an odd hybrid of alternative, drone-rock bands like Loop or Spacemen 3 with a kind of Prince vocal on the top.

"We sat down to jam a couple of songs," he says, "and as we were playing, he had an idea for something and I was just tuning my guitar in and out and we ended up getting something that sounded really good. He was just singing, 'Baby let's grind,' like Prince, or something."

In his art class, Thom was experimenting, too. Towards the end of the first year, when he finally came back to class, he discovered that they'd bought a load of Apple Macs. After that he spent most of his time scanning images, playing around with bits of text. Even then he felt that many of his fellow students were dubious that what he was doing was 'art' at all. One exception was one of his best friends at Exeter, Dan Rickwood. He had a similarly dark sense of humour to Thom and the same preoccupations with war and disaster. Talking to Craig McLean of the *Observer*, he remembered Thom later as, "mouthy. Pissed off. Someone I could work with!" Later on, using the name Stanley Donwood, he would collaborate with Thom on almost all of Radiohead's artwork.

"I think that my obsession with nuclear apocalypse, Ebola pandemics, global cataclysm and Radiohead's particular brand of unsettling melody have gone together quite well," he later quipped in an interview with *Antimusic* website. Like a lot of students, they relished the feeling of being outsiders. Thom still retained the distaste for students that he'd had at Oxford.

"I was embarrassed to be a student because of what the little fuckers got up to," he said to *Q*. "Walking down the street to be confronted by puke and shopping trolleys and police bollards. Fucking hell. I used to think, no wonder they hate us."

That hatred was directed directly at him on one occasion. He'd taken to wearing a long overcoat and an old man's hat. When a group of locals mocked him, he turned and blew them a kiss and they promptly pulled sticks from their own jackets and proceeded to batter him.

To begin with, Thom had managed to steer clear of most student clichés. He drank but he wasn't somebody who would have ten pints and then run amok with a traffic cone on his head. "He was a crap drinker!" remembers Martin. "He'd be asleep after a pint and a half. He was that kind of drinker. He wasn't a raconteur. He wouldn't stand there and entertain everybody. He was definitely somebody who was on the sidelines of things until he was onstage."

Thom had some of the best times of his life at Exeter. He was asked in a magazine interview years later about the best party he'd ever been to and he remembered one occasion where he was summoned to a kind of "happening" on a hillside outside Exeter. They were picked up at The Red Cow pub and driven to Dartmoor where, in the absence of any moon, it was almost pitch black. They then walked across the moor until they got to the edge of a deserted quarry. Then suddenly somebody switched on lights and the whole thing was illuminated. They smashed an abandoned car up and made instruments out of the pieces before crashing out in sleeping bags. Shaun, too, remembers it as being one of the highlights of their time at Exeter.

"'Info Freako' by Jesus Jones was a hit at the time and I recall trying to dance to it on very lumpy ground with Thom and other friends, surrounded by TV sets playing the cult film *Koyaanisqatsi*!" he remembers. "The rave was followed by some performance art around the quarry ponds and we slept in the open, huddled around bonfires."

It was the kind of thing that Thom might have sniffed at in Oxford a couple of years before but, despite himself, he was swept up in student life for a while. At the same time, music was still far more important to him than anything else. He would take his guitar with him to parties, he was writing constantly and his songs had reached another level. He was inspired by the new direction that REM had taken with a more mainstream, classic songwriting sound.

"I really noticed the passion in his singing in the student bar when I heard him singing the REM song 'The One I Love', says Shaun. "The way he sang it, that's when I realised how good his singing was. He did a really emotional performance of that with just him and his guitar."

Despite the fact that Headless Chickens were so popular, it was becoming very clear that, as he kept practising, Thom was beginning to stand out even among his talented peer group. At the end of Thom's first year at Exeter, Laura Forrest-Hay and Martin Brooks graduated and left the band, which carried on by recruiting a new drummer Lindsey Moore and a new bass player Andy Hills. Thom was starting to have a greater input.

"I just thought he was an incredibly talented musician," John says. "I don't know if you've ever been in the same room as him playing the guitar, but it's quite an awesome experience, really. A lot of the tracks that are on [Radiohead's debut album] *Pablo Honey* he would play at parties on acoustic guitar."

Among other songs, he would also play 'Stop Whispering', a particular favourite among his peer group. But it was at Exeter that he first came up with an even later Radiohead song 'High And Dry'. "At the time everything was flowing between all sorts of different projects and bands and things," says John Matthias. "They were just songs. Sometimes he'd say, 'This is a song I wrote with Jonny', or 'This is a song I wrote with my band at home'. We'd basically rehearse once and then do a gig at a party or a ball or something like that. Then we wouldn't see each other for ages and then we'd rehearse in a student house and do another gig. It was very ad hoc. But, for example, we played 'High And Dry' in the Headless Chickens.

This caused some confusion for fans of Headless Chickens when *The Bends* came out. "When I first heard 'High And Dry' I loved it and thought it sounded really familiar," says one Exeter contemporary of Thom's, Eileen Doran, "but I thought it was just one of those songs that strike a chord straight away. Then I realised that I had heard it many times! I've got a video of them doing it and it's a really interesting version. It was slightly faster and they had this black girl singing backing vocals and that added a different sound to Headless Chickens. When they did 'High And Dry' it had this really lovely backing vocal to it."

Increasingly Thom believed that pop music, with its directness and endless possibilities, had a lot more to offer than the elitist world of fine art. Although he would still diligently study his English Literature texts, he wondered what he was doing in his art class. Apart from anything else he just didn't have enough time. "That's the amazing thing," says Shaun. "He had his course and Headless Chickens and he was going back to Oxford to do On A Friday as well."

He'd always known that he wasn't a great artist technically. "He wasn't good at drawing," says Shaun. "He wasn't an academic, traditional artist. He was interested in outsider art. Art done by insane people, or people who are not conventionally trained. And all that comes through in the artwork he does with Stanley Donwood. It's 'badly drawn', scratchy stuff but it's wonderful. He was just interested in his own style. He was one of the few people who started to use computers in his art."

"They told me I couldn't draw at art college," Thom said to *Q*.

"At least I'm honest about it. My whole argument at art college was, 'What's the fucking point in painting or drawing this thing in this way when I can go and buy a camera for two quid and do it like that? Why should I bother drawing it?' I could never quite work out how I blagged my way into art college anyway."

Although he'd always had a strong sense of self, and of where he was going, at Exeter Thom's ideas about the world crystallised. He became disillusioned with the art scene, seeing it as an elitist, phoney playground for pseuds and their rich backers.

"I did a few things on computer," he said. "But I spent most of the time bragging about my future as a pop star."

This is no exaggeration.

"With Thom it was literally, 'What are you going to do when you leave?' 'I'm going to be a rock star'," says Martin. "That's an actual quote. I remember people asking him that and it was almost a standing joke, 'Oh, I wonder what Thom's going to be then.'"

Laura remembers that too, above everything else about Thom Yorke. "He was absolutely convinced, without any doubt whatsoever, that he was going to be a rock star," she says. "There was no question about it. He was studying art and a lot of people who were studying art would have been looking to that as a career of some sort. But I remember us all talking one night about what we wanted to do after university and Martin, I think, was into politics and various people had other ambitions and Thom just said, 'I'm going to be a rock star', and I thought, 'Yeah, right!' Looking back now he was completely focused on it and there was no suggestion that he was going to do anything else."

To people outside the band, this claim was starting to look more and more plausible. Eileen says that Thom always had something different about him. "It sounds like the sort of thing you say in hindsight," she says, "but one thing I really remember is that when we saw Thom onstage, we all thought he *was* destined to be a rock star. He just looked completely in his element. He was onstage with a few people who were talented. Him and Shack were joint lead singers and Shack went on to have lots of success as well, but there was something about Thom's presence onstage where he just came alive. He looked like he was in the right place. We used to say, almost laughing, how 'at home' he was onstage. We used to say, 'He's going to be a rock star'. He just looked like a rock star. But we had no idea that he'd be in this amazing band and go on to the level of success he's had."

"I think it's one of the most impressive things about his achievement," says Shaun McCrindle, "that he knew he'd be doing what he did. He knew he was destined for it all the time he was there. In the house you couldn't get away from the music. When we used to go out to parties it was like, 'Oh, no, he's getting his guitar out again!' It sounds funny now. He wasn't playing Radiohead classics but he was obviously honing his craft."

"When I heard of the success of Radiohead, I was thrilled for him but I was also surprised," says Laura. "I'd not dismissed him but I'd not taken him seriously. A few of us were doing things like that and there was a lot of talk and I was surprised it had gone so well. I always laugh at myself because I didn't take him seriously, when he obviously took himself very seriously. I always think, *Who's laughing now?* with me scoffing and going, 'Thom's saying he's going to be a big rock star! Give us a break!' The egg's on me. But I'm absolutely thrilled because he deserved it. There were so many others talking about stuff but he actually did it and it's fantastic."

Ironically, at the time, Thom was probably even more acclaimed for his sideline. He had a job as a DJ at Exeter University's main bar, the Lemon Grove. He would play a night of mostly guitar-based music called 'Shindig' on Friday evenings, while, on another night Felix Buxton, who would go on to be half of hugely successful duo Basement Jaxx, would play dance music. Thanks to the burgeoning rave and clubbing scene, DJs were now given considerable respect. The days of the middle-aged 1980s DJ with the flashing set of traffic lights and one bag of records were over. He would be bought drinks all night until, by the time the club was closing, he was so drunk he could barely put the records on the turntable. But, despite this, it was a career that would be surprisingly successful.

"When we were first at Exeter, the Lemon Grove wasn't a place you particularly wanted to go to," says Eileen Doran. "But when Thom DJ-ed it was really popular." When he started, there were only about 250 people and he just played the relatively limited selection of tunes he had in his own collection. This was only about twenty albums and a few singles. Then, as it became more popular and he played every week, he realised that people were very quickly going to get bored. He borrowed £250 from the bank and went record shopping. It was probably one of his shrewdest investments. A few months later there were about 1,000 people at the Lemon Grove and he was making a significant amount of money for a student.

Yet his set wasn't the selection of Joy Division or elitist art-rock bands that you might expect. Eileen remembers him regularly playing 'Push It' by Salt-N-Pepa. He had a knack for knowing what people wanted to hear and an innate populism which would mean that, years later, even when he was going as far 'out-there' as possible, there would always be a part of his music that was unashamedly pop, even when he didn't necessarily want it to be.

"He used to make a fortune," Colin Greenwood once said. "And he'd blow it all on crap records!" At the same time Headless Chickens was starting to fall apart. Right from the beginning they'd known that it wasn't going to be a long-term thing. There were too many obstacles in their way. "Thom always had On A Friday as his 'real band'," says Martin. "I remember there were times when we wanted to practise at the weekend and we couldn't because he'd gone back to Oxford to see Ed and the other guys."

At this time it also became clear that, although they never fell out, it wasn't realistic for Shack and Thom to be in the same band. They were both natural front men in very different ways.

"Shack was a music scholar at school," says Martin. "He was very technical. He could conduct an orchestra. Although he's since gone on to do many years of crazy grunge and quite niche stuff, the performing side of it and the whole rock star thing was nothing like as important for him as it was for Thom."

"We had two front men," says John. "That was one of the problems with the band, really. They kept talking over each other all the time. Which wasn't great in performance! They're both quite charismatic front men, which was one of the reasons the band wasn't going to go anywhere. They both needed their own band in a sense."

Headless Chickens wasn't the main thing in any of their lives, either. Shack was starting to become more interested in electronic music and, for Thom, On A Friday was always his main concern. "At university you get loads of bands but Headless Chickens was actually a really popular university band," says Eileen. "They had something that made you think they could have gone somewhere with it but Thom kept saying, 'No, I've got this band back in Oxford and I'm really serious about them.'"

"We didn't take it all that seriously," says Martin. "We took it seriously in that if we were going to play a gig we'd rehearse but we never had any pretensions towards serious recording. Good bands have to be about something. It's like any great art. You have to have an idea at the heart of it. And we didn't. We just did it because it was fun and we enjoyed it. And people came along and it was self-perpetuating. If we'd done three gigs and nobody had come or they'd gone badly, we'd have given up on it. It wasn't like we had a burning thing to express our teenage angst. It was just we were at university, in a band, and it was great fun. If anything, it was cool that Thom was doing this other thing as well."

Despite this, when Shack eventually got bored with their relatively generic indie and moved on to a new electronic band, Flickernoise, Thom and John joined him. When Flickernoise started, rock music was deeply unfashionable. Bands like the Stone Roses were the cool thing in the press and, in the UK indie scene, there was an undignified scramble for guitar bands to bring in turntables, electronic beats or other dance elements. The next big thing in rock music, grunge, was still very much an underground concern and it was only just starting to filter through to the UK with Nirvana releasing their debut album *Bleach*. It was still the time of raves and ecstasy and although none of Flickernoise were exactly ravers, they were heavily influenced by the scene.

"They had a track called 'MDMA'" remembers Shaun, "which tells you a lot about the time, the early 1990s. It was a really beautiful song. There was one song ('Apocalypse') where Thom did a guitar solo, which I was very impressed by. I thought, 'Oh, he can do that as well!' It was his singing that struck me but he was always a good guitarist as well."

"It was an amazing guitar solo that he did," agrees John Matthias. "Really quite astonishing." But Thom never felt entirely comfortable in Flickernoise and he only stayed with them for a handful of gigs. He described it later as a "computer-with-dreadlocks" band. However much he might have appreciated elements of electronic music, he was still an indie kid at heart and, having already written many of the songs that would later appear on *Pablo Honey*, he knew where his destiny lay and it wasn't with Shack.

"Shack didn't want to play guitars anymore," John says. "For a time we all worked together and then Thom went back to Oxford and … that was a fait accompli, really." Despite his keenness to get back to On A Friday, Thom's eyes had been widened by his experiences at Exeter. Although his new influences wouldn't come out in his own music for almost ten years, with 2000's *Kid A*, he'd already begun experimenting with new sounds.

"That was really the most influential period for all of us," he said to *Rolling Stone's* Mark Binelli later. "The Happy Mondays. The Stone Roses. At the end, Nirvana. It was just an interesting period of transition: lots of electronic stuff, lots of indie bands, and it was permissible for it to be all mixed up."

He also took part in a performance called the Contemporary Music Festival, set up by John Matthias, which was an art 'happening' far removed from the grunge bands he was increasingly listening to. John and Shack wrote a piece of music called 'Flickernoise', which was based on a mathematical formula that was found in many sounds in nature. It was semi-random and Thom's role was to sing behind a curtain, almost wailing his vocal over the top.

"It was interesting," Shaun remembers. "John, Shack and Thom worked together to create this semi-random music. It was determined by chance. Thom did an imitation of an Islamic singer calling people to prayer. He was doing it quite convincingly, standing behind a curtain."

In his third year at Exeter, Thom also became increasingly politicised. It was towards the end of Margaret Thatcher's time as Prime Minister and the country was changing. In 1990 she introduced the Community Charge, better known as the Poll Tax. Thom was one of approximately 200,000 people who congregated in Trafalgar Square in London for what turned into the biggest riot the city had seen in the 20th Century. What he saw shocked him. The police couldn't disperse the crowd and they were terrified that they would attempt to force their way past the newly installed gates in front of Margaret Thatcher's residence on Downing Street. They ended up charging the crowd on horseback and driving police vans right through the centre. Five thousand people were injured. It was unlike anything he'd ever seen before and the images stayed with him. Years later he'd use the footage in the video for his single

'Harrowdown Hill', using it as a symbol for on-going government oppression. Thom was also involved in the protests against student loans, which were brought in by the then Conservative Government in 1990. Thom's time at Exeter had an enormous impact on him in numerous different ways. He'd been introduced to new art movements, he became increasingly politicised and he wrote dozens of songs on the acoustic guitar. Jonny wasn't the only person who thought that many of them would stand up even now.

"He's probably got about twenty other songs that he wrote that will be on the next album," says John Matthias. "I wouldn't be surprised at all. He's got hundreds and hundreds of songs stored up and most of them are absolute classics. One of my favourites was 'Stop Whispering'. He used to play that a lot but I think they ended up ruining that song in the end. Or it wasn't as good a song as I thought it was when I was eighteen!"

He also, incidentally, passed both Art and English with reasonable ease. His early press releases with Radiohead seemed to imply that he'd failed art, perhaps to suggest he was that classic rock archetype, the "art school drop-out ". In fact he got a 2:1. For his degree show, he cleverly scanned a picture of the Sistine Chapel Ceiling into his computer and changed all the colours.

But the most important thing that happened at Exeter was his meeting with Rachel Owen. He would still be going out with her 20 years later and they would have two children. Almost every reference to her he's made in interviews has been to the fact that she has encouraged him on the frequent occasions when he's suffered a crisis of confidence. Intriguingly he met her at around, or not long after, the time he wrote 'Creep' – the second most important thing that happened during his time at Exeter. He'd written the song after a long obsession with a girl from Oxford. She used to hang around with the beautiful people who frequented the town's fashionable Clarendon Street quarter of Oxford.

"When I wrote it," he said to John Harris of *NME* later, "I was in the middle of a really, really serious obsession that got completely out of hand. It lasted about eight months. And it was unsuccessful, which made it even worse. She knows who she is."

He felt simultaneously attracted and repulsed by her, by her life and by her friends. "I feel tremendous guilt for any sexual feelings I have," he said to *Rolling Stone*, "so I end up spending my entire life feeling sorry for fancying somebody. Even in school I thought girls were so wonderful that I was scared to death of them. I masturbate a lot. That's how I deal with it!"

"I don't think he would have thought of himself as a creep then," says John Matthias. "But I think he could access a part of himself that could be a creep to write that song. I don't think it was a kind of: 'I'm a loser, so why don't you fucking kill me' kind of thing."

One legend has it that the song was written in a toilet cubicle at the Lemon Grove. This may or may not be true. Shaun definitely remembers him working on it at their shared house in Exeter. "He was singing at the top of his voice way down in the basement and I was on the top floor," he says. "I went down and asked him, 'Can you be a bit quieter? I'm trying to read up here!'"

Wherever and exactly whenever 'Creep' was written, it does seem like the song's genesis laid to rest the feelings of inadequacy that Thom had had since Abingdon. By his last year at Exeter, he was a successful DJ, had a girlfriend he'd be with for decades and his musical talent had reached new heights. He said later that admitting 'Creep' was about a real person got him in "a lot of trouble." By the time the song was finished, the 'obsession' was already history.

Yet that one song would soon blast Thom and his band into the stratosphere.

5

BACK ON A FRIDAY

Radiohead once said that their debut album, *Pablo Honey*, was a 'Greatest Hits' of their unsigned years. Throughout the period when they were at university and despite the distance between the band members, they'd continued to add to their stockpile of new songs. But, with so few opportunities to play live, the band weren't likely to go anywhere. Nevertheless, in the summer of 1990 they made one of their most important decisions when Jonny moved from keyboard to guitar. That was when they started playing songs for the first time that would, eventually, appear on Radiohead records.

"Phil was away for that summer and I was filling in and drumming for the band," says Nigel. "They did 'How Can You Be Sure?' which ended up as a B-Side for *The Bends*. The whole band was driving ahead and not wanting to look back so they did tend to kill off old material as new material arrived. It was that summer that they actually started sounding like Radiohead. At that point Jonny said, 'I play guitar as well, so maybe we could have three guitarists?' So they did and started coming up with this wall of sound thing."

"The early incarnations of On A Friday sounded like Haircut 100 or something," says Shaun McCrindle. "I remember Thom played me one of the On A Friday demos called 'What Is That You Say?' which I've seen listed as 'What Is That You See' and I think it was one of the first tracks that Jonny played guitar on. It had all this feedback guitar. That was massively different from the funky guitar, Haircut 100 thing they'd had before."

A tape of fourteen songs from that period, labelled On A Friday/Shindig demos shows the variation in their sound. The first track 'Climbing Up A Bloody Great Hill' is highly accomplished but rather cheesy funk-rock with a chirpy brass sound, a slick 1980s bass line and an incongruously louche vocal from Thom. If it had been a song like that which had propelled them to global stardom, Thom would never have had to worry about being seen as a moping miserabilist! Although it was recorded at Clifton Hampden Village

Hall in Oxfordshire, and despite some gloomy lyrics, it sounds like Thom had a Santa Monica beach on his mind.

The rest of the tape leaps around wildly: the highlights of 'The Greatest Shindig In The World' and 'How Can You Be Sure?' were later recorded as B-sides for *The Bends* singles (the former re-titled 'Maquiladora'). They were both songs that were recognisably Radiohead. Other songs, like 'Something' and 'Life With The Big F' sound like Headless Chickens. They have that same jaunty, Wonder Stuff-inspired late 1980s indie vibe.

Elsewhere, though, there are tracks like 'Rattlesnake In The Big City' and 'Everyone Needs Someone To Hate' that contain cheap, Casio beats and a kind of rap from Thom. Neither of them sounds particularly serious. One track 'Tell Me Bitch' is speeded-up ska with a chipmunk vocal that anticipates another Oxford band Supergrass's 'We're Not Supposed To'. These tracks show imagination but not much else.

Part of the change in their sound is explained by their decision to tell the horn section that their services were no longer required. It wasn't easy for Colin. "It was up to me to fire them since they were my friends – we're still friends, they still talk to me because they respected my honesty," he said later. "When things started to happen, it wasn't really practical to have three alto saxes."

"There were just too many people on stage," a friend of the band, Oxford act The Candyskins' Mark Cope told me. "What they were doing was more like guitar music anyway. They realised you could make all these different sounds with guitar and effects."

It must have been frustrating to have so many songs but so little opportunity to play them or work on them. Nevertheless, at the end of 1990 they started sending tapes out to labels and one of them ended up in the hands of Chris Hufford and Bryce Edge. The two of them had been in a band themselves in the 1980s, Aerial FX, but at the start of the 1990s they ran a recording studio in Oxfordshire called Courtyard. They'd twice had their fingers burnt by the music industry. Once when they signed a record deal and saw things fall apart after just one album and again when Courtyard started to struggle. They'd opened it in 1987 in the Oxfordshire village of Sutton Courtenay but, like many studios, it had been a battle to survive. Although there were many talented young bands in Oxfordshire in the late 1980s, few of them went on to enjoy commercial success. Ultimately they sold the business, rented Courtyard back off the new owners and set up their own production and management company. In 1990, when they first heard On A Friday, they were on the look out for a good band that they could help steer clear of the same obstacles.

Their first impressions weren't that positive. Fourteen songs was far more than most bands would put on a demo, and none of them stood out. Thom had been writing furiously but they realised that he still hadn't found a voice of his own. "There were some good tunes but it was all obviously ripped off mercilessly," said Chris in a *Q* interview.

When they got a chance to record another demo, Thom decided they needed to be more selective and get a proper recording done. During the Easter holidays in 1991, shortly before he graduated, they booked a session with local producer Richard Haines at Dungeon Studios near Oxford. The studio was built into a hill and the control room looked out over the rolling Oxfordshire countryside. By the standards of the places they would record at in the future, it was very basic but for On A Friday this was a major step up. Between them they'd saved £300, which was enough for three days and they had three songs ready to record: 'What Is That You Say?', 'Give It Up' and 'Stop Whispering'.

"Two of the songs were fairly unremarkable if not average 1980s rock," Richard Haines recalled for this book, "but 'Stop Whispering' had a verse that Thom sang that was just beautiful. It was one of those shivers-down-the-spine moments. I thought, 'Christ, that's quite special'. The other two tracks weren't special at all. Perfectly well done, very competent. But they were just glad to be in the studio. They were so into being in a band together. It was very harmonious. They got on really well. Thom was steering the ship, basically, which I guess he carried on doing throughout. But it wasn't antagonistic. He didn't have to push or pull them. They were quite cohesive and understood each other's roles in the band. It was pretty obvious that they were a great band in the making."

When Chris Hufford received the new tape, he still didn't think that they were anything earth-shattering but the dramatic improvement caught his attention nonetheless and he decided to go and see them at their next gig. "He heard about us through a mutual friend and came to see us at the Jericho," said Colin in that first interview with *Curfew* fanzine. "Afterwards he was almost shaking. He said we were the best group he'd seen in three years."

At the time Chris was best known for his work with Thames Valley band Slowdive. In 1991 he was producing their debut album and was used to seeing 'Shoegazing' bands with little or no stage presence. If there was such a thing as 'the Oxford sound' it was defined by bands like Ride who, while having a powerful style of their own, had no real focal point onstage. The vocal was just the crest of a wave of sound.

On A Friday were very different. Thom's vocals were much higher in the mix. He wasn't afraid to admit that he liked U2 more than My Bloody Valentine. In his own, highly idiosyncratic way, he was a rock star in a city that hadn't seen a rock star in years. When On A Friday finished playing that night, Chris was stunned. They'd not managed to capture their three-guitar sound on their demos in such an electrifying way – they were a very different proposition live. As soon as he could, he invited himself backstage and said, "I've got to work with you."

At this point, On A Friday were in an odd situation. They'd been together for five years and yet they were still relative unknowns on the Oxford scene. To many people in the city who saw them play the Jericho Tavern at the time, it must have seemed like they'd just emerged, fully-formed and ready. Thanks to Thom's prolific songwriting, they already had an extensive back-catalogue. They also had an energy borne of frustration at the years of waiting for this moment.

When all but Jonny had graduated, they made a decision to move in together. Inevitably they chose Oxford. They were very different to the other bands in the city but they had a growing fan base. In the rock scene, everybody knew everybody else but, unlike in many bigger cities, other bands were highly supportive.

"Everyone went out drinking and we'd go to [music venue] the Zodiac and various pubs. Everyone went out every night, all the bands, Supergrass and that, we all hung out together," says Mark Cope of The Candyskins. "Everybody was trying to get better and better. Everybody was trying to outdo each other and the music got better. It wasn't competitive in a nasty way but it was really nice. I remember listening to people from London and they'd be talking about what clothes somebody was wearing. For us it was about going round somebody's house with a guitar. It was all about music. There was a great atmosphere and nice people in Oxford then."

On A Friday weren't exactly cut out to be a 'scene' band. At that point it was unlikely that any scene would have accepted them. They'd been changing their style constantly for the previous five years. In retrospect, it was lucky that they hadn't been around for any of the trends that had caught on then. The bands that had leapt on to the dance rock bandwagon were seen as risible chancers while 'Shoegazing' had been and gone in barely a year.

"When we were off at college, Ride started up and the whole Thames Valley thing happened. By the time we got back it had all finished! That's called impeccable timing – we completely missed the boat," Colin quipped to *NME*. Dance music had taken over most of the charts with DJs commanding massive fees in the new, warehouse-style 'superclubs' and, with the success of Nirvana, rock music was back in fashion. Thom knew which way the wind was blowing.

"Thom was happy to follow fashion for a while, or try and be a little bit ahead of fashion," says Nigel Powell. "Like a junior Madonna, he'd always be trying to see what would happen next. I think the reason *Pablo Honey* sounded the way it did was because Thom got in early in seeing that the grunge thing was going to happen. I remember him playing me the first 12-inch that Nirvana released and going, 'These guys sound really great' and then, not long after that, their songs started getting noisier. At that point he was very ambitious. It might not have been quite that cynical but he was trying to strike that balance between doing arty stuff and doing stuff that was commercially viable."

John Matthias doesn't entirely agree with this assessment. "Their tastes were always very eclectic," he says. "A lot of the tracks that are on *Pablo Honey* he would play at parties on acoustic guitar. It wasn't like it was a means to an end. It was definitely what they were into at the time."

On A Friday couldn't help but be influenced by the fact that people were now appreciating a grungier sound. Even while Thom was still at university, they were heading that way. But between them they liked a wide variety of music and this was reflected in the kind of stuff they played. Right from the start there were creative differences within the band.

In contrast to Richard Haines' thoughts, Nigel Powell says, "I got the impression that there was a tension between the members. Ed and Colin liked stuff that's a little more straight-ahead where as Thom and Jonny liked stuff that was a little more skew-whiff." But they had to learn to live with their differences, particularly for the year or so they spent living together. "It was like some nightmare version of The Monkees," Colin once said. "I wouldn't recommend it."

Different members of the band drifted in and out at different times and, even if they weren't actually paying rent, they would often be found there anyway. Thom spent one summer sleeping on the floor because he was broke. He'd spent all the money he earned DJing on buying records.

"He'd blow it all on crap records," Colin recalled. "He freely admits it. He has the worst record collection ... I think he was actually going for quantity over quality. So I had him crashing on my floor!"

Most of the time it was Phil, Ed and Colin ("the sensible three" according to Colin) who shared the house but Jonny was there part of the time and Nigel remembers Phil moving out fairly quickly because, "he was too mature to muck in like that."

As in all shared households, there were domestic tensions. Nigel's main memory of their early days is the way they seemed able to deal with big things easily but would squabble over the most trivial things. "I just remember that things would sometimes suddenly sour and the atmosphere would get really difficult and there wouldn't be a good reason," he says. "It was very public school – somebody not apologising fast enough for spilling somebody's drink or something like that. Petty things. It would just be like, 'OK, what happened there?' Suddenly nobody's talking to each other."

On one occasion, Phil came home for the first time in weeks to find that Colin had eaten all his honey and, so Colin claimed later, he was furious. It was that kind of household. The band spent much of their time ignoring each other when they weren't rehearsing or writing songs but, despite the squalor, it proved a highly creative environment. The previous tenant had supposedly died there and they enjoyed scaring themselves with stories about what might have happened to her. One day they found a half-eaten pork pie down the back of the sofa and, "being morbid people," said Colin in an interview with *Select*, "we managed to convince ourselves that she'd choked on it."

Their experiences in the house were, in some ways, useful training for the long tours later on but they also picked up some bad habits. Rather than having major arguments, one or more of them would simply remove themselves from the house if things got too tense. This might have been why Phil – despite renting a room in the house – was almost never there. Thom had a flair for the grand gesture that was slightly different to the rest of the band. It's been said that he's incredibly sensitive, perhaps over-sensitive, but Nigel Powell thinks this is only half-true.

"In some ways, it's true, yeah," he says. "He liked things to be dramatic as well, which is a bad combination. He was fairly sensitive as a person but sometimes he would like things to be extra-dramatic so he'd find a reason to be excited about something if he wanted to. I couldn't say that he was just over-sensitive because sometimes big things would happen and they would just bounce off him."

For example, none of the band were particularly fazed by On A Friday's increasing popularity and industry interest. To Thom, in particular, it was obvious that they were going to be a successful band. Why not? What else was he going to do with his life? When he arrived back in Oxford, he spent a short time working in an architect's office but he had absolutely no serious Plan B. Every waking moment was taken up with writing songs, rehearsing or playing gigs. Most nights they would head to the Cold Room rehearsal studios at a fruit farm just outside Oxford and practise for hours while other local bands, often The Candyskins, practised next door.

"There was us in one room and them in another and we'd have a break and sit and chat and talk about music and what was going to happen us," says Mark Cope. "There was no pressure, we were just sitting there chatting and thinking about what could be."

Gradually they started playing gigs further afield and they'd come back to the Cold Room at 3a.m. to unload their gear. It helped that it all happened so slowly. There was no one moment when it changed from being their childhood hobby to some kind of career. 1991 just saw them continuing what they'd been doing since they were teenagers. It's just that now they were playing much more regularly.

The gigs at this point enjoyed varying degrees of success. At one gig a few miles away in Banbury, by the time they'd finished there was just one man left, a Noël Coward look-a-like according to Jonny, who supposedly said to Thom, "You were wonderful darling, you played that guitar like it was your penis."

In Oxford, their fan base was, very slowly, getting bigger. It was mostly made up of members of other bands to start with, but gradually they were bringing more and more friends. "There was no chance that there'd be a sudden, 'OK, now we're doing this,'" says Nigel. "They took it in their stride to some extent. Which was another thing they were good at, the five of them, going, 'Hey, it's another gig.' They were the kind of band who would take something completely stressful in their stride and then another day there would be some tiny little stupid thing that would make everybody freak out. But the fact that more people were coming to their gigs didn't faze them at all."

Nor were they fazed by Chris's invitation to come and record at Courtyard after the gig at the Jericho Tavern. What they came up with was still only a demo but it further boosted their confidence. They re-recorded many of the songs from the Easter 1990 demo – without the brass this time – and gave many of the tracks new titles. Later that year, they went back to the studio again to record a more professional demo that would be known as the *Manic Hedgehog* tape after the shop in which it was sold. It was to be the first recording that was unmistakably Radiohead. 'I Can't' was the closest they got to a 'Shoegazing' sound, with jangly guitars and Thom's voice sounding unusually breathy. Another song, 'Nothing Touches Me', was even more impressive. It was based on the story of an artist who'd been imprisoned for abusing children and who spent all his time locked away in a cell, painting. More specifically, Thom said, "it's about isolating yourself so much that one day you realise you haven't got any friends anymore and no one talks to you."

That was the song that convinced Chris Hufford and Bryce Edge to offer to manage them. Apart from anything else, it showed off the whole band's talents, particularly an alternately lithe and then heavy bass line from Colin. Although they'd never managed anybody before, Thom was impressed by their enthusiasm and ideas.

At the time, Colin worked in a branch of Our Price and one of the sales reps who used to come in regularly was Keith Wozencroft. One day Colin learned that Keith had got a job in A&R at EMI and he handed over a copy of the 'Stop Whispering' tape saying, half-joking, "You ought to sign my band!"

At that point, Keith was actively looking for bands to sign and so he listened to the tape. Like everybody he was impressed by 'Stop Whispering' and he arranged to come and see them play at an open-air show in a park near Oxford. They were playing in a tent with just a couple of their girlfriends watching but, just as it had for Chris and Bryce, the extra power they had live made a huge impression. The buzz about the band was growing rapidly. One night Keith was the only A&R man at a Jericho Tavern gig; two weeks later they played again and there were 25 of them. It was no less than Thom expected. This was what he'd been waiting for.

"I remember being at the Jericho Tavern when there were loads and loads of A&R people there. It just seemed like, 'Hey, this is what happens!'" says Nigel Powell. They may have taken their increasing success in their stride but as they improved as a band, Thom's expectations also rose. He found it hugely frustrating if he couldn't get the sound exactly right or if he or another member of the band screwed up a song. At one gig, they were supported by a band called Money For Jam and their bassist Hannah Griffith said to *Record Collector* magazine, "Thom was like a little kid, having tantrums all over the stage." He knew that they were close to breaking through and yet they still weren't the finished article.

When the *Manic Hedgehog* tape was released in November 1991, the band had their first interview with the highly prescient local fanzine *Curfew*. The editor, Ronan, was slightly surprised to discover the dark subject matter of 'Nothing Touches Me' because, at the time, most of their music was relatively upbeat or at least up-tempo and highly energetic. The article contained a quote from Thom that summed up their attitude so far.

"People sometimes say we take things too seriously," he said, "but it's the only way you'll get anywhere. We're not going to sit around and wait and just be happy if something turns up. We are ambitious. You have to be."

That was why, just over five months after Thom graduated from Exeter, they decided to sign with Keith Wozencroft and EMI. It was a more controversial decision than you might think. On A Friday were, in their sound at least, an indie band. In the early 1990s, for an 'indie' band to sign to a major label certainly wasn't unheard of but it was a definite statement of intent. To the guardians of indie purity at magazines like *NME* and *Melody Maker*, it was a major turn-off. It meant that they unashamedly wanted to be huge. This was distinctly uncool. It would cause them problems in the press later and, although they respected many of the people they worked with at EMI, would also cause many disagreements but, for now, it meant they had the chance to take the next step – a huge leap.

Their first meeting with their new collaborators wasn't entirely a success though. Label boss Rupert Perry stuck his head round the door and, according to an interview Colin gave to *NME*, said "'You'll never see me again until you sell 500,000 units and then we'll shake hands and take a photo. By the way, I really like that song 'Phillipa Chicken.'"

Typically, they would never play 'Phillipa Chicken' again.

It didn't take long for EMI to suggest they make some changes. There was one thing in particular they weren't happy with: the band's name. In an early *NME* review, the name On A Friday drew some scorn because the otherwise impressed reviewer, John Harris, thought that it was a laddish reference to going out boozing on a Friday night. He said they, "hinted at extremes that belie the just-got-paid/let's get pissed overtones of their moniker." If he'd known that it was actually a reference to the only day they could rehearse at public school, then that would have been much worse. The label was right. On A Friday was a terrible name.

"I remember them changing their name to On A Friday," says Mark Cope, "and everybody said to them, 'But everyone's just going to think you're playing on a Friday. If the gig's on a Monday, that's no good. It's like calling yourself 'Free Beer!' But when they called themselves Radiohead, everyone thought, *That's a rubbish name too! It's alright but it doesn't really mean anything*. But then all band names are rubbish until they get really big."

In 1991, it seemed like every new band had one word names: Ride, Lush, Blur, Curve. On A Friday were very different to all of those bands. They wanted something that would sum up their sound without being too specific. They'd already tried out dreadful names like Shindig and Gravitate before finally choosing 'Radiohead', the name of a relatively obscure song from the band's favourite Talking

Heads album *True Stories*. "We always felt this massive affinity with them," said Ed O'Brien, "because they were white folks grooving in a 'college geeky' way and still making records as good as Al Green."

A&R people regularly get a bad press, taking all the blame for bad advice and getting none of the credit for good advice; however, the band realised that this time EMI knew what they were talking about. "Radiohead was cool and it's still cool," said Thom, "because it just sums up all these things about receiving stuff. All these people in America have teeth you can pick up radio on. They have this metal on their teeth and some of them can pick up radio with it."

At this point Thom also took the opportunity to have singing lessons. He'd been a great, instinctive singer since he was very young but the teacher, although extremely impressed by the quality of his voice, was appalled by some of his habits. At that point Thom still smoked. He had no idea how to look after his voice and his teacher would end up shouting at him every time he turned up for a class stinking of tobacco. He explained to Thom that if he wasn't careful, he wouldn't be able to sing at all in a few years.

Jonny, too, had a decision to make. While the rest of the band had acquired the safety net of university degrees, he was still studying music at Oxford Brookes when the band started to go places. As they began playing more and more gigs and spending more time writing and rehearsing, it was becoming increasingly difficult for him to study as well. Particularly now they had a major record deal. Since he'd moved on to guitar, his role had expanded and he was Thom's key songwriting partner. He brought something to the band that wasn't quite like any other guitarist. He had none of the traditional qualities or drawbacks of a virtuoso. He never saw himself solely as a guitarist and he didn't fetishise his instrument in any way. Later on in his career, a journalist from a guitar magazine was shocked to discover that he didn't even know what make his guitar was. To him it was just a means to an end. The EMI deal meant that Jonny, who'd always had tremendous faith in Thom's songs, was able to quit college to join the band full-time.

6

RADIOHEAD

The first thing Chris and Bryce did for Radiohead was send them back into Courtyard Studios to record some more songs. It wasn't an entirely successful experience. The problem was that Chris and Bryce had never recorded anything quite like Radiohead before. For his part, Thom had never had anyone tell him how his songs should sound before. He wasn't sure he liked it. With great honesty, Chris described the situation later as, "a huge conflict of interests. I think Thom was unsure of my involvement … (and) I can be quite overbearing and opinionated in the studio."

Nevertheless, the resulting *Drill* EP had its moments. Opening track 'Prove Yourself' sounds very much of its time, now. It could have been the work of any number of indie bands, with its mixture of British and American influences, but it had a strong chorus and a haunting central refrain. The problem with the other tracks 'You' and 'Stupid Car', in particular, was that the three guitars, which made them such an exciting proposition live, just sounded cluttered and messy.

They knew that they could do better. The songs on the *Drill* EP were never supposed to appear in that form. Originally they were just going to be demos to get a record deal. The experience of launching their rough sketches into the world via a major label wasn't what they'd expected at all. The transition from being a little independent band to having the advantages and disadvantages of big money backing took some getting used to. Before pressing the *Drill* EP, Thom got in touch with his old friends from Exeter Art College asking for ideas for the sleeve design. A few years later Dan Rickwood would get the job full-time but at that point Radiohead weren't sure what or who they wanted.

"He asked a few of us if we wanted to do a cover for the *Drill* EP," says Shaun McCrindle. "He wrote letters to all of us to see what ideas we came up with." But either EMI dissuaded them or else the ideas didn't quite work. In the end, they used a professional design company. It cost them many thousands of pounds and they still weren't happy with the results. Then, bizarrely, the first three thousand copies of the record were lost, just as most of the copies of the *Hometown Atrocities* EP had been. The release ended up having to be delayed by two weeks. Even worse, a promo was sent out bearing the brand new name 'Radiohead' but the actual music was by another EMI artist: Joe Cocker. It wasn't an encouraging start to their career on the major label.

When it finally came out, the *Drill* EP was met with relatively little interest. Steve Lamacq, then at *NME*, was the most positive: "Does this mark the end of the shoe-gazing era?" he asked after announcing that it had been stuck to his stereo for two weeks. Yet it received almost no radio play and peaked at number 101 in the charts. Still, although it seemed like an anticlimax after the excitement of being signed, nobody was expecting Radiohead to break through straight away. At that point, in the early 1990s, bands were given a little more time than they would be in later years. Nevertheless, EMI weren't particularly pleased. They didn't think that the production on the record was right for a major label band.

By now grunge was exploding, EMI wanted Radiohead to be a British version of Nirvana and Thom and the rest of the band seemed only too happy to concur (at least on the surface). "'Smells Like Teen Spirit' had the kind of feel we're after," Thom said to John Harris later, during their first national press interview. "When it came on the radio, you had no choice but to listen to it. You couldn't just drive along and ignore it, it came out at you. I hope we'll come out of people's speakers in the same way."

Thom was still a fan of bands like The Pixies and Throwing Muses and he wanted Radiohead to have a similarly collegiate take on rock music. If British indie bands in the 1980s and early 1990s were stereotypically lightweight and fey, and American rock bands stereotypically lumpen and one-dimensional, then bands like The Pixies had found a third way. The problem with On A Friday, prior to this, was that they were never quite sure what kind of band they wanted to be. John Harris told *Q* magazine that, when he was first taken to see them by their new PR team, Hall Or Nothing, they seemed somewhat erratic. "They looked awful," he remembered. "Thom was wearing a brown crew neck jumper, had cropped hair and looked very small with none of the presence he has now.

Musically they were all over the place. They'd start with something Rickenbackery that sounded like *All Mod Cons*-era Jam and then they'd flip it with something that sounded like The Pixies. All the raw material was there but they hadn't found their feet stylistically." But his actual review at the time was much more positive. "Promising seems something of an understatement," he said.

Their biggest selling point live was the way they interweaved the three guitars of Jonny, Ed and Thom. Thom later described his musical contribution to the band as "inaudible guitar" – when they were mixing the sound there was rarely much space left for him. But the three very different styles gave them a unique sound at a time when, in many ways, they were still pretty derivative. This was what they wanted to capture on record but nobody was quite sure how to do it.

By sheer chance, at this point two American producers, Paul Q Kolderie and Sean Slade were in the country. They were from Boston and had produced records for The Pixies as well as Throwing Muses, Dinosaur Jr and Buffalo Tom.

"We flew over to England," Paul Kolderie told me for this book, "and a record we'd done for the band Clockhammer was on (EMI director of A&R) Nick Gatfield's desk and we said, 'We did that!' And he said, 'You did all of it?' In England at the time, it was very common for people to take credit for doing something when they didn't do all of it. You'd mix it and say, 'I did that record'. He said, 'Did you get the guitar sounds?' We said, 'Yeah' and he said, 'Well, we have this band and we're trying to sort out the guitar sounds and I like the guitar sounds on this record. Maybe you could try to work with them?' We said, 'Sure, that sounds good.' So he played us a couple of songs. I think they were demos that Chris had done. I think that song 'I Can't' was on there.

My first impression was that the kid [Thom] had a great voice, sort of an angelic, choirboy voice. That was something that struck me. You're always looking for a singer. There are enough bass players in the world, you know! You're looking for a lead singer. I had no idea what they'd be like or sound like or anything like that but we said, 'Sounds great, we're looking for a job, if you think we can do something for them, great.' So they brought us back over."

"If you'd asked me the least likely place we'd have got a job, I'd have said EMI," says his co-producer Sean Slade. "Showing up at the fabled office building there, I said, 'OK, these guys are the total rock establishment of England.' I don't know what they're going to think. We'd made a bunch of American indie records and I didn't know if that counted for anything."

But Sean, too, was hugely struck by one thing. "Nick played us two songs," he says, "and I remember being immediately impressed by Thom's voice. I was just sitting there going, 'My God, this guy can sing. This isn't gonna be that hard!'"

The first time Radiohead met Paul and Sean, neither side knew what to make of the other. Thom was impressed that they'd produced Miracle Legion, as well as The Pixies, Buffalo Tom and the others. But the Americans were very different characters to Radiohead. They came from similarly privileged backgrounds – both Harvard educated – but they were confident and outgoing where the band were reserved and reticent. To begin with, the Americans found it hard to get a sense of what Radiohead were all about. The five of them were much less experienced than most of the US bands they'd been recording.

"Initially it was pretty tough," says Sean. "They were very, very young. They hadn't gigged that much. They had a kind of basement band kind of thing. They were all friends. They grew up together and they dug each other. I got that vibe immediately. I thought, 'This group has a chance', because these guys really like each other and they want to play. But they hadn't played in front of that many people. They were just starting out. Just getting a feel. Also, the fact of our 'American nose' struck them as being a little strange. They gave us the chance to do it because we had done these indie records, which had made an impact in England. But at the same time, there was something about our general demeanour that was very American. Sometimes I'd catch the guys and they'd be on the phone to the managers and they'd say (posh English voice) 'Oh, the Americans ...' I think there was something about our whole trip, we had a certain swagger and I think they kind of liked it but they might not have ... I don't know! There was a little bit of a gulf there culturally. But I think they appreciated the fact that we did want to go in there and make a rock record – three guitars – that was how Nick Gatfield laid it out to us."

"The first time we met them, I don't remember thinking anything really good or bad," says Paul. "They looked like a bunch of friends from school, which is what they were. They were sort of a motley crew. You've got Ed who's tall and handsome, Thom who was kind of cool looking and short, the Greenwood brothers had a very English look with shaggy hair on their faces; they were all over the map. But they were obviously friends. They got along well at the time. And they were definitely keen to get on with it. They were itching to get moving and make a record: 'Let's do this!'"

But after the relative failure of the *Drill* EP, EMI weren't taking any chances. Rather than hiring Paul and Sean to make a whole album they gave them two songs to work on. "When they first hired us, they asked us to produce 'Inside My Head' and another one," says Paul. "They weren't great songs. I was very disappointed. They'd already played us a few. We had a tape of some of the better songs and all of a sudden it seemed that we'd been assigned to do the worst songs as a kind of safety measure maybe, to see what we could get from them. It turned out later that Wozencroft really liked one of them but that was my subjective feeling – that they weren't very good songs."

"Keith Wozencroft thought that 'Inside My Head' was a hit," says Sean. "It wasn't." Thom was starting to think the same thing. When they tried to record 'Inside My Head' and the other song, 'Million Dollar Question', it just wasn't happening.

"I was really stuck and it wasn't going very well," says Paul. "They weren't playing very well and nobody really wanted to do these songs, everybody was just going, 'Uuuuughh.'" 'Million Dollar Question' was a long way removed from the kind of stuff they'd been doing as On A Friday. It didn't have much of a tune. It simply rattled and clattered along without pausing for a chorus. At best it was the kind of thing that would make you think, *Well, they might be good live*. 'Inside My Head' was much better with an impassioned, almost gruesome vocal from Thom and some vicious guitar from Jonny, but it wasn't exactly going to change the world.

To loosen everybody up a bit, Paul suggested that they play the Scott Walker cover that they'd done when they were rehearsing. At least he thought it was a cover. "Before we started the record, we went to pre-production and they just started playing this song and Thom mumbled, 'That's our Scott Walker song'," says Paul. "But I thought he said, 'That's *a* Scott Walker song.' There are a lot of Scott Walker records – I don't have them all. Slade actually looked over at me and said, 'Too bad their best song is a cover!' So when I told them to play it. I said, 'Play that Scott Walker song that you played the other day.'

The song, of course, was 'Creep'.

"They only played it once," Paul says. "One take and then everybody went to lunch. Then when they came back from lunch I said, 'Let's work on this.' When they finished the take, there was a moment of silence and then everybody in the studio applauded. It was one of those weird moments where you're like, 'Wow, what just happened?' So I worked on that for the rest of the day and I called Wozencroft and told him to come up from London because we had another song. But he was suspicious because we were only being paid to do two songs. I don't blame him. It sounded like we were trying to get more money out of him. So he was a little suspicious."

"When we went to Keith at EMI and told him that we'd got this song that was an actual hit, as opposed to the two songs that we'd been assigned to do, he thought we were just trying to make more money," agrees Sean. "Because we were getting paid on a per-song basis that if we just added song number three that was our sole motivation. That wasn't the case at all. It was just that we were frustrated with the two songs that had been given to us."

But Keith drove up to Chipping Norton studios after work to listen to what they'd done so far. His radar was typically sharp and he agreed that it was better than the other two songs they'd done. "When [Keith] took it to the office and played it for people," says Paul, "everybody was jumping up and down. The first thing we did was kind of an audition – we didn't really have the job producing the record. So pulling 'Creep' out of them was the thing that made them say, 'OK, we'll hire these guys to do the rest of the record.'"

EMI agreed that they should go into Chipping Norton studios to make their debut album. It was a step-up from the Courtyard but, once again, nobody in the band was fazed. "Paul and Sean were both very chilled Boston Americans," says Nigel Powell, "so they made it easy for them. Chipping Norton's a nice place. It's a very bright, happy studio to be in."

"It was a pretty famous residential studio in the 1980s," says Paul. "It was built in the late 1970s and they did Stealers Wheel's 'Stuck In The Middle With You' there and Cutting Crew's 'I Just Died In Your Arms Tonight'. It was a well-established, quality studio with 24 tracks and all that."

It was, in other words, very much a major label environment. Later on, Radiohead would become slightly sick of such places. "It's just very depressing," said Jonny in 1997. "You turn up at most studios, you still have the body odour or the copies of *Playboy* of the previous band, and you just want to start from scratch."

Back then, when they went into Chipping Norton, however, they were just delighted to be there. In some respects, with EMI looking over their shoulder, it was like being back at school, but they were still grateful to have been signed at all and they weren't about to make a fuss. And they had the confidence of youth on their side.

"They were not intimidated by it at all," says Paul. "Jonny's just completely a musician and all of them were good players, so their instruments were under control and the technology they left to us."

But, in a way, both sides were making it up as they went along. Paul and Sean came from a very indie background. They were used to making raw alt-rock records in a fast, no frills fashion and, perhaps luckily for them, that style had suddenly become the biggest thing in rock. Nevertheless, Sean says it was never explicitly suggested that Radiohead should be the "British Nirvana".

"I never thought about it like that," he says. "It wasn't calculated. The main thing was that they seemed to be interested in that kind of sound. They were into Sonic Youth, the whole idea of the extremities of the noises you could get out of an electric guitar and an amplifier. We'd done Dinosaur Jr and Buffalo Tom, both of which used excruciating guitar volumes as part of their musical expression. The other thing about making that record was that, even though it was for EMI, the approach that we'd taken up until that time was to make records very quickly. We did it for a number of reasons. We were used to working on low budgets. There was a certain aesthetic to it where you went in, you played, banged out the tunes and that was your music. That was what happened. I know that Paul and I have been criticised for that approach, but that's the way it turned out."

But this was why EMI had hired them. That way of working was suddenly much more lucrative than it had been. There was undoubtedly a culture clash between their loose, raw style, the perfectionism of Thom and the controlling nature of EMI but 'Creep' proved that the partnership could work. Even when it was still a demo, most people who heard it agreed that it was a big step up from anything they'd done before. Colin said that it was hearing Thom's demo of the song that made him decide that he had to take the band seriously.

"I remember an acoustic version of 'Creep' he sent me a cassette of from Exeter University," he said. "I listened to it and said, 'This is what I want to do. This is my destiny: to help disseminate this music and propel it directly into contemporary popular culture, because it's so important.'"

It's hard to tell how serious he's being here. He later said that the lyric of 'Creep' made him 'chuckle' but he was undoubtedly impressed. They all were. All except Jonny. He found the song too weak and simplistic. When they played it, he would get frustrated and attack his guitar, blasting out squalls of angry noise. But, by the time Paul and Sean came to hear it, the rest of the band had already decided that it actually sounded a lot better with a bit of an edge.

"When we actually did the song, we were very matter-of-fact about it like, 'Time to do the noise!' says Paul. "It was one of the last things we did. The first take we did was perfect and it took him, like, a hundred tries to get the second one. Nowadays, of course, we'd have just sampled it but back then you couldn't do that."

It was a pivotal decision in the band's career. "If the guitar hadn't exploded where it exploded, there's just no way it would have got on alternative radio," Thom told *Rolling Stone* in 1997. "And we wouldn't be anywhere."

Thom always had reservations about 'Creep'. It exposed the kind of feelings that most people have every now and then but nobody likes to talk about. To put it in a song for the whole world to hear made him feel highly exposed. By now he'd been going out with Rachel for some time, too, and the spark for the song – his obsession with some girl he'd never even spoken to – seemed ridiculous and embarrassing.

"That song was where he was at, at the time," says Paul. "It expresses a real feeling but it's kind of an ugly thing that nobody wants to get trapped in their whole life. It's high school, basically, or college. He wrote it at college about a girl who wouldn't give him the time of day and you'd like to feel that you'd moved on from that. It was sort of an adolescent expression. I wouldn't say it was tongue-in-cheek. He was torn about whether to put it out because it just wasn't him anymore, even at that point."

It also expressed something very ugly. Although, on the face of it, it's a twisted love song there's a lot more hate than love. He almost seems to be blaming the object of his affections for making him feel like a 'creep'. This view of the song is backed up by Thom's famous – and famously regretted – assertion that he'd never met a beautiful woman he liked.

In an interview with *Melody Maker*, he said, "Confronted by a beautiful woman, I will leave as soon as possible or hide until they leave. It's not just that I find them intimidating. It's the hideous way people flock around them ... Beauty is all about unearned privilege and power."

Later, although he admitted that he'd said this, he took it back. "It's as arrogant as you can possibly get," he said to *Q*. "Rude. Silly. I do have a genuine, normal awe of beauty, a feeling that it's completely unapproachable and intimidating and it's at its most extreme in women."

'Creep' expressed the same sentiment in a much more powerful way. It was about *resentment*. Fittingly, then, he would later come to bitterly resent the song itself. But before that it essentially saved Radiohead's career and it certainly saved their debut album, *Pablo Honey*.

7

PABLO HONEY

Pablo Honey is now like the orphan of Radiohead's career, almost disowned by its parents, yet it sold over two million copies and made them a genuinely big band. When second album *The Bends* came out, it was initially seen as a flop in comparison, selling far fewer copies in its first month. However, like all their records, it was a struggle to record it. The problem was that they simply didn't have enough good songs. Thom refused to put forward many of his old On A Friday tracks. He was determined that they should move forward with the new, grungier sound.

"I'm not saying we were scraping the barrel, but we didn't have a lot of stuff," says Paul. "We didn't sort through a lot of things and say, 'This is what we're going to choose for the record', it was more, 'OK, this is what we've got.'"

Also, the band weren't as technically accomplished as they would become. Thom occasionally struggled to reach the vocal standards that he'd set himself and Phil wasn't yet the drummer he would be later. "They were young. They were inexperienced," Sean says. "Although Colin's amazing, we had some problems getting tracks that had groove to them and that was part of their inexperience."

"For a while [Phil] lagged behind," says Nigel. "I do remember visiting the studio and Paul and Sean being locked away with long strips of tape dangling round their necks as they put together various drum takes. That kind of thing is pretty standard for making any record. Even if you've got Phil Collins behind you, you're probably going to edit together a couple of drum takes to get the one that actually goes on the album. Phil was very sensitive about it, which made it worse. Honestly, he was a fine drummer, it [just] made him a bit nervous."

However, Thom, too, would feel tremendously frustrated if he couldn't get things right. "Thom's a very emotional person and if you got him in the right frame of mind, the vocal would come very easily," says Paul. "If he wasn't in the right frame of mind, it would be hard. But he's a fantastic technical singer. He had training as a child in choirs and stuff like that. But that's the hardest part of being a producer – getting a good vocal out of the singer. When we did 'Creep', it just sort of happened. It was one of those things. There was something weird going on there. It was strangely effortless. It was one of those things you look back on and think, 'Something was going on there.' Because the rest of the album wasn't that easy. It was hard to finish."

Thom admitted later that he was "unbearable" during the *Pablo Honey* recording sessions. The rest of the band knew about his perfectionism and hyper-critical approach, but it was the first time they'd had to deal with it in such an intense, confined period of time. In contrast to every other album they'd record, they were on a tight schedule. There wasn't too much time to worry about things. They had three weeks. They just had to blast it out and if they weren't entirely happy with something, too bad. And, partly as a result perhaps, they had a huge amount of fun on some of the tracks. They weren't quite the straight-laced puritans of legend.

"[First track] 'You' was one of those instances where we were stuck," Paul remembers. "We couldn't quite get it off the ground. I remember a friend of theirs' showed up with some hash and … we had the greatest time. All of a sudden, Ed's guitar started making sense. He played this cool part that went all the way through it and all of a sudden that tune got going that day. I'm not saying drugs are a good thing but sometimes they will inspire you!"

Another time, on 'Anyone Can Play Guitar', they decided to find out whether the sentiment was actually true. "Every single person in the studio got a track on that," says Paul, "even the cook. Everybody we could find, the gardener, the assistant engineer. Everybody had to play a guitar part because the whole concept was that anyone can play guitar. It was funny to see what everybody's approach was. Some people did more of a straight guitar part; Sean went for pure noise and ripped the strings off the guitar. It was kind of a Rorschach test for personality. Jonny got out a coin and used that. I think I tried to play a rhythmic thing. You can't hear anyone particularly, it's just a big mishmash of stuff. That was a really fun day. We weren't really approaching it technologically. It was just an Eno-esque approach to having fun with it. We weren't jaded old fuckheads who go, 'Let's fuck off to the pub, I hate this!' We were really into it. We knew we had a good band and we were trying to do a good job. Those guys are smart and they learned so much from that experience, being in a good studio, seeing what worked and didn't work."

The experience of recording *Pablo Honey* was a steep learning curve for Thom and the rest of the band. That, too, made it a frustrating experience. Thom was starting to write better songs but they were on a tight schedule and an even tighter budget and there wasn't time to work these new tracks out and put them on the record. Some songs like 'Prove Yourself' had seemed like Radiohead's best work when Paul and Sean first heard them, but they were rapidly superseded by newer, better tracks.

"I think that was one of the first songs we heard from the demo. At first it was one of the best things we'd heard but as the record went on we thought 'It's alright," says Paul. They knew they were starting to get somewhere when Thom finally managed to get the high-pitched vocal on 'Vegetable'. "We were struggling with it and one night Thom finally just got it right. That was one of the hardest ones for him to sing. I don't know why. We had a break-through one night when we nailed that one. It was like a hump that we had to get over."

But there were other tracks that, even at the time, nobody liked all that much. A particular bugbear was the noisy, abrasive track that appeared after 'Creep', called 'How Do You?'.

"There were some songs that the band didn't like right from the beginning," says Nigel, "Even today, on the last couple of albums, I've talked to Jonny and he'd say, 'Yeah, we're just trying to decide what songs to put on the new album. Just playing the game of 'Spot the 'How Do You?'". Nobody enjoyed that song. They realised that wasn't their finest hour."

"To me that song is a fun track but the British press tore us to shreds over that one with 'fake punk' and the like," says Paul. "It's just a short, little crazy song. I think we put it after 'Creep' to get the album moving again. It would have been better if we'd moved it away from 'Creep' because it was too jarring for people, I guess. I remember the press gave us enormous amounts of crap about that one. They weren't having it."

In a throwback to their earliest demos 'How Do You?' was a song with a very Oxford subject matter. Nigel says that's why Thom decided to keep it on the record. "I think Thom liked the lyrics to that one. It was about Kevin Maxwell, Robert Maxwell's son (who lived in Oxford) and Thom liked the angriness of the lyrics but I don't think the music really kept up."

The last track they recorded was also the last track on the album, 'Blow Out'. It was a fittingly chaotic end to what had, at times, been a chaotic process. They were adding the final touches when their friends, Oxford band The Candyskins, arrived. The studio was packed and noisy and, somehow, in the chaos the monitor speakers perched on top of the console fell on to the control board with a massive crash. A whole row of switches were completely sheared off.

"It didn't blow up the board but it messed up a lot of the console," says Paul. "We had to call the engineer and he was shocked. It was kind of a chaotic session because we had other people around and the board was kind of crippled. It was fun. That was I think about the last thing we did on the record!"

But although the band and producers had, mostly, got on well during the sessions, the next stage began to strain their relationship. All the way through recording, Thom had been able to cling to the belief that, if things didn't sound quite right, they'd be able to sort it out when they came to mix it. In practice, it wasn't quite like that. When they heard what was coming out of the mixing desk, they were all a little disillusioned.

"We weren't having fights but there was a lot of [tight-lipped], 'Well, we don't really like this mix,'" says Paul. "When you make a record I don't like to say, 'We'll fix it in the mix' but there are always a lot of things where you put it off and say, 'I know you don't like that but we'll fix it later', but eventually it comes down to the point where all those things have to be done. If somebody then realises that, 'Woah, I still don't like it!' sometimes there's a limited budget for changing it. If Def Leppard and [producer] Mutt Lange want to go back and re-do a song, nobody's going to go crazy but at that point, for us, the budget was pretty much done."

The only thing they did go and record again was 'Creep'. It was pointed out to them that there was absolutely no chance that it would be a hit because of its lyric. In 1993, the lead lyric's profanity would never get played on the radio, not even with a bleep.

Sonic Youth had changed their lyrics in similar circumstances, so why not Radiohead? It was a bit of a 'sell-out' they admitted, but

Thom duly went back into the studio to record a radio version where he'd sing a vitriolic, "very" instead of "fucking". Ironically the version with "very" sounds even more antagonistic towards the subject – now he was clearly just being sarcastic. The only advantage of the re-write was that it gave him a chance to go back and improve the first verse of the song, too. At the time it had a different lyric to the one that would ultimately appear.

"It was a filler lyric," says Sean. "You know how The Beatles' 'Yesterday' originally had those lyrics about scrambled eggs [before Paul McCartney came up with the finished version]? It was like that."

"We actually had an argument," says Paul. "I said, 'Now's your chance to make it better,' and Thom said, 'No, it's done, it's written, we can't go back to that.' But I kind of leaned on him, as much as I ever leaned on Thom. I said, 'I think the song could be huge but I don't think the leg of lamb is going to make it.'"

Thom wasn't impressed. He thought he'd finished the song. He'd had enough of it. He didn't want to go back and do it again. "He kind of got this funny look," says Paul, "and he went away and came back with that first verse, which is much better. That's the most producerly (sic) thing that I can remember doing."

"I understood why Sean and Paul said, 'Maybe we should try some different lines there', to make it less obscure," says Nigel. "But I think I asked Thom about it and he said it was a reference to domesticity, just thinking about being married to somebody and being in the kitchen – nice stuff!"

By the time of the mixing process, the fun part of recording was most definitely over. The band listened with increasing gloom to what they'd done and tried desperately to change things but it was too late. At one point, Thom decided he didn't like the sound of the record. It was too much like other indie albums at the time. In a panic he instructed the producers to change course.

"It was when we were mixing 'Blow Out'," remembers Sean. "Thom came in that morning when we were starting to mix it and said [abruptly] 'No reverb!' And we said [glumly], 'Oh, alright'. And since reverb is the body and soul of recorded music, it was kind of tough. So we did this mix that was dry as a bone and then the record company guys show up and we play it for them and they're sitting there scowling and I'm going, 'I don't like it either, man.' So I had to talk to Keith [Wozencroft] and say, 'This isn't adding up'. We did the mix at this terrible, terrible studio," he continues. "The console was terrible, the vibe was terrible, the record company showed up en-masse to criticise. The whole thing was fucked. I remember turning to Keith and saying, 'Listen, man, I know nobody's happy with this shit. Just let me and Paul go back to [their home studio] Fort Apache and we'll mix the stuff and you take it from there. And that's what *Pablo Honey*' became."

"It was a hard record to finish," says Paul. "We were mixing and we had people coming up behind us and going, 'Could we just change this? And what about my part?' At that point 'Creep' was already mixed but we went back to Fort Apache without the band there and they were basically forced to accept it and they weren't very happy about it. At that point the label had spent a good amount of money and they needed a product. The band didn't want *Pablo Honey* to come out the way it came out, as far as I know. We never really discussed it because at that point relationships were a little strained, after that long working on the record. They didn't want it to come out like that because they knew it wasn't great but the record company – as record companies do – kind of stepped in and said, 'Guys, we've got to get you out there, we've got a single, let's get you out there and get moving on it.' I think ultimately they were right. You only get one chance to make a first record and if they didn't have 'Creep' it would have sunk like a stone but they did have it. The label knew that they had something going and it was the touring and the playing that made them mature as a band."

The somewhat rushed nature of the *Pablo Honey* sessions comes across in the album title. It sounds very much like the first thing that came into their heads. It didn't mean much or have anything to do with the record's content. It was inspired by 1990s phone pranksters The Jerky Boys. One of their calls featured them impersonating an elderly Hispanic mother calling somebody she apparently thought was her son. "Pablo, honey, come home", she begged. Radiohead had been given a tape by fellow Oxford band Chapterhouse and they'd got hooked.

"Some of it's really sick," Thom said to *Select* magazine. "Some of it I can't cope with. But the notion of phoning people up cold is so 1990s. It's just the ultimate sacrilege. Turn up in someone's life and they can't do anything about it."

It's funny, considering how imaginative and inventive Radiohead are, that they've always been so bad at titles. The long struggle to come up with a decent band name tells you that. You get the feeling that if they'd been listening to something else on the bus when EMI demanded they come up with a name for their debut album, then it could have been very different. But by then, perhaps, they'd had enough. It had only taken three weeks to record (nothing compared with the time they'd put in on later albums), but they were a little disillusioned. Only the thought that they'd soon be able to record a vastly better follow-up album kept them going.

They appreciated *Pablo Honey* for what it was, a crash course in how to be a rock band provided, in part, by Paul Kolderie and Sean Slade. In an interview with *Mojo's* Nick Kent years later, Thom was asked. "Would you have preferred a different producer?" "Oh no," he replied. "That was great. They were rock 'n' roll. They were brilliant."

Their long-term producer Nigel Godrich has also defended Paul and Sean from the accusation that they somehow let Radiohead down. The problem was that Radiohead simply had no experience of making a record at that point and there was no time to learn. "They'd been signed very quickly and put in a studio very quickly," he told journalist Nick Paton Walsh. "The situation required somebody to take the situation in hand or the record wouldn't have been made. As a result, they felt, quite justifiably, that they hadn't had as much of an input as they'd have liked. They hadn't made a record they felt was completely theirs – even the artwork was done by somebody else."

But Paul and Sean had the same frustrating yet encouraging feeling that Radiohead were capable of much more. "When the guys put me in their van and took me to the airport, I remember thinking, 'These guys really have what it takes and if they could just go out there and play on a regular basis, then they will become a mighty band,' says Sean. "I definitely had a very strong intuitive feeling that they were capable of it. Then all I can say is that 'Creep' was so God-damned powerful and hit the zeitgeist at the exact right time that it enabled them to go out and play and become the mighty band that created *The Bends*."

It's no coincidence that it came out the same year as 'Loser' by Beck," says Paul. "There was a lot of that kind of thing around.

The thing about the first record was just that they needed to get off the ground. They needed to get up in the air. It got them a tour and that took them around the world and made them play together a lot and really gel as a band."

Both producers accept that *Pablo Honey* was nothing compared with what Radiohead would come up with next. But they make the fair point that it was the process of recording the debut that helped push them on to the next level. Still, it must have been a little frustrating when, right at the end of the sessions, when it was too late to record anything else, Thom played them two other demos that he had. They were 'The Bends' and 'High And Dry'.

One thing *Pablo Honey* and its subsequent tour taught Thom was how not to do things. It taught him not to listen to the record label. Not to try and copy what was going on elsewhere. Not to listen to what the press said or what other bands said. It was like one of those disposable rockets that they used to use to blast the Space Shuttle into orbit. It served its purpose. It got them off the ground, but once they'd finished recording and touring it, they didn't want to think about it again. "When I hear the singing, I just don't recognise myself at all," Thom said to Nick Kent. They certainly didn't realise that they would have to spend the next two years playing the same songs over and over, before they could go back into the studio and try again.

8

CREEP

'Creep' was the first single to be released from *Pablo Honey* and, after the *Drill* EP's poor performance, expectations weren't all that high. Even so, when it only sold 6,000 copies initially and peaked at 78 in the UK charts, the band, their management and the label were all disappointed. The problem was that it received very little radio play. BBC Radio 1, in particular, decided that it was just too dark. Other bands in a similar position have been helped out by the music press but, although the single enjoyed mostly positive reviews, the band weren't given many column inches. They were in the unfortunate position of being seen as too weird and out-there for the mainstream and, as a major label band, too corporate for the alternative.

Luckily, a series of support slots kept them from thinking too much about commercial success (or lack of it). As they played more and more gigs, they were getting better and better, even if the British music scene hadn't realised yet. First they went out with Kingmaker, a band best known for their quotable front man Loz's regular appearances in the press. Then they headed out again with Irish band the Frank And Walters. It was on that tour that they took another major step forward. In retrospect, the combination of the happy-go-lucky Frank And Walters and the 'dark' Radiohead seems highly bizarre but at the time nobody found it odd. The Frank And Walters were on a roll with their records selling quite well and earning highly positive, if slightly patronising, coverage in the press.

"It was a sell-out before it started, so it was a good tour to get," Frank and Walter drummer Ash told this author, "and there were a few bands in for it. We saw Radiohead at The Venue in New Cross and they were really good. So we said to our managers 'Let them do it.' It was the song 'Creep'. They played it third song in or something and it was like, 'Fuck!'"

"It worked really well!" says Nigel Powell, who did the lighting for Radiohead on that tour and many others. "The Frank and Walters were lovely fellas. They were really friendly. This was the time before Radiohead were the most respected band in the world! They were just another band who'd signed to Parlophone and tried to break through."

To the Frank And Walters, meeting a band like Radiohead was something of an eye-opener. The Irish band were very young, too, and they'd always seen rock 'n' roll as, essentially, a mobile party. Meeting somebody like Thom, who was so desperate to continually improve his songwriting and play better shows was, according to Ash, an inspiration.

"They were definitely different from any other band we'd ever come across," he says. "We moved to London in about 1990 and most of the bands we met were into the usual rock 'n' roll stuff of getting drunk and meeting girls, but they were very different. Most other bands were thinking, 'This is great, we're on the gravy train, the record company are giving us money to go and tour and have a good time.' But, with Radiohead, you suspected that they had the recipe for success in their back pocket. Over the whole tour there were only maybe two nights when they'd go and get drunk and let their hair down. They used the soundchecks for what soundchecks are supposed to be used for, practising the songs and getting things right. Other bands would get dragged up there by the tour manager suffering from a severe hang-over, just bashing out some noise for the soundman and hoping he could work with it. They were different characters to most other bands we'd come across, alright."

It was during the Frank And Walters tour that 'Creep' came out for the first time. Ash thinks that its relative failure hit them pretty hard. "It was a bit odd," says Ash. "They were with EMI and there were a couple of A&R guys at the shows and they were getting mid-weeks [sales figures] through for the single and all wasn't rosy. They were under a bit of pressure because, I suppose, if you're on EMI, there's some expectation on you because it's such a huge company. I've been there myself when you're in the van and the call comes through that the single's peaked at 61, you start thinking to yourself, *Oh, right, that's the career over now then. We'll just pack our bags and head off.*

We played Oxford, which was their hometown gig, on a Saturday night and I think the 'Creep' single had been released on the Monday and they got the midweek on the Thursday, so they knew it wasn't charting. The tour manager at the time said the people at EMI weren't very happy with it."

It was the worst time for them to hear bad news. The first few dates of the tour hadn't gone badly but they weren't blowing anyone away and now they had to play their hometown gig with a cloud hanging over them. They knew that EMI's patience was in short supply. They also knew that 'Creep' was the best song on the album and if that wasn't going to chart then how well were the follow-up singles going to do?

"The band could have gone into their shell and felt sorry for themselves," says Ash, "or they could do an amazing show and I think that was the first time I saw them and thought, 'Jeez, these guys are something.' For the previous gigs, they were OK but they didn't quite let fly. Jonny Greenwood took the band to a different level. Back then Thom wasn't that charismatic. Jonny seemed to carry the band. That was the first night I saw him going from one of two guitarists to the main attraction. It was the same songs but it was completely unlike the previous sets they did.

When the tour started they were a bit stand-offish with the audience. It was as if they didn't know how to interact with an audience. But that night in Oxford and for the rest of the tour, it was weird; it took the single not doing well for the band to step up to the mark. For the next twenty-odd dates of the tour, they were amazing. I remember a gig in Glasgow, which is one of those areas of the UK with a big Irish population [and] so a lot of people who'd known us from Irish radio [came]. They had an audience who didn't know them and didn't really care about them. But one or two songs in, you could watch them become instant fans."

Radiohead's live show was very different to the other bands that were popular at the time. There was an intensity and a fervour to the way they played that lifted even their lesser songs. At a time when most other big-selling indie acts were all about a good, beery night out, Radiohead were trying to create something closer to a spiritual experience.

"I suppose back then, '91, '92, it was an era of 'Let's all jump up and down together and hold hands and won't the world be a great place?'" says Ash. "Gigs were all about moshing and jumping around and having fun. Ned's Atomic Dustbin and Carter and all that sort of stuff. Radiohead were playing music that you couldn't really mosh to. They weren't being all, 'Let's clap hands for this bit.' There was no 'You fat bastard' song (the opening tune for Carter USM)! They were very different to the bands that were touring but they were still able to win over an audience. And I'd always assumed that to win over an audience they had to be jumping around and stage-diving and doing all the mad stuff. But for the first time I saw that a band were able to win over an audience who were just watching the performance of the songs."

As the tour went on, Radiohead were becoming a much bigger band almost surreptitiously. Although 'Creep' hadn't sold well, Radiohead now had an ardent fan-base who were busily proselytising on their behalf. It was as though everybody who saw them play went home and told three more friends that they *had* to catch this band.

"Word spread," says Ash. "I don't know how it spread, because it was pre-mobile and pre-internet and stuff, but I think when the tour started off, somewhere like Cheltenham, there were 200 people at the gig and 30 of them were watching Radiohead and 170 were in the bar. Then everything changed after that Oxford gig and the audience wanted to see them. I'm not sure why. Because I think the problem with 'Creep' from day one was that it didn't get the radio play. EMI [struggled to] get it on the radio so it didn't filter through but it seemed like by the end of the tour they were a really big band. Rather than people popping in for 'Creep' and then going back to the bar, people were there for half an hour before they went on. We used to try, where we could, to have a local act and the local act would be on and there'd be 300 people in the hall watching them because they didn't want to miss Radiohead. We were just worried 'Would they stay for us?' I'm not sure how it happened, it must have just been word of mouth, unless people were sending smoke signals or writing to each other. We finished the tour at the Astoria in London and it was a sell-out gig and a great vibe and there were 1,500 people in there and they were all watching Radiohead, the whole gig, from start to finish. There wasn't the usual support band chatter. People were watching and they were watching vigorously. It was a great tour. It was a great tour for us as well. Sometimes you don't get the support band right but that time we got it right!"

But Thom remained something of an enigma. He appreciated the friendliness of the Irish band but, at the same time, a tour for him was a kind of mission. It wasn't about partying and socialising with the support band. It was about the music. Nothing else.

"The other lads we knew quite well," says Ash, "but we'd get to a venue and Thom would take himself off with his guitar to some corner and change the strings and be strumming away and getting ready for the soundcheck. And they'd put as much effort and enthusiasm into doing a song at the soundcheck as they would at a gig, which is admirable. Because when you're touring for a long time, you're fed up with music and you're just going through the motions. But you could see they were really honing the whole thing and working on their craft.

But he wasn't odd or rude or anything. If you chatted to him, he'd chat back and I'd have full-blown conversations with him but he wouldn't instigate a chat. He didn't seem like a, 'Let's have a chat over a cup of tea,' kind of bloke. He seemed quite reserved. I guess he was just shy. It's hard to think of someone who's a huge rock star and an icon to millions as shy, but I guess looking back he was just a shy, young guy who was just trying to get on with his life and write songs and play music as well as he could."

Ash says they couldn't help but be influenced by Thom and the rest of the band's dedication. "By the end of the tour, we were pretty much taking the lead from Radiohead, getting home, getting a good night's sleep, and then getting up and eating a good breakfast," he says. "Instead of busting open the tin of Tennent's Super in your anorak pocket! With Radiohead it was very much back to the hotel early. They used to take their instruments with them and start working on stuff. Jonny was always fiddling with the guitar and anything else. He had that sort of brain. He wanted to know how things worked and how he could get them to work so they'd suit him. I'd imagine he was up in his room taking the trouser press apart and getting it to work more efficiently. Or he'd have his guitar and he'd be writing the intros for the next twenty albums. They were always up early, always got breakfast, always at the venue before time. They were like the model band. At that time, being in the music industry was something you did while you were waiting to grow up, but they were different."

But Radiohead learned from the Frank And Walters, too. At a time when things didn't seem to be going according to plan, with their records not selling and EMI breathing down their necks, the successful gigs gave them a massive confidence boost. Frank And Walters also, perhaps, taught them the importance of relaxing every now and then. Certainly on later tours, they weren't always back to the hotel room straight after the gig to work on songs. And there was one thing about the Irish band that Radiohead would always appreciate. At a time when it was the norm for support bands to have to buy their way on to a tour, the Frank and Walters refused to take a penny.

"EMI got on to us saying, 'How much do you want for the tour?' says Ash, "and we'd never encountered that before, paying to get on to a tour, we were shocked, we thought there's nothing worse than a band having to pay to play. So we went, 'Jesus! Nothing! They're a great band, we don't want anything.' [People were] going 'Fucking idiots! You could get ten grand or fifteen grand for this!' We were like, 'No way.' It was nice, a couple of years later, I read an interview with them where they name-checked us and said that bands toured with them on merit, nobody ever had to pay to play on their tours. It was nice that a tiny bit of their inspiration for that decision came from us."

An indication of the way their audience had grown over the course of the tour came with the release of next single, 'Anyone Can Play Guitar'. It wasn't bad but it was no 'Creep' and yet it was much more successful, giving them their first Top 40 hit. It was a song that, lyrically, summed up Thom's already ambiguous attitude to the concept of rock stardom. He's complained in the past that it's been taken as an entirely sarcastic sentiment when, in fact, he meant it as a celebration of the guitar. But it seems to be both. "I do want to be in a band when I'm in heaven," he said in an interview, "it's the best thing you can do with your life." But he also said that, "rock 'n' roll just reminds me of people with personal hygiene problems who still like getting blow-jobs off complete strangers."

Just like 'Creep', 'Anyone Can Play Guitar' exhibited a simultaneous fascination with the beautiful people and the glamorous life, and a contempt born out of knowledge that he would never feel part of it. There was a small part of him that really did want to be Jim Morrison but, increasingly, it wasn't a part he had a lot of respect for.

Not long afterwards, the debut album *Pablo Honey* was released. It did pretty well too, peaking at 25 in the charts. But they still weren't shifting units in the way that EMI hoped. It didn't help that they insisted on releasing a single that wasn't on the album, 'Pop Is Dead'. It was their first real dash for independence and it wasn't a great success. They decided to produce it with their live sound engineer, rather than using, as Thom put it, "expensive producers". In consequence, it had a powerful, raw guitar sound but it was a little muddled. It sounded like it was something that Thom just needed to get off his chest. The lyrics were all about record labels killing pop by concentrating on their back-catalogues rather than new music. It was something he felt passionate about but the record buying public as whole probably didn't. It was a flop, causing an outbreak of gloom in the band.

"Nobody saw 'Creep' as a failure when it first came out," says Nigel. "The *Drill* EP went in at 101 and 'Creep' went in at 88 so it was like, 'Hey, we're twenty places higher than we were last time!' Nobody saw 'Creep' as a problem. The thing that deflated them and made the atmosphere get a bit darker was 'Pop Is Dead'. 'Anyone Can Play Guitar' went in at 35 or 38 I think but then 'Pop Is Dead' didn't make the Top 40. They did a tour in slightly bigger places and they weren't full. Everybody had expected 'Pop Is Dead' to do better than it did and so they booked them into bigger venues and there weren't quite so many people there and they all thought, 'This isn't quite as much fun!'"

To some insiders, it looked like there was a real risk that they would get dropped if things didn't improve but the man who signed them, EMI's Keith Wozencroft, denies that this was ever on the cards. "Parlophone and EMI generally were always known for sticking with their artists and growing over a long period," he says. "I don't believe that we would have dropped a band after one album, especially a band that were very good and had built a solid fan-base."

EMI could also have argued that they'd advised against releasing a single that wasn't on the album. It seemed like they were right but Radiohead's managers Chris and Bryce always had their eyes on the long-term. Paul Kolderie believes that their contribution to the band's success has been much underrated.

"The strategy that the managers were pursuing from the start was to hire an American producer and maybe focus a little bit more on America at the time," he says. "They went to America first and kind of worked it back that other way. The one thing I would say, and I think it's really important if you're going to write about Radiohead, is that the managers have been there from the beginning. When we first met them, Chris and Bryce drove me around and they told me their whole story of how they'd been in bands in the 1980s and they'd gone for the whole ride ... they were hip to the game. They weren't going to let Radiohead get screwed ... they were letting me know right away. It was kind of like parents letting me know that if I was going to take [their] little girl out, I'd better behave. I'd better do a good job!

Everybody says you've got to have a great drummer to have a great band, and you do, but you've also got to have a great manager. It's no accident that U2 have a really terrific, smart manager. Even The Beatles. Every band that's successful has somebody doing that job because if they don't, they're not going to make it. They're not going to have the direction and they're going to blow it. It's a marriage. Those guys couldn't have managed just anyone but Radiohead could not have done it on their own either."

But before anything happened in America, and while they were still despondent from the relative failure of 'Pop Is Dead', success came from an unexpected source. "Luckily that's exactly the time when 'Creep' got big in Israel," says Nigel, "so we went out there. And that was when it was still a really dangerous place to go. There was fierce airport security. Lots of people with guns on the streets. It was weird, you'd chat to teenagers at the shows afterwards and say, 'What have you got coming up?' and they'd say, 'Oh, I'm joining the army. I've got to do that for six months.'"

As it was such a small country, individual DJs had a great deal of power in Israel. When their equivalent of John Peel got hold of 'Creep' and started playing it all the time, it became a big hit. In Israel, all of a sudden, they were pop stars.

"I think the fact that very few people played gigs there helped," says Nigel. "All the gigs were sold out and we got treated really well. You can tell when a band gets successful because even the crew gets treated well. That came immediately after the 'Pop Is Dead' tour when everyone was down and [Israel] picked everybody up again. From there, there was a European tour and that went straight into a US tour. That was good for the band because it didn't give everybody a chance to dwell on 'Pop Is Dead' doing a bit shit. It was just a case of, 'More stuff to do, forget about that, carry on!'"

Before the first gig in Israel, they were approached by a fan asking if he could play the bass on 'Creep'. It was their first indication of a different kind of fan than they'd had before. They were taken aback but Colin cautiously let him take over at the soundcheck. He realised what it would have meant for him to be able to play bass on one of New Order's songs. That night there was an air of hysteria in the crowd before they even went onstage. When Thom leaned into the audience halfway through a song, he had clumps of hair pulled out by over-enthusiastic fans and his favourite bangle broken around his wrist. It was unlike anything they'd experienced in the UK. They had 1,200 people at their biggest gig and they were told that there would have been more but Israel's equivalent of Glastonbury was happening at the same time. 'Creep' eventually went to Number 1 in that territory and *Pablo Honey* peaked at Number 2. For Thom, it was simply proof that if people got to hear his songs then they would like them.

And Nigel agrees with Paul Kolderie that Radiohead's success overseas was more than just a stroke of good fortune. "I think Chris and Bryce were very good for them," he says. "They saw exactly what was happening and they thought, 'Right, we've got to really push in another territory now, because we've done everything we can in the UK. We've got to go elsewhere and try and make it happen there to convince Parlophone that it's worth doing another album. So after that they concentrated a lot of their time on America. It was only after 'Creep' was a hit there that they re-released it in England."

'Creep' arrived in America when a DJ on San Francisco's Live 105 radio station got hold of a copy on import and started playing it. The phones then lit up with more requests for the song and the station put it on heavy rotation. Within a few days, it had been picked up by other stations on the West Coast and on the highly influential KROQ station it was the second most requested song. This meant that their American record company, Capitol, got behind them in a far bigger way than EMI had in the UK but it also meant they expected far more. As far as they were concerned, there was no time to lose. Radiohead had to go out to the States straight away. From a gig in Paris they were driven to the ferry at Calais, then straight to Heathrow in London where they took a plane to New York. When they got there, they were astonished to be picked up in a white stretch limo with a bar in the back. At the Capitol Building itself, the staff were all wearing Radiohead T-shirts. From New York they then had to take a coach to Boston. When a completely shattered Thom arrived in his hotel at 7a.m. in the morning, he switched on MTV and there was 'Creep'.

All the attention, the praise and the hyperbole didn't come without a price. They were expected first to schmooze the executives of various retail outlets and radio stations. Then they had a packed schedule of interviews where Thom would be asked over and over again about the girl that he'd successfully forgotten about years ago. In the end, he just insisted that people should decide for themselves what the song was about. Amusingly, in one interview he anticipated music file sharing by about seven years when he joked: "What's vinyl? We're experimenting with fax machines at the moment. I think that people should sort of just be able to fax songs as well as listen to them. You should be able to plug your fax into your hi-fi."

At another interview with KRoq he was asked to sing a jingle about how "special" the radio station was to the tune of 'Creep'. When he refused the DJ twisted his arm by asking, 'You did actually sing on the song, right?' In the future, nobody would ask him to do anything quite so ridiculous but Thom gave in. It was one of many "never again" moments that they went through on that tour.

Most of their interviews were even less entertaining and the gigs weren't quite what they'd hoped for either. They were playing shows to a crowd who were only interested in one song. In retrospect, they've painted it as a grim experience and, in some ways it was, but it was also everything Thom had always wanted. Still, their marketing executive Carol Baxter later said, "I'll never make my bands do this again." But at the time Thom and the rest of the band did everything that was reasonably asked of them.

And Capitol knew what they were doing. MTV's decision to playlist the video was crucial and 'Creep's popularity rocketed. They were invited to play MTV's 'Beach Party' where they played the song while bikini-clad models jiggled behind them. It was, in a funny way, a highly appropriate setting for a song about feeling inadequate and resentful in the presence of beauty.

"I don't think the irony was lost on people," said Thom, "all these gorgeous bikinied girls shaking their mammary glands and we're playing 'Creep' and looking terrible."

Luckily "looking terrible" was all part of what being "that 'Creep' guy" meant. They were even invited on to the popular *Arsenio Hall* show. Backstage, before they went on, Thom was so nervous he was actually shaking, but he gave an extraordinary performance of the song, rasping the words and coming across like a hybrid of the Hunchback of Notre Dame and the Phantom of the Opera.

The fact that America had accepted them when it had rejected other bands such as Suede was a massive vindication. This was even more the case when they re-released 'Creep' in the UK and promptly had a Top Ten hit as the radio stations who'd ignored it the first time were forced to admit they'd been wrong. It seemed like the weaker they got the stronger 'Creep' got. They would finish touring the song in one territory only for it to become a hit in another. While 'Pop Is Dead' had sank without trace in the UK, *Pablo Honey* was racing towards eventual sales of over two million copies (much of them in the US). But the live shows, half the reason they were in the band, were becoming increasingly demoralising.

"There was a marked difference between the US and the UK," says Nigel, "which was that even though the audiences were smaller in the UK, everybody stayed for the entire gig, where as in America, certainly some of the co-headline tours, Radiohead would play 'Creep' halfway through the set and 100 or 150 people would go, 'Hey, 'Creep', I like that one,' and then they'd leave as soon as they'd played that song. They were a 'pop hit' band. They'd had the one big song and the follow-up in America didn't do as well as 'Creep' – they released 'Stop Whispering' but it didn't have the same impact as 'Creep', [so] there were quite a lot of people who only knew that one song."

The band always felt that their success in America at the time of 'Creep' was somewhat exaggerated in the press. "Things became polarised between us being extremely famous, megastars in America and utterly unknown in England," said Jonny in a TV interview. "It's somewhere between the two really."

They occasionally liked to point out that the first time 'Creep' was released in the UK, it ultimately went on to sell 20,000 copies over the course of their tour, which, while not a big hit, wasn't bad. It didn't quite justify the *Evening Standard*'s headline 'British Pop Unknowns Storm The USA."

THOM YORKE

The *Pablo Honey* tour lasted, in various guises, for the best part of two years and it almost broke them. For the first time since they'd been signed, they wondered whether it was all worth it. "Immediately towards the end of the *Pablo Honey* tour, it seemed like there was a little bit of fatigue and uncertainty about what to do next," Nigel says, "but I think all they needed was a break. I think the long history helps at that point. When you get to that kind of point of feeling angry and frustrated and thinking, 'Do I want to carry on with this?' if you've been in a band for six months you go, 'Bollocks, I'll get another band.' But if you've been in a band for eight years or whatever, there's a little bit more to lose."

The most frustrating thing about the *Pablo Honey* tour was that they had new songs, better songs, than the ones on their debut album and yet few people were interested. They'd had 'High And Dry' for ages and other songs were also falling into place.

"They'd been playing 'The Bends' from the 'Anyone Can Play Guitar' tour," says Nigel. "In fact they might have even been playing it on the 'Creep' tour. That was the earliest one they ever played. I hung around the studio when they were demo-ing 'High And Dry' and I thought it was a really great song. That was the point when Thom went, 'Now I just want to do what I want to do.' Whereas *Pablo Honey* was more like, it needs to be a bit grunge to fit in with what the industry expects. *The Bends* was like: 'No, I want to do it this way …'"

But, for a long time, nobody would give them a chance to do it their way. 'Creep' had created an image of the band – and of Thom in particular – that was almost more powerful than the reality. But if the success had its downside, in the end, its upside was much more significant. 'Creep' is still an incredible song. The problem with it now is that so much of its impact came from sheer shock value. It was a classic tune with an instant hook, perfectly tuned to the MTV era. This was captured by the famous Beavis and Butt-head sketch at the time when Beavis explained why the song needed "the bit that sucks" and, by inference, explained most of the great rock of the 1990s. With familiarity 'Creep' lost much of its impact, but go back to that extraordinary bit where Thom sings "Ruuuuuuuun!" and holds the note for so long that it sounds like he's going to explode … and be blown away all over again.

9

IRON LUNG

On August 27, 1993, Radiohead were due to play the Reading Festival. Instead Thom Yorke woke up with laryngitis, his voice reduced to a feeble croak. Rachel phoned up Chris and Bryce to tell them that he wouldn't be able to play, while he sat there gloomily plucking at his acoustic guitar, composing a new song. The melody that came out was characteristically pretty but the lyrics that followed were anything but. They were a bitter take on the last few months of Radiohead's career, tearing into 'Creep', the song that had saved them, and dubbing it with an unforgettable metaphor, 'My Iron Lung'.

It was an image Thom had stored in his head since he found a picture when he was at university of a child in an iron lung. These devices were respirators that were frequently used during the polio epidemics of the first half of the 20th Century. The unfortunate child would be placed inside a giant metal tube with only their head outside and a vacuum would be created inside the tube to cause the lungs to expand and suck in air. They saved lives but some people were stuck inside them for years.

In September 1993, when 'Creep' was re-released in the UK and Thom was fully recovered, Radiohead didn't even bother to stay in the country. They went back to America where Thom spent much of his time at the back of the tour bus working on songs. By now the band weren't talking to each other much. When he went back to 'My Iron Lung', Thom decided that the melody was much too pretty for the lyrics. With perverse glee, he added a second half to the song, which was as brutal and unrestrained as the words. It was, many people noted later, the same thing that Kurt Cobain had done with *In Utero* – mixing the sugar of his melodies with broken glass as if to deliberately sabotage any possibility of mainstream success.

At the end of the year, when Radiohead finally made it home for a sustained period for the first time in two years, Thom bought "the house that 'Creep' built" on the strength of the royalties that were now coming in. But he was shattered.

"As soon as you get any success, you disappear up your own arse and lose it forever," he said in an interview with Stuart Baillie of *NME*. "When I got back to Oxford, I was unbearable. You start to believe you're this sensitive artist who has to be alone, this melodramatic, tortured person, in order to create wonderful music. The absolute opposite is true. All these things happen to you anyway, you don't have to sit there and make them happen. Otherwise you're not a human being."

The pressure on Thom as "that 'Creep' guy" was very different to what the rest of the band experienced. "Ed and Colin and Phil have stayed refreshingly the same," says Nigel Powell, "because they've had less of the limelight, they've all dealt with it very well. They're all still as charming and humble as they need to be. Thom, maybe, his moods got slightly amplified by all the attention but it's not like his personality changed overnight."

Colin later described the period at the end of the *Pablo Honey* tour as a kind of "break down" rather than a "break up". They weren't falling out. It was just that after two years on the road there was nothing left to say.

They'd been waiting for months to get back into the studio but when they got off tour they were in no fit state to record. Luckily the success of *Pablo Honey* had bought them time. They were also able to call on the services of one of indie's key figures, producer John Leckie. He hadn't been that impressed with *Pablo Honey* but the demos they sent him of early songs like 'High And Dry' and 'The Bends' were a different matter. He was fresh from the gruelling, massively extended recording sessions for the Stone Roses' tardy second album but if he was looking forward to an easier challenge, it wasn't to be. At the end of February 1994, Radiohead went into RAK studios in west London but almost immediately things turned sour. They weren't listening to each other.

"We had one song that had loads of strings and heavy guitars. It was very epic and sounded like Guns N' Roses' 'November Rain'," Ed O'Brien said to Steve Malins of *Vox*. "By this time, Thom was trying to shut off from everything. There was a lot of pressure for us to make a loud, bombastic record and all I ever wanted to do was the exact opposite."

Initially, of the tracks that would eventually appear on the second album, they just had a demo version of 'High And Dry', which by then was stuck in a drawer somewhere, virtually forgotten about, and a very rough version of 'Nice Dream'.

"We were really scared of our instruments," Thom said in the same interview with *Vox*. "That might sound over-dramatic, but that's how it felt. It must have been tortuous to watch. I know it was very hard on John Leckie, who didn't know what the fuck was going on. We'd be going to him: 'So what do you think? What shall we do?' He was like: 'Well, I don't know, it's up to you. You can do what the fuck you like, just do it rather than sit there thinking about it.'"

Luckily for them, John Leckie had seen it all before. He'd worked with everybody from solo members of The Beatles to The Verve and he knew he just had to wait until they were ready. The record couldn't be forced.

"John Leckie seemed to be about the most relaxed human being you could meet," says Nigel Powell. "At the time I questioned what he did because every time I'd pop round, I saw him at RAK Studios and a couple of other places, and it seemed like the only thing he did was sit at the back of the control room … while this other, small, short-haired guy called Nigel Godrich (who at the time nobody knew) was doing all the work rushing around setting up mics. But now, looking back, I can see what John Leckie was doing. He was just keeping it chilled. He'd be sitting at the back going, 'Yeah, it sounds alright …' He was making sure the hammer wasn't down. He'd say, 'It sounds alright. Maybe we can do one more.' He was still driving the record on but he was trying to do it in the most relaxed way possible."

But the label certainly weren't relaxed. One executive supposedly left the studio after listening to what they'd come up with so far and raged, "Look, I don't intend to take some fucking prog rock album. What the fuck is going on?"

By contrast, EMI's Keith Wozencroft says now that it was always clear that *The Bends* was going to be a great record. "Songs like 'Street Spirit', 'Nice Dream', 'Fake Plastic Trees' etc were testament to that," he says. "I don't recall ever hearing any comments along those lines. Also, it wasn't a prog record anyway."

But, whether or not the label meant to pressurise them, there was a definite sense that they needed to produce another 'Creep'. John

Leckie says that EMI wanted them to write another hit single before they did anything else. "It kind of affected the first few weeks of recording," he said to *Melody Maker*. "Because every three or four days, the record company or the manager would turn up to hear these hit singles and all we'd done was got a drum sound or something." Thom ended up simply refusing to take the label's calls, causing even more concern, but John dealt with that as well.

"He viewed everything with a lack of importance," Thom said to Nick Kent of *Mojo* later. "And thank God he did! He's been doing it for so long he realised sometimes a producer is simply someone who just creates the right atmosphere for things to happen. In a way, he was like a caring uncle. He might see you as his little nephew who's in a right fucking mess – but he still lets you get on with it."

"He's a wonderful man," Thom also said in a TV interview. "When we went in to do this album, we were in a pretty bad state really, fragile to put it mildly, and he was able to make the studio a place conducive to work. A lot of producers tell you what to do and you scurry around and go, 'OK'. We'd run around the studio and go 'What do you think John?' and he'd go 'I don't know, you decide, you're the band! I'll tell you when you're going wrong.'"

But, in America, Capitol wondered if they'd already gone wrong. There were rumours that they wouldn't even release Radiohead's second album. It seemed like the band had had their day in the sun with 'Creep' and they might have run out of steam. The problem was that the lack of communication on tour continued into the studio. Thom needed somebody to bounce ideas off but the tension was crippling. He's described the decision-making process in Radiohead as, "like the UN – and I'm America" but this was one moment when the rest of the band rebelled. They couldn't take anymore.

At that point, they had a world tour booked. It had originally been intended to promote an album that they'd barely started recording. Thom wanted to cancel it and stay in the studio until they'd got things right but Jonny, Colin, Phil and Ed suggested that they go anyway. John Leckie agreed. It was clear they were getting nowhere. A couple of months break would do them good.

"Towards the end, we had all these tour obligations and I thought, 'Fuck it, no, I want to stay in the studio for three months', Thom said later. "Everyone said no, you've got to get out of here and they were absolutely right."

However, when they hit the road, the atmosphere became unbearable. Their friendship had always felt like an accident of circumstance. Initially they'd chosen to hang around with each other because they were musicians, not because they had much else in common. They'd always dealt with things in a very English way, holding back and swallowing their feelings. There were no arguments, there was no strife as Jonny told *B-Side* magazine. It was just that they'd forgotten that they used to be friends.

"'Strife' implies arguments and things being thrown," he said, "but it was worse than that. It was a very silent, cold thing, away from each other. No one was really talking to anyone, and we were just trying to get through the year … there were never rows or anything, which is worse in a way. Everyone withdrew away."

Halfway through the tour, in Mexico, something snapped. They hadn't been sleeping. There were twelve people crammed into a small tour bus. Thom had suddenly decided that they weren't a good live band anymore. Their first gig was in a tiny, filthy club that was very different to the venues they had been playing. It had a low stage with tables placed in front of it as a barrier between them and the small crowd. They had to clamber out of a small window at the back to get offstage. A few months before they would have found it an amusing, exciting experience, but now they were too tired, sick and bored of each other to take anymore.

"It all just came out," Thom said to Andy Richardson in *NME*. "Years and years of tension and not saying anything to each other, and basically all the things that had built up since we'd met each other, all came out in one day. We were spitting and fighting and crying and saying all the things that you don't want to talk about."

They could have broken up right then but instead everyone knew exactly where they were for the first time in years. At the end of the tour, they went into another studio, the Manor in Oxford, in the knowledge that everything that could be said had been said. The barriers were down and *suddenly* the record began to take shape. They realised that if they were getting upset about the way the record was going, it was only because they all cared about it so much.

"If someone disagrees with Thom, he only gets upset because he trusts them," said Jonny much later in a radio interview. "It's not like he's saying, 'No, it's great, I'm not listening to you.' He goes,

THOM YORKE

'Maybe you're right, maybe it is no good.' It's upsetting. Sometimes your judgement's wrong and sometimes it's right."

10

THE BENDS

Their decision to go back out on the road was vindicated by a May 1994 performance at the Astoria in London. Most of the fans would have been expecting a run-through of *Pablo Honey* but what they got was over half of *The Bends*. It's odd now to think of Radiohead playing a show where 'Street Spirit' would get a less rapturous reception than 'Pop Is Dead', but in the DVD of the show, the audience simply look stunned at what they're hearing. They wouldn't hear most of the songs again for almost a year until *The Bends* finally came out.

"This is yet another new song," Thom half-smirks before introducing an astonishing version of 'My Iron Lung'. It was so good that when they listened to it afterwards they decided that they weren't going to top it in the studio. Thom just re-recorded his vocal and they kept the rest for the EP and the album.

"They always seem to work their best when there's a certain moment when they all get into the flow," says Nigel. "It just seems to take them a long time to get there. Once they'd got 'My Iron Lung' down suddenly they were like, 'Hey, maybe we can do this,' and it all went quite quickly from there I think."

What at the time seemed like an agonising combination of paranoia and creative paralysis would turn out to be merely Radiohead's normal working method. This would only become clear when they tried to record subsequent albums. *The Bends* was the first time they'd had absolute freedom to do whatever they wanted. It turned out that was a lot harder than they'd thought. It was perhaps their hardest album to record because they had no idea what to expect. Revealingly, Thom once named a painter called Alan Davie as one of his heroes because, he said, Davie wasn't afraid to admit that art could be a frustrating, gruelling experience.

"He always talks about how he finds creating a really painful experience," he said to *NME*. "How he really despises himself when he's creating and how it always takes him ages, how sometimes he won't think of anything good for six months and then it all comes pouring out; I really identify with all that."

The second breakthrough on the album came when they went back into the studio to record 'Fake Plastic Trees'. It was a day, Phil said later, when they just couldn't get anything done. Characteristically Thom put it in more melodramatic terms. "I had a complete meltdown," he said. John Leckie suggested they take a break to go and see Jeff Buckley at the Garage in Highbury, London.

Inspired by Buckley's extraordinary vocals, Thom went back to the song afterwards and came out with the beautiful, keening falsetto that's on the album. After months of indecision and paralysis, most of *The Bends* then came together in one or two takes. When they knew what they were trying to achieve, it suddenly seemed much easier. Opening track 'Planet Telex' was recorded with Thom, drunk, spitting out his vocal while crouched in a corner, barely able to stand. 'Bones' was captured in one go on the same day as 'The Bends'. 'Black Star' was recorded while John Leckie was away with, according to Jonny, "a real 'teacher's away' larkiness" to it. From being barely able to pick up their instruments, suddenly they were recording a song a day. "I went into The Manor and did the whole fucking album in two weeks – having realised what we were doing wrong," Thom said later. "That easy, but sickening!"

In retrospect, the moment they knew they'd really done something special was when they recorded *The Bends*' last track, 'Street Spirit (Fade Out)'. It was initially another day of going round in circles and feeling that nothing was going to happen. Then suddenly the melody came pouring out. Those were the moments, Thom said later, that justified everything else. Those two or three minutes of complete happiness when the song came together made the long nights on the tour bus and the weeks of studio madness worthwhile.

At that point, they also went back to 'High And Dry'. Thom said later that he had his "arm twisted" to put it on the album. Perhaps somebody at the record label thought that they needed something simple and straightforward as a counterpoint to songs like 'My Iron Lung'. The band weren't convinced but, for the only time on *The Bends*, they gave in, much to Thom's consternation. He was perhaps put off the song later by the fact that it provided a blueprint for the many bands, such as early Muse and Coldplay, who were openly influenced by this period of Radiohead. But, after the magnificent

'Fake Plastic Trees', it has one of the best lyrics on the record, seemingly a thinly veiled band biography disguised as the story of a dare-devil motorcyclist.

"It's about Evel Knievel, but not really," Thom said in a TV interview when it was released as a single. "One of the first things I noticed when we started doing this was that people around us, other bands and ourselves, were changing into complete idiots, losing their friends and losing their connection with reality very fast. I saw us doing that."

This doesn't sound quite right. When he wrote 'High And Dry', Thom was still at university and Radiohead didn't even exist. In an interview with *Billboard*, he admitted that, "the words were originally about some loony girl I was going out with, but after a while, they got mixed up with ideas about success and failure."

But then many of the lyrics on the album seem eerily prescient. 'The Bends' sounds like it's an autobiographical description of what happened when 'Creep' took off. It's clearly an allegory about a band who rose too quickly and became ill from the pressure. Except that, too, was written long before they'd ever had any kind of success, long before 'Creep' made them stars in America.

"I had a four-track of it when we were doing *Pablo Honey*," Thom said in a 1995 TV interview. "I don't know why we didn't do it really ... I poured all this rubbish out into the song. Then it all started happening, which was a bit odd. I was completely taking the piss when I wrote it. Then the joke started wearing a bit thin."

By the time *The Bends* was finished Thom felt like they were back on track. "Somewhere along the line," he said in another interview, "the enjoyment went out of what we were doing and it all got a bit silly. But by the time we finished *The Bends* we thought, 'Yeah, this is why we started this."

Another exciting moment came when they added strings to 'Fake Plastic Trees'. It was the first time they'd ever recorded with other musicians and they went for the unorthodox combination of Caroline Lavelle, the cellist who'd played the haunting strings on Massive Attack's 'Unfinished Sympathy' and John Matthias, the young violinist Thom had met at Exeter.

"It was the first time on that album that they'd used other musicians," John Matthias told this author. "And I think that helped make it real for them in some way. I got the impression that it brought the process to life." John has since gone on to make highly regarded music in his own right but at the time he was aware not everybody was delighted that Thom wanted to employ an old college friend.

"When they arrived I realised we had this violinist who was a student from Oxford, and probably the best cello player in the world," said John Leckie in a *Melody Maker* interview. "So there was a slightly uneasy atmosphere to it."

"I wasn't a student," says John, "but I wasn't a regular professional and she [Caroline Lavelle] was brilliant. She was an amazing musician. Thom had to stick his neck out to get me on board, I think. I think he had to argue with EMI. He said, 'No, I want John Matthias.' Which was pretty brave at the time for someone in his position. I was a completely unknown quantity. He probably had to argue with Jonny as well I should think! I was really appreciative of that."

On the morning of the session, John met Thom at an exhibition by photographer Annie Leibovitz. He was struck by how excited and upbeat the singer was at that point. There was no sign of the angst or confusion that had been the hallmark of earlier sessions.

"I don't know what the atmosphere had been like before," John says, "but I got the impression that the sessions hadn't been easy and there was a lot of pressure on them to get the album right. But certainly they were very excited about it. There were some tracks that just ended up as B-sides that sounded great."

However, just as with *Pablo Honey*, the pain wasn't over yet. They still needed to get the record mixed. At first, the mixes they were hearing just didn't quite sound right. The band and the record label weren't at all sure what to do. Then somebody had the counter-intuitive idea of calling *Pablo Honey* producers Paul and Sean to see if they'd do it. It was a controversial decision because, although they liked the two Americans, the process of mixing *Pablo Honey* had not been smooth either. Remember, towards the end of their relationship things had got a little tense. It was only in retrospect that they started to think they might have done a pretty good job, considering the material they had to work with.

"It was one of those things where they were kind of thinking, *What the fuck, who can do this?*" says Paul, "and somebody raised his hand, I don't know who it was, and said, 'Well, these guys mixed the million-selling hit that we had. Let's call 'em'. I think they were just taking a shot … they were just trying anything they could think of and it just happened to work pretty well.

The first song we mixed was 'Bones' and we went, 'Yeah, this is like the Pixies' and mixed it like that and sent it back to them and it was a home run. They started pitching them at us and we started hitting them back. The whole process took a while and several of them were done several times. 'Just' we must have mixed five times. The band … would say, 'No, try again, this part should be louder, or whatever.' So we'd send it to them again and pretty soon they were all in the 'Done' pile. It was over a long period of time and we were doing other things." Some of John Leckie's mixes were also used – for example, 'Street Spirit' and 'Iron Lung' – and so the record ultimately came to have a fine balance.

Regardless of their own part in the process, Sean admits that Leckie's production skills and those of his (then unknown) engineer, Nigel Godrich, were one of the key factors in the success of *The Bends*.

"One of the reasons working on *The Bends* was such a thrill and a pleasure was that the tracks were immaculately organised," he says. "I think to an extent Paul and I might have got a little too much credit for mixing it, because the tracks were just there. It was just 24-tracks. No fucking Pro-Tools and we cranked it through our board and said to ourselves, 'Let's make this sound like Van Halen!' I'm being a little facetious when I say that, but I think they did want to showcase the guitar power that they had. When they started to work with Nigel they said, 'We don't want all that guitar stuff anymore.' Which is great. *The Bends* is the penultimate Radiohead, guitar-band album. That's how Paul and I entered the situation because we had this skill of recording loud rock 'n' roll guitars."

At one point during the mixing process, Ed flew out to America on holiday and while he was there he visited Sean and Paul's Fort Apache studios. They were shocked when he told them how close they'd come to losing it while making the record. "They nearly packed it in making *The Bends*," says Paul. "The way Ed described it to me was that, 'We thought we'd made the worst record. We had a chance and we lost it.'" "There was that panic," admitted Jonny later, "when we thought, 'oh no, we're rubbish after all, our music's shite! It's a disaster."

"They went through that thing that's so prevalent in the studio where the thing you didn't pay any attention to turns out good," says Paul. "The harder you try the worst it gets. *Because* they truly believed they'd lost it, they won. They truly believed it. They weren't just like, 'Maybe we've fucked it up?' They were like, 'We have screwed it up and lost. We're over. Radiohead is finished.' Right then the mixes started coming back from us in America and they were like, 'Wait a minute – maybe it's good!' And everybody started pounding each other on the back going, 'This is good!' And everything changed. But they really got so far down. They really came close to breaking up. The fact that record came out as good as it did and did as well as it did is a miracle. It's similar to the miracle of 'Creep' – how the hell did that come out when the rest of what they did was still forming? The real important story of the band is how they fought their way out of that trap."

Although Sean was joking when he said they wanted it to sound like Van Halen, the album undoubtedly rocks. Paul thinks that *The Bends* is defined by the fact that many of the songs were written when their primary means of winning new fans was simply by playing live. They needed an album of songs that would work well in that context. They wanted to redefine stadium rock from something bloated and vacuous to something intimate and warm.

"I think it's because they were in a cycle of touring and playing and they wanted to really kill people," he says. "They wanted to hit them hard. A song like 'The Bends' – Thom would never write a song like that today. That kind of heraldic, anthemic guitar part. He wouldn't have a need for that. But because they were out there playing [live] they needed ammunition. Some of those songs, I think, it was Thom saying, 'Well, if I've got to drag my body round the world and try and grab people's attention, I've got to have a body of songs that's slamming.'"

When they got the mixes back for the first time, Thom was convinced he'd got exactly that. For the first time since they were kids, he and Jonny listened to the finished work over and over again. They'd hardly ever listened to *Pablo Honey* after recording it, but this one he knew was good. It was *really* good.

However, when the new material from the second album – *The Bends* – was released, it was met with an initially disappointing reaction. First of all they released the *My Iron Lung* EP and, just as they had with 'Creep', radio programmers took one listen and said a definite 'No'. They'd listen to the first two minutes, nod happily along to the gentle melody and then abruptly switch it off as it exploded into the warped, violent guitar assault of the last two minutes. "I wrote the verse," Thom said in a TV interview, "and thought, *That's great, that's beautiful*, so we just had to screw it up by putting the other bit in." He had intended it to make people forget 'Creep' but it didn't quite work out that way.

"There was one press junket they did when 'Iron Lung' came out, [and] Thom and Jonny flew out to the US do a live show," says Paul Kolderie. "I was in the truck with them because I was friends with the DJ and the woman said, before we went on, 'Is there anything you want to talk about or not talk about,' and Thom said, 'Whatever you do, don't talk about 'Creep', I don't want to play it tonight, I want to play our new stuff.' So she goes 'OK'. Then the interview starts and the first thing she does is say to the crowd watching us outside, 'Hey, they say they're not going to play 'Creep' tonight! What's up with that, people?' So of course everybody goes 'Boooo! Fuck you!' Thom just went completely white. First he turned red then he turned white. Then he goes, 'I've got to get out of here!' So he jumped up and ran out of the interview. Me and Jonny finished the interview but it was one of the things where you go, 'We just talked about this! What, you think that's a scoop or something?' He was completely pissed but he ended up giving a really good show. It sort of energised him in a strange way, I don't blame him. Different people might have dealt with it in a different way but it was Thom's way to just run out and go, 'Agghhhhh'. But it worked for him."

"The main thing that we wanted to do was not repeat ourselves," Thom said in a TV interview. "It would have made certain people very happy if we'd done twelve versions of 'that song' but by that point we'd really had enough. Even if we'd wanted to, we can't repeat ourselves."

This was the point when many 'Creep' fans started to disappear but a new breed of Radiohead fan was slowly replacing them. Despite muted radio support, sales of the *My Iron Lung* EP were better than the worried record label had expected and it became clear that, even without the backing of the radio or much of the press, they had a loyal fan base. It was an important boost after an extraordinary, confusing couple of years and it helped fire them up for the release of *The Bends*.

11

COMING UP FOR AIR

Radiohead's second album bears none of the signs of being recorded over such a long period of time. It's as taut and powerful as a clenched fist. Despite its recurring themes of sickness and physical decay, it exudes all the energy of the great live band they'd become.

"The whole concept of *The Bends* goes back to 'My Iron Lung' and that weird breathing thing," says Paul. "I don't think he meant to do a concept album but in a way he kind of did. It's about claustrophobia and feeling hemmed in and unable to breathe."

Songs such as 'The Bends', 'Fake Plastic Trees', 'Bones', 'High And Dry' and 'My Iron Lung' could be seen as throwbacks to Thom's childhood hatred of hospitals, but he would always angrily deny that the record was autobiographical.

"It's not my fucking day-to-day," he said in a *Melody Maker* interview. "It's not my life. These lyrics aren't self-fulfilling. *The Bends* isn't my confessional. And I don't want it used as an aid to stupidity and fucking wittery. It's not an excuse to wallow. I don't want to know about your depression – if you write to me, I will write back angrily telling you not to give into all that shit."

He's always insisted that many of his lyrics are written in a spirit of sarcasm or outright humour. "The biggest battle I have at the moment," he said in a late 1990s TV interview, "is to persuade people that a lot of the lyrics I write are very funny."

At the time, many people might have gone along with Colin's wry response to this: "Funny peculiar – not funny ha ha". But undoubtedly there is humour in many of Thom's best lyrics on the record. Even 'My Iron Lung' is obviously blackly comic. Not many people would have the brazen ingratitude to slag off their biggest hit in such a way. Thom has the ability of many creative people to simultaneously feel an emotion and to mock it.

This was an ability he shared with his old college friend Dan Rickwood. Dan's art, too, often dealt with serious subjects by making them absurd. At university he was regarded as "a good laugh" by friends and his artwork had a similarly spiky sense of humour. Thom hadn't been happy with EMI's early decisions on their record sleeves and therefore when they came to do the *My Iron Lung* EP, he gave Dan a call.

"Radiohead were unhappy with the amount of money they'd had to pay for design," says John Matthias. "[Before now] it was music industry people trying to be grungey. It was only really with the 'My Iron Lung' EP that they started becoming much more autonomous. I think when they first got signed they did what they were told and it was a bit like being at school. They gradually realised that EMI didn't know everything; they didn't know what Radiohead wanted to do. It was a very gradual movement away from them in a sense. The realisation that they were actually in control of their own stuff."

This was when they started to make decisions about more than just the music. They'd been disappointed with the artwork and the videos as well as the way they were promoted generally. The cover of *The Bends* then, was the first album that came under a broader aesthetic of which Dan – now working under the name Stanley Donwood – was very much a part. It featured a doll that Oxford hospital The John Radcliffe used for resuscitation practice. Thom and Dan liked the way its mouth lolled open. It was hard to tell whether it was in ecstasy or in agony, the perfect Radiohead image.

From then on the artwork and the music would be tied together as closely as possible. Often Dan would join the band in the recording studio, coming up with ideas as he listened to them play. "He's either in a little room adjacent or above us in the mezzanine, or in the shed at the bottom of the gully," said Ed O'Brien to *AV Club*. "He's always with us, and we need him in that creative process. Not just for his artwork, but because he'll say, 'I know nothing about music, but that was fucking brilliant!'"

When *The Bends* was released, most critics thought it was brilliant, too. It received rave reviews in the two main music papers, *NME* and *Melody Maker*, and later on appeared in numerous 'Album Of The Year' lists. Despite this, in 1995, Thom's relationship with the press, never exactly warm, hit a new low. The first bruising encounter had come in 1992 with an early live review in *NME*. Writer Keith Cameron famously described them as a, "a lily-livered excuse for a rock band." This was just his opinion but the knife was twisted by a montage of unflattering pictures of Thom captioned:

"Uglee – Oh yeah!"

They could cope with that. They even took the "lily-livered excuse for a rock band" moniker on board as a kind of ironic mission statement. Then, in March 1995, Thom – who'd always been a vociferous reader of the music press – was shocked to see a *Melody Maker* feature that asked its readers whether he was likely to be the next great rock casualty after Kurt Cobain and Richey Manic (then missing for just a month).

"I stopped reading the press when they printed I was going to top myself," Thom said to *NME* at the end of that year. "And my girlfriend rings me up, really, really upset, saying, 'What's all this, what have you been saying?' You know, that's when I stopped reading it. That was enough for me."

In reality, writers The Stud Brothers didn't say that he was going to top himself. Buried in the text was the line, "Thom Yorke, 26, is already marked for destruction. But Thom doesn't see it like that. And frankly, neither do we." Their piece was a deliberately provocative attempt to look at the unfortunate obsession of rock fans and the media with martyrs like Richey and Kurt. Unfortunately any subtlety that the piece might have had was overshadowed by the line below the heading which described Thom as, "a man who will soon know the price of fame, and who already knows the cost of being born ugly."

The music press's obsession with Thom's supposed "ugliness" was always rather vicious. By "ugly" they just meant that one of his eyes didn't open properly. That kind of gratuitous abuse was the real "price of fame."

In fact *The Bends* came out at a time when the music scene was moving away from the darkness of albums like *In Utero* or the Manic Street Preachers' bleak classic *The Holy Bible*. The big albums of the era were Blur's *Parklife* and Oasis's *Definitely Maybe*. They had an upbeat, optimistic sound, which was far removed from *The Bends*. Still, at least people weren't talking about the fact that they didn't always play 'Creep' anymore. Their decision to – temporarily at least – drop it from their live sets, no longer seemed like the act of precious prima donnas.

"It might have seemed [like that] at the time," says Paul, "but then you realise later on that it's just having the courage of your convictions. It was like, 'We've got to get past this!'"

And get past it they did. And they were still as ambitious as ever. Following the release of *The Bends*, they headed back to America for an astonishing *five* tours. When asked why they did it, Thom said, "Don't fucking ask me, it wasn't my idea!" In the USA, *The Bends* was a definite flop in comparison with *Pablo Honey* for the first couple of months, yet they were determined to prove themselves all over again. In the summer of 1995, they had their best chance when REM invited them on tour. It had been a running joke that the only bands they would support were U2 or REM. When they got the call from Michael Stipe's band, Thom couldn't believe it. Stipe had been one of his biggest heroes since he was at school.

"I was absolutely terrified of meeting him," he said later, "because I projected so much stuff onto him when I was a kid." But when they met it was Michael who was more effusive. "I'm really glad you could do this," he told Thom. "I'm a very big fan." Thom was stupefied. "I've never believed in hero worship," he wrote in his tour diary, "but I have to admit to myself that I'm fighting for breath."

REM acted like a crash course in 'how to be a big band' to Thom. He was astonished at how good they were at schmoozing without losing the plot. "It seems you have to be nice to people forever," he mused. "I may as well get used to my cracked smile."

But it didn't take long before he realised that REM were just ordinary people. It helped him realise what other people felt when they approached him for an autograph. "Now Michael and I have quite a good relationship," he said to Alex Ross in the *New Yorker*. "Making friends with your idol makes you realise how fucking important it is to stay on this side and never go to that side."

It helped that REM were so supportive. Michael Stipe declared one night on tour that Radiohead were so good "it's frightening". On another date, Thom was mortified when a girl approached their table in a restaurant when the two bands were eating and asked for his autograph and not the REM front man's.

He'd never liked supporting other bands as much as playing headline shows. He kept having to tell himself that he couldn't expect the same reaction from the audience. As long as they were facing the right direction and they "had their eyes open" it was OK. But the REM tour was different. Everything seemed to be going well. After one show in Norway, he played the rest of the band a new demo he'd written on the acoustic guitar. It was called, he said in a tour diary at the time, 'No Surprises Please'. Colin, he reported, "went nuts."

By then the sheer effort they were making was starting to pay off. *The Bends* eventually went Top Ten in the UK and was selling steadily, by word of mouth, around the world. It was one of those albums that many people didn't get at first, yet it sounded better with every listen. Even Paul and Sean admit that they didn't realise what a great album it was initially.

"When we got the tracks, they were well-recorded but it was one of those things where you're so close to it that you don't really get it," says Paul. "I thought it was good. I thought it was a step forward. I didn't realise how big a step forward it was until I saw that record go out and work its way into the culture. 'Creep' was a hit but it was one of those hits where the first time you hear it you're like, 'Wow, that's crazy,' but after a few times you don't want to hear it again. I got to the point where I didn't want to hear it again. But *The Bends*, when it came out and had worked its way into the culture for about a year, was one of the most successful records I'd ever worked on because it was just everywhere. You'd go to a party, you'd go to a club, you'd go to a restaurant, every party you'd go to it'd be playing because it was the record that everybody could agree was good."

When *The Bends* came out, a small hardcore of fans rushed out and bought it straight away. Radiohead already had a fan base for whom it didn't matter whether their songs got played on the radio, or their videos appeared on TV. They would search out and buy everything that the band put out. "The album came out and within two days everyone knew all the words of all the songs," said Thom in a 1995 TV interview. "That's why we do it, it's wonderful."

A year later, that hardcore was much, much bigger. The bedrock of support they now had made it possible for them to go on and be the experimental band that they were for the next ten years and more, without having to worry about what the industry or the media would think.

But towards the end of the last tour following the album, they all just wanted to go home. They were enjoying the live shows again but were finding the promotional treadmill draining. Some interviewers still knew little about them except that they were "that 'Creep' band".

Luckily there was a much easier way of promoting their music. They'd always been highly ambivalent about music videos. Thom didn't like the fact that they were blatantly just adverts. On MTV, 'High And Dry' would be followed by Coca Cola and Nike and there seemed little difference between them. But one great video could easily do the work of a year-long tour in terms of promoting the record. When they came to promote *The Bends*, they seemed to accept this. Arguably the first in a long list of great Radiohead videos was 'Fake Plastic Trees', a surreal vision set in a supermarket where Thom and the rest of the band were pushed around in shopping trolleys. It was the first single to be released in the States (the second in the UK where 'High And Dry' appeared first) and the video had a big impact on MTV. But it was the video for the third single, 'Just' that gave *The Bends* a massive boost when it appeared.

It was filmed outside Liverpool Street Station first thing in the morning and featured an apparently distressed commuter giving up, lying down in the street and refusing to move. To the consternation of passers-by, he refuses to tell them what's wrong. When he finally gives in at the end of the video and tells them, they all lie down with him. It was shocking, clever and funny. Everything that Radiohead was about.

"The idea for the video was originally going to be for my next short film," the video's director Jamie Thraves explained to this author. "As I was listening to the song over and over, trying to come up with an idea, I was also thinking about my latest short, I was definitely treating the two things as separate entities but the song started to creep into my film and vice versa, then suddenly they fused together, it was a very exciting moment. Radiohead were brilliant and very supportive, they took a risk with me, they gave me complete freedom to make the video I wanted."

This was the way Radiohead always worked. They treated other artists as creative equals. For Jamie Thraves it was a fantastic experience but, in some ways, the success of his video was a mixed blessing. It made his reputation but it also meant that, for years afterwards, he would be asked what the man says at the end of the song. Many people have suggested that the video doesn't have any kind of 'meaning' as such but Jamie denies this.

"The truth is I actually do have something the man said," he says. "I don't think the video would work without there being something.

I've never told anyone, not even my wife. From the get-go the idea always included the subtraction of the man's last words creating a conundrum, some characters are undone because of their desire to know the unknown and anyone who watches the video is taunted by that same desire. I did not imagine the video generating the speculation it has though. The funny thing is, I'm actually quite bad at keeping secrets; I usually blurt things out without meaning to. The truth is I'd like to reveal the answer because I'd like to share it, it's a burden of sorts, but I know that if I reveal the answer the video would be dust, so I have no choice, it's almost a curse really. I feel like Patrick McGoohan in *The Prisoner*. The reaction to the video was brilliant afterwards. People continue to ask me what the man says at the end which amaze me. I went through a small phase of getting a bit annoyed but I don't mind anymore, I quite like it, I have my rehearsed lines, 'Don't make me tell you, you don't want to know, please believe me.'"

And, as always, if Thom believed in something he was prepared to go all the way to make it work. On the day of the set, despite the band having a supporting role in their own video, they threw themselves into it with abandon.

"Everyone talks about the man and what he says, or doesn't say, in this video," says Jamie. "Very few people actually discuss how great a performance it was from the band and Thom in particular. Radiohead performed the complete track a 100 times over but they always kept it fresh and exciting each time. The band had all agreed that they were really going to go for it. Thom had just started doing his twitchy psycho thing at a few live gigs, they wanted to commit it to celluloid, it was mesmerising to watch. It was a 360° set; there was only room for the cameraman, grip and focus puller so I tended to watch everything on a monitor outside the room. Every time the song ended, no one said anything for a second or two, it rendered everyone speechless. When I walked into the set, I remember there would be this strange kind of charge in the air and there'd be Thom still twitching."

This may have been part of his problem with the whole concept of music videos. He resented putting so much effort and energy into what he saw as essentially another branch of a sales job. But Radiohead's best videos were works of art in their own right. Jamie still won't reveal what the man said and apparently Radiohead have agreed to keep the secret, too. All he will say is that "lip reading won't help you."

Gradually, bit by bit, Radiohead were becoming as big as they were at the peak of 'Creep's success. *The Bends* ultimately went gold worldwide and, just as they had with 'Creep', the band found themselves in the bizarre situation of being invited, albeit cautiously, into the mainstream. One particularly strange experience was being asked to play teen pop magazine *Smash Hits*' 'Poll Winners Party'. Naturally, with an audience of young children and their anxiously watching parents, they chose to play the raucous, disturbing 'My Iron Lung'. "Little children were crying," said Thom, "and you should have seen some of the parents, it was wicked! It was great. I was really proud we did it."

A year after *The Bends* came out, it went back into the Top Ten in the UK for no obvious reason. It was the definitive word-of-mouth success. But one problem with Radiohead's slow, gradual progress was that it meant they kept touring. There were always new fans who wanted to see them. During the last months of the tour, they desperately wanted to go home but as soon as they did they found it difficult to adjust. It was difficult to return to reality when Thom got home.

"A lot of it's down to the fact that towards the end of a tour, it's just drink yourself stupid all the time," he said to *Select* magazine. "And then you go home and carry on. 'Wahey! The end of the tour's coming up. Wahey! The tour's finished!' It just carries on, and you don't really know what to do afterwards."

He occasionally regretted the fact that, early on in their career, they'd played up to the middle-class, tea drinking image. He knew it wasn't an accurate representation of what they were like. Most of the lyrics of *The Bends*, Thom said later, were written when he was drunk at the back of the tour bus during the long, post-*Pablo Honey* tour when nothing seemed to make sense.

"The reality is that we were probably doing as many drugs as everybody else," he said in an interview with *Vox*. "I wouldn't go on a chat show and talk about it, because it's purely recreational. I love getting stoned, it's the best thing in the fucking world."

They would sometimes record while stoned, which could be helpful, but which also, perhaps, contributed to their painfully slow progress and occasional outbreaks of paranoia. When they came to record their next album, the revered classic *OK Computer*, any additional source of paranoia was the last thing they needed.

12

OK COMPUTER

In 1996, when they started working on their third album, *OK Computer*, Thom had been doing Radiohead as a 'full-time job' for five years. It sometimes made him feel like he was losing touch with the real world. For large chunks of the year he found himself in an environment, on tour or while carrying out promotional duties, where he felt like a salesman or a politician. Even when he got home, he sometimes had to remind his friends that he was the same person. And, sometimes, they had to remind him. These were the experiences, combined with the 20th Century's background drone of computers, TV and radio – what he called "fridge buzz" – that would help shape the next album.

Radiohead started by promising themselves that, whatever else happened, they would do things differently this time. There would be no long, sterile sessions stuck in a recording studio glaring at each other. They wouldn't go running to the producer every time they ran out of ideas. John Leckie had taught them that a producer wasn't there to tell them what they should or should not do. They had to work things out for themselves.

"One of the things I'm eternally grateful for," said Thom in a TV interview, "is that he made it so the studio no longer seemed like some kind of science lab. John took all the mystery out of recording and made it something you could enjoy, just like playing."

What they needed, they thought, was somebody who knew how to press the right buttons. In Nigel Godrich, the engineer from *The Bends* sessions, they'd found just the right person. He'd become a friend during the long, fraught time at RAK and The Manor. He was the same age as them so they didn't see him as an authority figure. Having him around would remove the temptation to ask somebody else what they should do. Also, their most enjoyable experiences during *The Bends* sessions had come when the pressure was off and they were recording B-sides. One of those tracks, 'Black Star', was so good that it made the final cut of *The Bends*.

Dragged out of bed to sing at Courtyard Studios in 1992.
Ian Patrick/Retna

Thom and Jonny prepare to 'prove themselves' at Courtyard.
Ian Patrick/Retna

Thom, live in 1993.
Ian Patrick/Retna

'I don't belong here!' – Jonny, Colin and Thom at the 1994 *NME* Brat Awards.
Steve Double/Retna

'Ruuuuuuuuuuun!!!' Thom at the Reading Festival, 1994.
Brian Rasic/Rex Features

Preparing to lose another bangle, live in 1994.
Hayley Madden/Rex Features

Rocking out in Germany, 1995.
Brian Rasic/Rex Features

Radiohead 'High And Dry' on *Later With Jools Holland* in 1995.
Niels Andre Csillag/Rex Features

Considering changing the name to Rain-io-head at T In The Park, 1996.
Sutton-Hibbert/Rex Features

Radiohead in 1997: Ed, Phil, Thom, Colin and Jonny.
Roger Sargent/Rex Features

Thom, inspired, at the Free Tibet Concert in New York, June 7, 1997.
Jay Blakesberg/Retna

Staring into the void at Glastonbury, 1997
Hayley Madden/Rex Features

Taking a break in New York, 2003.
Greg Allen / Rex Features

Thom says no to the 'Star Wars' missile defence system
in North Yorkshire, September 25, 1994.
Sarahphotogirl / WireImage

Thom gets coy for Rosanna Arquette's *All We Are Saying* documentary in 2005.
Everett Collection/Rex Features

Yes it is annoying ... he sings, plays guitar and piano.
Malahide Castle, Dublin, Ireland, June 6, 2008.
Kim Haughton/Rex Features

Nigel Godrich also shared Radiohead's antipathy towards studios. "I hate studios myself," he said in an interview on his website (www.nigelgodrich.com). "The idea of going somewhere where you know 200 million people have done the same thing – it's like using a public toilet. You don't feel like it's your space."

They really thought that if they just avoided the elementary mistakes that they'd made with *Pablo Honey* and *The Bends*, then the next album could be a much less painful experience. They'd already had a taste of how simple recording could be when they came to do 'Lucky' for the Bosnian War Child charity record *Help*.

They'd been playing it for months on tour and, when they were asked to contribute a song, Jonny suggested it. Thom wasn't sure. He wasn't a fan of many of the other bands on the *Help* album and he didn't like the back-patting element that's always present with charity records.

"We did it because we were asked to do it and because Ed studied the Balkans," he said. "We just felt it was a good idea to just make the gesture. We realised that there would be a lot of back-patting but we knew it wasn't going to end up like *Live Aid*. To be honest, we were really itching to record the song anyway and we just didn't see why we shouldn't put it on this record."

When they went into the studio with Nigel, they were conscious that they didn't have long. The idea of the charity album was that every song would be recorded and mixed in one day. It didn't seem like a massive task. When they were on a roll, as the song 'Lucky' put it, they were perfectly capable of blasting songs out. But when they got there, they found that the first part of the day was taken up with talking to press and TV. Thom kept looking at his watch, thinking anxiously to himself, *Erm, shouldn't we be making this song at some point?*

But, when they came to do it, it was almost effortless. The song was what you might call one of Thom's many "crash ballads", the story of somebody crawling out of the wreckage of an aeroplane, and it just came pouring out. "It just happened," he said, "writing and recording it, there was no time, no conscious effort."

To be able to record a song like that, without the stress of constant revision and critical analysis, was a rare joy for Radiohead. By this point, Thom was looking back to their earliest days of recording, just him and Jonny and a four-track, as some of his happiest moments.

Although in those days he'd dreamt about being given the keys to a professional studio, he hadn't realised how debilitating they could be.

"We didn't want to be in the studio with A&R men coming around, nice air-conditioning, staring at the same walls and the same microphones. That was madness," he said to the *Launch* website. "We wanted to get to another state of mind – one that we understood."

Their trust in Nigel Godrich was such that they handed him $140,000 of EMI's money in order to buy them a state of the art mobile studio. Nigel had the rich-kid-at-Christmas role of going out and buying whatever he thought they would need. It was an approach that had been pioneered by Thom's early heroes U2 on their *The Unforgettable Fire* album. It meant that they could record in different locations without having to start again with new technology every time.

Initially it even seemed like the whole of their next album would be almost as simple and easy as 'Lucky'. In an interview with a Canadian radio station in early 1996 Jonny thought the album was almost finished already.

"We were aiming to be kind of self-indulgent and spend a year recording," he said, "but we did four days in a studio and we've already got three songs so I think it's going to be horribly quick again."

"I remember going to early sessions for *OK Computer*, which they did up at the Fruit Farm near where I live," says Nigel Powell, "and in the first weeks I heard versions of 'Paranoid Android' and 'No Surprises' and I thought, 'This is going to be easy, they've got half of it already.' Then nine months later, they'd recorded four other versions of 'No Surprises' and somebody had gone, 'Shall we listen to that first one again?' and they listened to it and went, 'Actually that's really good isn't it?' That's the way they seemed to approach things."

While at their rehearsal space, an old apple storage barn at the fruit farm called Canned Applause, they spent much of their time playing with tape loops, perfecting the background buzz that would form such a major part of the eventual album. For the first four months they mostly just rehearsed, practising until they got things right. They could have just used samplers but they preferred the more organic, analogue sounds of the tape spinning. Then, with four songs almost finished, they decided to do the same thing they'd done during *The Bends* sessions – perfect the tracks on tour. This time they played the European festival circuit and then went out as support act to Alanis Morissette. It was an odd choice of tour, although highly lucrative given how successful she was at the time. With the enormous sales of her debut album, *Jagged Little Pill*, she was either a warning or an example of what Radiohead could become if they wanted it badly enough. Thom wasn't sure if he did.

Nevertheless, they were starting to warm to the idea of being a stadium band. Playing the new songs in vast, sterile concrete boxes gave them a new sense of direction. "A lot of the songs needed to sound quite big and messy, like they were bouncing off the walls," Thom told *Jam Showbiz*. "When we went back into the studio, we were actually trying to recreate the sound of a shed soundcheck, or a baseball stadium thing, without sounding like bloody Def Leppard or something. That was really important to the songs."

When they got back they moved into a mansion called St Catherine's Court in a secluded valley just north of Bath. Completed in the 16th Century it was an extremely imposing building, grey and gothic with ivy hanging beneath the windows. It was owned by actress Jane Seymour who'd bought it for £300,000 in 1984 and then spent £3,000,000 doing it up. In the last few years it had mostly been rented out for grand weddings and corporate events but in 1996 The Cure had hired it to make their *Wild Mood Swings* album. When Radiohead got there, with all of the shiny new equipment that Nigel Godrich had bought, they immediately felt much happier than they had done in any professional studio. "You don't feel like lab rats, like you're being experimented on all the time, which you normally do in studios," Thom said in a TV interview.

The house had large stone rooms and beautiful wood panelling. The acoustics and the atmosphere were very different to any other studio they'd ever been in. Among other things, they were amused to find pictures of the proprietor in her underwear in the bathroom. The Cure had used the dining room as the control room but there was also a vast wood-panelled ballroom and an entirely stone-clad room that gave a completely different feel to the acoustics. Phil set up his drum-kit in the children's playroom, surrounded by soft toys. The sessions there were instantly much more laidback than on *The*

Bends. Almost too laid back. The Cure had ended up spending sixteen months at St Catherine's Court, making an album that was far from their best. It seemed quite possible that Radiohead might do the same. "We had as much time as we wanted to do it and that kind of got out of hand," Thom said.

After the trauma of trying to record *The Bends*, they wanted to make a simpler, more stripped-down record this time. There wasn't to be the endless analysis and self-criticism. There wasn't to be the darkness of *The Bends*.

"You know, the big thing for me is that we could really fall back on just doing another moribund, miserable, morbid and negative record, like, lyrically," Thom enthused to *NME* before they started recording. "But I really don't want to, at all. And I am deliberately just writing down all the positive things that I hear or see. But I'm not able to put them into music yet. I don't want to force it because then all I'm doing is just addressing all the issues where people are saying that we're mope rock."

But as the sessions started, Thom realised that the record wasn't turning out quite how he'd expected. It was as if it had a life of its own. They just had to follow wherever it wanted to go. It became a running joke in the studio, when things got too complicated, Thom or Jonny would say "Didn't we say we were going to make an album like *77* (Talking Heads' stripped-down debut album).

That was never going to happen. Thom wasn't listening to that kind of music. He was obsessed by Miles Davis's *Bitches Brew* album. At the time, none of the band were listening to pop or rock. Jonny had got into dark, atonal classical composer Penderecki, best known for the use of his music in films like *The Exorcist* and *The Shining* and for his incredibly harsh and harrowing, *Threnody For The Victims Of Hiroshima*. The idea that they were going to come up with something light and accessible was, looking back, absurd.

The songs Thom had written depicted the weird, depersonalised world of airport lounges, hotel rooms and bars. They had been his home for much of the last three years. It was a world where people alternately worshipped and preyed on celebrity and where constant travel by car and by plane meant, for Thom, a constant low-level fear of death. It was, he said later, "everything I never thought I'd write an album about."

Some of the most violent imagery on the record came directly out of an experience Thom had one night in LA in 1996. He went to a bar and was immediately surrounded by a group of coked-up, hysterical and over-ambitious wannabes in expensive, designer clothes. One woman had a drink spilled over her and Thom was astonished and shocked by her transformation from glamorous clothes-horse into howling harpy.

"There was a look in this woman's eyes that I'd never seen before anywhere," he said. "Whether that was down to me being exhausted and hallucinating ... no, I know what I saw in her face. [I] couldn't sleep that night because of it." She would later be immortalised by Thom as a so-called Gucci little piggy. Other hangers-on were skewered with 'Karma Police' – the woman with the Hitler haircut and the man who buzzes like a fridge.

But if the subject matter was vicious and unpleasant, the experience of recording 'Paranoid Android' was anything but. It was everything they loved about being in a band. The way Thom has described it at times is reminiscent of the way an inventor might describe the process of creating a miraculous new product. As well as the sheer joy of artistic expression there was an element of solving a technical problem, finding the perfect balance between harmony and chaos. As 'My Iron Lung' had done, the song started with a beautiful melody, before taking an abrupt left turn, and then another one and then another one, until it finishes by thrashing around like a fish on dry land.

In some respects, *OK Computer* was a continuation of the themes of *The Bends*. Travel was still a major preoccupation, with tracks like 'Airbag' and 'Lucky'. It was an album that could only have been made by people who'd spent an awful lot of time in the last few years getting in and out of cars, buses and planes. There was also a major supernatural or alien presence with tracks like 'Subterranean Homesick Alien'.

"I'm like most people; I'd love to be abducted," Thom said to the *Yahoo* website. "It's the ultimate madness. So many people go loopy when they're abducted, whether you believe it or not. But if you take away the word 'alien' and replace it with the word 'ghost', it becomes less hysterical. Everyone believes in ghosts. Surely that is more significant than little green men, isn't it?"

Jonny preferred a more logical explanation of the same song. "I'm an enormous cynic," he said to *Launch*. "That song is more about how for every generation, it's a different thing. Before UFOs it was the Virgin Mary, and before that it was something else. People flock to the same places with their cameras and hope to see the same things. And it's just about hope and faith, I think, more than aliens."

For Thom, too, it was half-joke ("in as much as my jokes are ever funny") and half-metaphor for loneliness and isolation. It was about the same craving for something extraordinary to happen that is the hallmark of the song 'The Bends'. But the songs he'd written were, seemingly, much more outward-looking than the tracks on *The Bends* album, and much less introspective. 'Electioneering', for example, was about the cynicism and mendacity of politicians. However, underneath there was surely still an autobiographical element that Thom didn't seem to be able to get away from. It was based partly on his experiences on tour, constantly saying hello to new people and feeling like a fraud.

"I went through this American tour where we just seemed to be shaking hands all the time," he said to *Jam Showbiz*, "and I was getting a bit sick of it and upset by it. So I came up with this running joke with myself, where I used to shake people's hands and say, 'I trust I can rely on your vote?' They'd go 'Ha, ha, ha' and look at me like I was a nutcase."

One of Thom's main aims when he was writing the lyrics of *OK Computer* was avoiding the trap of easy sentimentality. As a result songs like 'Karma Police', 'Paranoid Android' and 'Electioneering' have a tone, superficially, of dark sarcasm. There's very little 'emoting' except, perhaps, on the heartbreaking 'Exit Music (For A Film)'. And even there the protagonists of the song, apparently running away in some kind of suicide pact, refuse to let the listener indulge in pity, finishing with the infamous line, later included in the album's artwork, about choking.

Yet, somehow, as they recorded the album the songs were developing their own undercurrent of deep sadness. "*The Bends* was a record of consolation," Thom said afterwards. "But this one was sad. And I didn't know why." Despite these dark thoughts, the initial stages of recording were a huge buzz. The 'teacher's away' vibe that they'd felt when John Leckie disappeared during *The Bends* sessions seemed to be there to stay. They had Dan Rickwood with them as well as Nigel; they were all in their mid-to-late-twenties and all heading, initially at least, in the same direction.

The first two weeks were among the most enjoyable experiences Radiohead had ever had while recording. During that time they essentially finished recording the whole album and then, in their usual fashion, they set about pulling it to pieces. "It was heaven and hell," said Thom.

The house, from being a friendly, welcoming place suddenly seemed weird and sinister. They started to notice strange things going on. "There was a very odd presence in the house we were recording in," Thom said in an interview with *The Times*. "I just didn't sleep at all. I started seeing things, hearing things … I mean, we made jokes about it, but there was fear everywhere, coming out of the walls and floors."

Part of the problem was that the house was in a deep valley and it was incredibly quiet. Thom, who lived in the centre of Oxford, wasn't used to the deathly silence. All night he'd lie there worrying about the sequencing of the tracks or about particular sounds. That might explain why he started crediting the house with its own, malevolent personality.

"The house was oppressive," he said to Pat Blashill of *Spin*. "To begin with, it was curious about us. Then it got bored with us. And it started making things difficult. It started doing things like turning the studio tape machines on and off, rewinding them."

But then Radiohead had never needed ghosts for things to start getting difficult. The closer they got to finishing a record, the more they started getting distracted by thoughts of what other people would think of it. Thom described the experience of making *OK Computer* as being like a man building a spaceship in the shed at the bottom of his garden. At first they were completely absorbed in the task at hand. They took great pleasure in every little effect, making Colin's guitar sound like a car crash at the beginning of 'Airbag' or like a child's toy in 'No Surprises'. At some point, though, they came out of the trance and looked up, blinking, at what they'd created. How were they going to finish such an enormous project?

The songs they had were extraordinarily complex and multi-textured. The lyrics were loaded with references to aliens, death and violence. All those "positive" things that Thom said he'd been writing down seemed to have been either thrown away or spliced with irony or confusion. By October 2006, they were painfully close to the finish line but they couldn't get it quite right and, as they listened to it, they were concerned about what they'd created. It was, Thom sometimes thought, a little bit disturbing. "At the eleventh hour, when we realised what we had done," Thom says, "we had qualms about the fact that we had created this thing that was quite revolting."

It's an incredibly harsh verdict. It's typical that the first person to come out against the view that *OK Computer* was the best album of the 1990s and, perhaps, of all-time, was the man who wrote it. But then again, if you listen closely you can hear what he meant. If *The Bends* had been about illness then this album sounded ill. It was woozy, disconcerting and claustrophobic. "I think people feel sick when they hear *OK Computer*," Thom said later. "Nausea was part of what we were trying to create."

It made the final weeks of the recording incredibly difficult. The doubts he had about the album, not about whether it was any good but about whether it could be polished and put out as a normal product, made sequencing and mixing it a huge headache. "Making this record was really good fun but finishing it was a fucking nightmare," he said in a German TV interview. "Everything was really spontaneous and then we had to mix it and everything went wrong."

For two weeks before mastering the record, Thom got up at 5a.m. every day and agonised over the track sequence, playing the songs in different orders on his Minidisc player. "I couldn't find the resolution that I was expecting to hear," he said. "I just went into a wild panic for two weeks. I couldn't sleep at all, because I just expected the resolution to be there ... and it wasn't."

By now the rest of the band knew very well that they just had to let him get on with it. He kept compiling discs for them and they would politely take them and then throw them in the bin later. "They knew I'd fucking lost it!" he said later.

And yet there is a resolution in *OK Computer*. Like *The Bends*, it's another concept album where the 'concept' is almost subliminal, conveyed by the strange textures of the music as much as by the words. It's that "fridge buzz", the static of the end of the 20th Century, transformed into something beautiful and moving. The most obvious resolution is the one that they say they didn't even notice at the time. It starts with 'Airbag' and a man pulling himself out of a car crash and it finishes with 'The Tourist' and somebody pleading to slow down.

For the recording sessions, there was to be no definitive, obvious end. In January, Jonny had simply had enough. While Thom was still worrying about whether 'Fitter Happier' should come at the beginning of the album, halfway through, or maybe at the end, he walked into the studio and told them that they had to stop. Thom was still uncertain whether *OK Computer* was really finished but, at the same time, it was a huge relief that somebody had called a halt. He wasn't sure what they'd done, or whether he'd still be "electioneering" after radio programmers got to hear it. Just as after recording *The Bends*, he thought that nobody would be interested in shaking his hand anymore. And maybe that was no bad thing.

"When we finished it and were putting it together, I was like pretty convinced that we'd sort of blown it, but I was kind of happy about that, because we'd gotten a real kick out of making the record," he said to *Launch*.

That was initially many other people's reaction, too. When Capitol got hold of the initial mixes, they immediately halved their projection of how many copies it would sell. And, just as with *The Bends*, the final mixing process proved more difficult than expected. Once again they sent Sean and Paul at Fort Apache tapes but this time they weren't the only people the band tried. "They were sending the tapes around," says Paul. "We did a mix of 'Climbing Up The Walls' and I remember thinking, 'This is weird! Is this their new record? I don't get it!' It was very murky and kind of a mess."

After the satisfaction of finishing the record, Thom felt slightly sick that it was no longer in his hands. From purely having to think about whether he liked a song – and whether the rest of the band liked a song – he was suddenly back to having to think about whether the outside world would like it.

"Suddenly you're presented with it as a finished thing and you have to start thinking about the bullshit that goes with it," he said in a TV interview. "You have to start thinking about the British press and you have to start thinking about how something you may have meant completely genuinely will be taken as something else. It's out of your control and you have to say goodbye to it."

Nobody was more shocked than Thom when they saw the reviews. They almost all acclaimed it as a masterpiece. Suddenly, from having been ignored and occasionally derided in the UK, they were being hailed as the world's greatest rock band. Thom was even more surprised at how many people seemed to have really listened to it and picked up on all the little nuances of texture that they'd put so much time into perfecting. Nevertheless, they couldn't help but be cynical after the experiences they'd had in the past with the press.

"In terms of people saying it's the album of the year, people say that all the time," he said to *Launch*. "In Britain, it's great – in the space of two weeks, our album was the 'Album of the Year' and so was Prodigy's. Two weeks from now it will be another album. It's just what people say."

But two weeks after the album was released, Radiohead played Glastonbury. It was their first public performance of *OK Computer* in the UK and their agent had spent a year negotiating a headline slot. Many people were still highly suspicious of them. Their aesthetic didn't exactly fit the peace, love and hippies vibe of the festival. And it didn't help that, for the first time in a decade at Glastonbury, it had rained solidly and the field in front of the main stage had turned into a swamp. Two stages actually sank and some people caught trench foot, a condition more commonly associated with World War I. Thom must have thought back to his old Headless Chickens, hippy-bashing song 'I Don't Want To Go To Woodstock'.

When they started their set, everything seemed OK. Two songs in and they'd already won the crowd over. Then Thom's monitor blew up. He stared out at the dark mass of the crowd in a blind panic but soon he couldn't even see them. The lights had gone wrong and were glaring directly into his face.

"I was going to kill," he told *Q* later. "I was going to kill. If I'd found the guy who was running the PA system that day, I would've gone backstage and throttled him. Everything was going wrong. Everything blew up. And I was the one at the front standing in front of 40,000 people while that was happening. You're standing there: 'Thanks very much for fucking my life up in front of all these people.'"

They played six songs unable to hear themselves properly and unable to see a thing. Thom turned to walk off, feeling that probably the most important gig of his life had been ruined. Then he had second thoughts. He screamed at the lighting guy to turn the lights around so that they were pointing at the audience instead of him. To his complete shock, there was an expression of rapture on the faces of most of the sodden, muddy crowd. The band carried on, confused but determined to finish the set. Then, when he walked off at the end, Thom decided to find out what had gone wrong but before he could find the soundman he bumped into Rachel.

"I thundered offstage, really ready to kill," he told writer Andrew Mueller for the website, www.thequietus.com, "and my girlfriend grabbed me, made me stop, and said, 'Listen!' And the crowd were just going wild. It was amazing."

From feeling like they'd royally messed up, Thom had to accept the word of thousands of fans that it was one of the best gigs they'd ever done. "I said to them afterwards, 'That was the best I've ever seen you,'" says Mark Cope, "but not one of them really enjoyed it. It's horrible to play a gig like that and not enjoy it. It's strange. But I think they learned from that. What's really good is that they're very humble. They still don't believe that they're as good as they are. That's one of the things that's kept them going and kept them in front of everyone else."

That performance consolidated Radiohead's position as the most acclaimed band in the country. If many music magazines had overlooked *The Bends* then they were rushing to catch up now. Perhaps there was a degree of over-compensating. For several years, *OK Computer* was acclaimed in various polls as the best album of all-time. This, typically, made all of Radiohead feel uncomfortable. But, then again, it is an extraordinary album. It combines gorgeously simple, nursery rhyme tunes like 'No Surprises' and 'Karma Police' with complex, disturbing prog-rock like 'Paranoid Android.'

"When I heard it, after a couple of listens, it became one of those things where it was all I could listen to for a month," says Paul Kolderie. "I'd run into people and be like, 'What are you listening to?' *OK Computer*. Only. That's all I listen to.' Everyone would be like 'Yep, that's me, too.' It was one of those things where, man, they just nailed it to the wall. If *Pablo Honey's* a 'one' and *The Bends* is 'ten' then *OK Computer* is '100'. A factor of ten every time."

The first single to be released from the album was the brilliant, decidedly loopy six-minutes plus of 'Paranoid Android'. This time Thom was determined to underline the fact that the song was supposed to be, among other things, *funny*. The band were all big fans of animator Magnus Carlsson and his late-night cartoon Robin.

Robin was an odd, slightly random character who wandered through his brightly coloured life with odd, slightly random things happening to him. They approached Magnus to see if he'd make a video for 'Paranoid Android' featuring Robin. He accepted, locked himself in a room and listened to the song over and over again. "We had really good fun doing this song," Thom said, "so the video should make you laugh. I mean, it should be sick, too.

The result was both – a brilliant, comic, surreal vision. It featured a man being dismembered, rescued by mermaids and then turned into a baby to be fed by a bird, among other highly memorable images. Typically, when it came out, MTV were happy to let all the violence appear but they insisted that the bare-breasted mermaids needed to be given bathing suits.

In the UK, one sign of Radiohead's new status as, in Nigel Powell's words, 'RADIOHEAD', the most important band in the world, came with BBC Radio 1's decision to playlist 'Paranoid Android' in the daytime. "Each time I'd hear it, I'd keep thinking about people doing intricate jobs in factories," joked Thom to Nick Kent in *Mojo*, "working on industrial lathes – getting injured from the shock of being exposed to it."

It meant that the song was Radiohead's biggest hit so far in the UK, reaching Number 3 in the charts, although it was less successful in the rest of the world. Originally they'd planned to commission videos for every track on the album, but the relative commercial failure of 'Paranoid Android' in America meant the plans had to be scaled back. In the end, they only made videos for the singles, which were, first, 'Karma Police' and then 'No Surprises'.

"I think they had about half a million quid set aside to do every video," says Grant Gee, who directed 'No Surprises'. "The first video was Magnus Carlsson's 'Paranoid Android'; the next one was Jonathan Glazer's 'Karma Police'. They'd done two and spent [most] of the 500 [grand] and I think then it was like, 'Oh shit!'"

The video for 'Karma Police' wasn't as striking as 'Paranoid Android' but was also a work of art in its own right. It features a car slowly following a man who's growing more and more tired as he runs along a deserted road. Halfway through the video, the camera pans to the back of the car where a completely blank, dismissive Thom is sitting occasionally mumbling the lyrics to the song. Director Jonathan Glazer later described the video as a "complete failure". He'd tried to make it as minimalist and subjective as possible but he felt that it didn't have the dramatic power that he wanted. Nevertheless the way it switches your sympathy between the runner and the car is highly effective. To begin with it seems like the car represents Karma, chasing down an offender, but as the terrified man turns the tables on his pursuer, lighting a trail of petrol and blowing the car up, it seems like it might be the other way round. It was typical of Thom that, rather than being the man chased, he preferred to portray himself as the chilling figure in the back of the car. His blank expression might have owed something to the fact that, as he sat there lip-synching to the music, something went wrong with the car and it started filling with carbon monoxide.

But it was the 'No Surprises' video, a genuinely minimalist affair, that was to be the most memorable and significant video to come out of *OK Computer*. The disturbing image of Thom, with his head in a glass bowl slowly filling up with water came to represent in the public mind exactly what being in Radiohead was like for him. This image was reinforced by the documentary made by the same director, Grant Gee, the ironically titled *Meeting People Is Easy*.

13

MEETING PEOPLE IS EASY

They must have wondered what they were thinking. At a hotel in Barcelona, Radiohead were literally surrounded by journalists. There were journalists walking down every corridor, sitting in the lobby and waiting by the bar clutching Dictaphones and swapping notes. For the launch of *OK Computer*, they'd decided to get all the interviews out of the way in one mighty splurge but they hadn't realised quite how many there would be. It was the equivalent of a child eating their greens by piling them high on a fork, covering them in ketchup and wolfing them down all at once.

"They were doing this crazily intense launch scene in Barcelona," says Grant Gee. "So while they were off touring if anyone asked they could say, 'Fuck off, we already did the interview.' It was something like a hundred interviews over three or four days and two shows. All in one hotel. It was something to see – corridors full of journalists!"

Grant was in an odd position. He was part of the media scrum yet not really. His role was to film the chaos for some, as yet unspecified, future DVD. At the time he was relatively unknown. He'd directed videos for the band Spooky, who Thom really liked, but he wasn't (yet) a big name like Jonathan Glazer. Nevertheless when they were looking for somebody to shoot some footage of the press day Dilly Gent, who commissioned videos for EMI, suggested Grant.

"They knew it would be very crazy with hundreds of cameras pointing at them and their commissioner, Dilly, who's a very smart woman, very important to the whole thing, said, 'Why don't you get somebody who's going to be on this side of all those cameras with you.' So I got the job."

It was just supposed to be a one-off thing but when he looked at the extraordinary footage that he'd got in Barcelona, Grant realised that there was something bigger there. "I just had this four day job and I got all this footage and showed it to Dilly and she really liked it," says Grant. "And I said, 'Look, if you keep me on this job I can do something really good.' And then it took about another four or five months before anybody said anything and I wrote a proposal saying, 'This is what I want to do' and after four or five months they said, 'Alright, come and film them on tour.'"

It was a brave, even perverse decision, for a band who'd largely managed to preserve a degree of privacy. Apart from Thom and perhaps Jonny, the rest of the band were rarely recognised even in their hometown of Oxford. Nevertheless, when they met Grant, they liked and trusted him. So much so that, as with everybody they worked with, they gave him free rein to do whatever he wanted. It helped that Grant was, in some respects, a similar character – polite, diffident and middle-class.

"It was little things like they're from Oxford and I went to college in Oxford," says Grant. "Ed said he remembered seeing me at this indie club that we used to go to. He's about four years younger than me and he said, 'Yeah, I think I remember you.'"

When they went on tour, Grant came with them and it wasn't what he'd expected at all. "It was sort of insane," he says. "It was situations designed to make you mad, the repetition, the long stretches of boredom ... the repetition. You meet someone new and they say the same things to you. You go to a new city and it looks the same and people talk to you the same. I know it's what anyone who goes on tour says, but I'd never seen it before. Because of identifying with them as sensitive twenty-something blokes, and being able to see it through their eyes, and because it was all kicking off and spiralling very quickly, how big a band they were over that year, it really sharpened what happened."

The resulting documentary, *Meeting People Is Easy*, shows them struggling to cope with the endless demands of the promotional machine. Even little things seem too much. At one point, recording a thank you for an *NME* award, Thom looks like a little boy being forced by his parents to thank a distant aunt for a hand-knitted pullover. It's hard to tell whether the rest of the band, sitting behind him, are more frustrated with him or the situation.

It looks like a kind of hell but Grant has always admitted that there were plenty of good times. "The shows were great," he says. "I had a nice time. We listened to music, went to bars and things like that but as an activity you just realised that this is not good, this type of behaviour all the time. As sensitive and intelligent men, you could really see it affecting them. But it certainly wasn't awful. The hotels were really nice, the food was really good."

Jonny said later that the film was accurate in that it emphasised the parts of touring that somebody who'd never done it before would find surprising. "Obviously it isn't like that all the time," he said to *JAM*. "Sometimes you are sat on the beach in Australia having a day off, thinking *this is the greatest*. I think he was surprised to see what goes on, so he made a film about it. That is always going to be far more interesting than the guys having a beer backstage and laughing." "We could've edited it to make it look like we were having a really good time," said Thom in a TV interview, "there was just as much footage of that."

The main problem, for Thom in particular, was that he'd never been somebody who could just unquestioningly accept being told what to do without good reason. A large part of the promotional process seemed to consist of doing ridiculous things over and over again with no obvious purpose. Like many people who've met Radiohead, Grant remembers the rest of the band as incredibly nice, friendly characters but Thom, while perfectly courteous and accommodating, was never so easy to figure out.

"He could seem quite intimidating because he's so intense," Grant says. "I don't know what he's like now, but then I'd never met anybody whose nerves were so much on display. It was as if he had no skin at all. Whatever anyone else was feeling, he was feeling a few times more intensely. Which was the great thing about him. Which was why he was such a fantastic rock star."

But it was also why he has always found elements of the job so difficult to deal with. At times, the whole band did. Nigel Powell is dubious about how accurately *Meeting People Is Easy* portrays life on the road with Radiohead but he admits that there were moments when it's extremely odd.

"I'm sure that given the amount of footage that a documentary maker shoots, if he'd wanted the make the tour look like the fun-est (sic) time you could have with your clothes on, then he probably could have," he says. "There was an editorial bent to it of emphasising what a load of old bollocks it can be. The only time I got the impression that Jonny was really hacked off with it all was when they went out to America to do two weeks straight of promo, no playing, just talking to people and I talked to him halfway through that and he said, 'This is awful.'

"I can understand because I've done a similar kind of thing myself [in the Unbelievable Truth] and you almost forget why you're a musician. You can do eight or ten interviews a day and everyone's asking you the same questions. It gets very strange."

Eventually Radiohead would come up with games to make even more interesting. Just to keep themselves sane. "They'd set little rules for each other in phone interviews like: 'In this one you have to say the word 'no' fifteen times in a row. So at some point they'd go 'No, no, no … no, no, no, no, no … no, no, no, no, no, no, nooo.' Just stuff like that," says Nigel. "One particularly classic one was Ed doing an interview with a magazine called *Good Times* but I think Jonny told him he should do it as if he was talking to (marijuana subculture magazine) *High Times*, so throughout the interview, he was making reference to that kind of thing, trying to make the interview relevant to the demographic of the magazine!"

It was always much easier for the rest of them than it was for Thom. He was the leader of the band, the face of Radiohead and the person everybody wanted to talk to. Even playing live, the part of the job he loved most was hugely draining.

"You have to go into this completely different mindset," he told *Pitchfork*. "It's great, but you are exposed to all this extra stuff that you don't have to deal with when you stop. I'm getting used to it now, but it's kind of just the fall-out. It's really weird. It's not a natural situation to be in. It sounds like moaning, because I know that's what I'm supposed to do, and I'm not moaning."

"You can say what you want about Thom's fragile persona," said Colin in an interview with *Yahoo*, "but someone who works as hard as he does and then performs in front of 10,000 people every night and reveals his emotional candour – physically, he is a strong person and emotionally, he is very sensitive, too. People think he is fragile and fucked up, but not really, don't think so. Do an eighteen-month tour around the world and see how you feel."

After eighteen months, Thom felt wrecked. After the jubilation of Glastonbury he just wanted to go home. He didn't think they'd ever be able to top that. Every other day he would say to the rest of the band "I don't wanna do this!" And the management or the band would coax him on. People would tell him that if he did it just this once, he'd never have to do it again. It was the opposite of the normal situation in the band. Normally, Thom would be the one driving everybody on, telling them to try that bit harder when they were ready to give up.

"I guess they were right," he said to *Q* afterwards. "Go and flog yourself to death, make the most of it. But I think it was unwise. Because we were playing badly, we weren't interested. By the end we weren't listening to each other. If you want the truth!"

One problem was that, having had the kind of highs they'd experienced making the record and playing enormous gigs, going back to normality felt like an equally enormous low. "Everything that's happened after Glastonbury has been a let-down," Thom said to *Melody Maker's* Neil Kulkarni in 1998. "The feeling when I shouted at the lighting engineer to turn the lights on the crowd so I could see at least one person, 'cos we couldn't see anything … there were 40,000 people up the hill, holding lighters and fires burning, and tents pitched, and I don't think I've ever felt like that in my entire life. It wasn't a human feeling, it was something else entirely."

After that, the relatively run-of-the-mill gigs on tour, night after night, couldn't quite match up. And Thom always had a horror of going through the motions. This is captured at one point in *Meeting People Is Easy* where Thom tells the rest of the band that he's struggling to cope. Grant's not sure whether his presence there influenced how the band felt or not. "There's a scene in the film where Thom says 'Why don't we just call it off. I don't know if I can do this anymore'," says Grant. "In retrospect, I'm not sure how much of that was because I was there. I could be completely wrong but it might be that Thom wanted to say that and have it recorded. But I didn't have any doubt at the time that it was the real thing."

He's adamant that there was no editorial bent to *Meeting People Is Easy* but his status as an insider within the Radiohead camp meant that he was careful about what he shot. "That's the interesting thing," he says. "When is it OK to turn the camera on and when should you really turn it off? How much trust do you have with someone in that situation? There were a number of times when stuff was happening and I just couldn't turn the camera on. I know it's awful because you should be like one of these war guys who go, 'Just get in there, film everything!' There was lots of funny stuff. There were things I filmed literally like that [holds hands up as if unable to look through the viewfinder]."

One thing he left out of the film was the appearance of Marilyn Manson backstage after a show. They got a message from the American star's 'people' just before they went onstage that he'd like to see them. When he turned up later they were relieved to see that he was perfectly nice and normal. Until, bizarrely, he gave Thom a present. It was a piece of jewellery.

"It was this sort of Gothy, batty thing," says Grant. "It was one of those things where Thom was just a bit bemused and Marilyn was trying to be nice. Nobody was quite understanding each other. It was really funny but if we'd put it in the only way of seeing it would have been that we were taking the piss out of the American rock star. But it was funny."

Thom still hadn't got used to the fact that major stars wanted to come and meet him. Radiohead were on a different plateau than they'd been on before. Even when 'Creep' went global they weren't courted by celebrities. They were playing bigger venues than ever before and it looked like they were on the verge of becoming a stadium band like U2. It was a situation that Thom half-dreaded. He'd always been terrified of developing stage fright. He sometimes thought it could happen very easily. At one show in Ireland, it almost did.

It was in front of about 33,000 people, by far their biggest headline show. Thom told *Hot Press* that he was 'absolutely cacking' himself. The night before he had an incredibly vivid dream that he would later describe as the most distinctive memory of the year. He was running down the River Liffey in Dublin, "stark bollock naked, being pursued by a huge tidal wave."

Grant didn't know the state Thom was heading for but the video treatment he wrote for 'No Surprises' could be seen as a metaphor for somebody who's starting to go under. The out-takes that appeared in *Meeting People Is Easy*, of Thom soaked, gasping for breath, became perhaps the most striking image of the singer at the time. Grant just hadn't realised how difficult it would be for him to hold his breath underwater with the camera on him.

"He's not precious," says Grant. "All he cares about is whether it's a good piece of work. But I felt bad when he came to do it. All he cared about when I was talking about it was, 'How long do I have to hold my breath for?' 'About fifty seconds.' 'No problem.' He didn't care. Until he had to do it."

When he came to do it, things were very different. For take after take Thom attempted to hold his breath but every time he came up spluttering after fewer than thirty seconds. By the end, he was swearing furiously. He couldn't understand why it was so difficult.

"It wasn't that difficult if you weren't under any pressure," says Grant. "But as soon as you get any adrenaline, your breathing goes shallow and quick and that's just what can't happen. So we had these stand-ins who could do it. We *knew* that Thom could hold his breath that long. But as soon as you put lights on somebody and go 'Action!' you can see in the film what happens. It was really horrible. He started doing it and had four or five goes and it became apparent that it was nowhere near it. He'd be able to hold his breath for about ten seconds."

The atmosphere in the studio got progressively worse as the crew sat there not knowing what to do, not knowing whether it was OK to put somebody through this. "It was horrible for me because I didn't have anything to do," says Grant. "My whole thing with that was not to direct. Because I'm not a very good 'proper' director in that way. I just like setting situations going and then recording them. It was like designing a machine that will make a pop video. Then you just turn the camera on. So I had nothing to do after I'd given the lighting guy the cues. All I said to Thom was, 'If you feel chuffed when you come out, don't be afraid to show it.' I said, 'Don't sing your heart out, you just need to talk through it.' But it was unpleasant watching it because he was *suffering*. The more he couldn't do it when he knew he should be able to do it, the more upset he was getting. He was shaking with rage. It was not nice to be around." Ever the perfectionist, even at a personal cost.

But by then Thom trusted Grant and he didn't want to let him down. Part of the reason that, in their early days, they hadn't enjoyed making videos was that they just didn't like working with people they didn't know.

"The thing that always kills me stone dead about making videos is they cost so much money and you meet the director once and you never see him again," Thom said to *Spin* magazine. "It's like sleeping with someone and never seeing them again. Videos should be much more about having a group of people who hang out and do stuff whenever. I find it very destabilising to constantly have to work with different people."

"There was that American video woman," Jonny Greenwood remembered of one video. "She came over with us on a video shoot and said, 'Can't you make the little chap jump up and down a bit?'"

At least Thom knew Grant by then. He knew that if he could get through it they'd have something startling and different for the video. That was all that mattered. And, finally, he managed to triumph. "The Assistant Director on the shoot was this larger-than-life avuncular American character called Barry Vasserman, who's a great pop video AD," says Grant. "He sat with Thom all day and said, 'OK Thom, we're gonna do this, ten seconds at a time, five seconds more each time. Here we go, 'OK, Tommy, and you're out. OK, five!' They got up to about 45 seconds and he said, 'OK, we're up to 45 seconds. We're gonna do a take. Next time you're gonna do a take Tommy. You're gonna make it boy!' It was that sort of thing. So he did it and, boom! *Perfect.* Then he did it again and I said, 'OK, the first one's better' and we used the first one." In the end it looked easy but it had taken almost two days. Thom later said it was "the most terrifying thing I have ever done in my life."

The famous video worked partly because the relief on Thom's face when he finally managed to get through fifty seconds without coming up for air is genuine. The result, for all its simplicity, was mesmerising.

Thom would have similar feelings two or three years later when he finally managed to deal with the fall-out of *OK Computer* and their endless tour schedule but, in 1998, the worst was still to come. "On the *OK Computer* tour," he told Andrew Mueller, "we were in a situation where people were trying to persuade us to carry on touring for another six months, we should have said no but we didn't, and I went bonkers."

It was a deliberately glib assessment of the way he felt but Thom was starting to feel distinctly uncomfortable again. He said that he was seeing things out of the corner of his eye. He couldn't deal with the fact that so much of his time and of the band's time was spent dealing with things that seemingly had no relevance to music, or to anything else that he cared about. What made it much, much worse was that he felt like *OK Computer* was a dead end. After that there was nowhere else to go. During 1998 they only played one gig, a benefit for Amnesty International. It was the longest period of inactivity they'd had since they started the band. Even when they'd been away at university, they'd managed to play more often. At the start of 1999, for the first time in his life, Thom felt like he couldn't express himself the way he'd always been able to express himself – through music.

"New Year's Eve 1998 was one of the lowest points of my life," he told Danny Eccleston in *Q* magazine. "I felt like I was going fucking crazy. Every time I picked up a guitar I just got the horrors. I would start writing a song, stop after sixteen bars, hide it away in a drawer, look at it again, tear it up, destroy it ... I was sinking down and down."

It wasn't the first time he'd struggled with feelings of doubt about what he was doing and where he was going but it was undoubtedly the worst. "I was a mess, a really bad mess," he said later in a Dutch documentary. "I found myself in a place I didn't want to be and I didn't recognise myself and I wasn't sure what it was we were supposed to have done. I didn't have much to hold on to. Two year writing block, writing stuff and throwing it away. It's like losing someone you love."

He ended up spending a lot of time walking around Oxford, just watching people, trying to get back some idea of what 'normal' meant. "It was bad," he said later. "The ultimate reality check."

Unlike before and during *The Bends*, though, there was no question that the band were about to split up. They'd been through that stage and they knew that they were stuck with each other.

"They gave the impression of having known each other forever," says Grant. "They'd been together for about twelve or eleven years. People would sigh rather than get angry. They were a very mature band. You hear bands now when they get to their forties and fifties go, 'I used to hate him but we've got over it now.' Or if that doesn't happen, the band splits up. They seemed to have got beyond that already by 28, 29."

But if they weren't going to split up and Thom had no desire to be a rock star or write rock songs anymore, then what were they going to do? It was something that he had to decide for himself. The rest of the band were left in a position where they didn't know what would happen next. The massive acclaim that *OK Computer* received should have helped … but it didn't.

"There's a pervading sense of loneliness that I've had since the day I was born," Thom said in an interview with *Rolling Stone*. "Maybe a lot of other people feel the same way but I'm not about to run up and down the street asking everybody if they're as lonely as I am. I'd probably get locked up."

And Thom had still not got used to being a rock star. He didn't like the feeling of being public property. "I went to the supermarket the other day," he told *Launch*, "and it was a really shitty day, and I had been drinking all day, which I don't normally do. And I went shopping and I was walking out with all these bags, growling, and this middle-aged lady came up to me, and said, 'It's really good. You don't have to worry. It's a really good record. You don't have to worry.' And then she wandered off. That was strange."

Another time a fan managed to trace his email address, despite the fact that he was using a pseudonym that he thought nobody knew. On another occasion a stalker turned up at his house and demanded to see him. "He said, 'What shall I do?' remembers Mark Cope, "and I said, 'Tell her to fuck off or you're not going to make any more music.' He said 'why didn't I think of that?!'"

But not everybody was so easy to get rid of. At music industry parties, celebrities would suddenly demand to be his best friend, purely on the strength of the fact that they were both in the public eye. At one party an unnamed celebrity gave him a lecture about the way he behaved after he rudely refused to acknowledge his gushing compliments.

"I couldn't do it, you know?" he said. "I wasn't really able to communicate with anyone except for people I really knew. I suppose the novelty of these people has worn off and I just sound like this sulky kid who has had a big birthday party but didn't get the present he wanted and, you know, someone should just slap him around the face. And this guy was quite prepared to do that."

Thom suspected that the person in question would never have been interested in talking to him if it wasn't for the fact that he was a star. He felt like a millionaire who wonders whether people are only interested in them for their money. "The sickness of it for me," he said in a TV interview, "the bit that I couldn't deal with, was that somehow this is a reason to exist. You get to a certain level of exposure or fame and then suddenly you can communicate with other famous people on a higher level and waft around going [airily] 'Hiiii!' I just thought that was a bit peculiar."

The way Radiohead worked also increased the pressure. They once read that Brian Eno had a card pinned to the wall of his recording studio reading, "Whatever worked last time, never do it again." It had become their mantra, too, but it meant that every album was a massive full-stop. It meant that they had to go back to square one each time. After *OK Computer*, the only agenda Thom had was the same one he always had after an album was completed: next time everything should be completely different.

14

KID A

"It sucks, fucking rock music sucks," Thom said in a TV interview in 2000. "I hate it! I'm so fuckin' bored of it. It's a fuckin' waste of time."

He didn't mean that playing music with guitars, bass and drums was a complete waste of time (although he wasn't quite as keen on that as he used to be). He meant everything that goes along with rock music: all the mythology and the marketing. On every album so far, he'd forced Radiohead to reinvent themselves but by this point it was hard to see where they could go. Thom even found it difficult to listen to *OK Computer*. He'd read all the press hailing it as the best record of the year, and then the best record ever made, but by now Radiohead's influence was audible in many new records and he didn't like what he was hearing.

"I had this moment after *OK Computer* when I heard other people imitating what we'd done and I really didn't like what it sounded like," he told a German TV interviewer. "I had this moment of, 'My God, this is really self-indulgent. Have I been responsible for this? That's really awful.'"

"Hearing people like myself on the radio made me not want to sound like me," he also said. "I'd do anything to not sound like me." Of course, he wasn't responsible for people trying to imitate Radiohead and, in reality, *The Bends* had been much more influential than *OK Computer*. *The Bends* was a record that musicians listened to and felt that they could emulate if they tried hard enough. Not many bands tried to copy 'Paranoid Android'. Talent spotter Simon Williams of the Fierce Panda record label has said that, after *OK Computer*, he came across noticeably fewer new indie bands. It wasn't until The Strokes made it OK to make simple, three chord garage rock songs again that there was another surge in guitar sales.

In 1995, even before they recorded *OK Computer*, Thom was already saying that he wanted to move towards electronic music.

"I get really envious when I hear good jungle or stuff on Warp or the Tricky album," he said to Ted Kessler in *NME*. "I get this sense that they made it in isolation and that there wasn't this need to be in a bollocks guitar band going, 'I want my guitar solo.'"

However, the reaction to *OK Computer* completely freaked him out and, even after a year of inactivity, he still wasn't ready to start making music again. Nevertheless, in February 1999 the five members of Radiohead met up at a studio in Paris. It was the first time they'd gone into the studio without any idea of what was going to happen. Ed and Colin wanted the next album to go back to something simpler. "My suggestion for *OK Computer*'s follow-up had been to say, 'Let's go back to the well-crafted three-and-a-half minute song,'" said Ed. Colin, meanwhile, felt the kind of electronica that Thom was now listening to sounded pretentious and emotionless.

It made their meeting awkward and uncomfortable and the sessions were the worst they'd ever had. Thom had no idea what he wanted them to do next but he was very clear what he didn't want them to do. They would start trying to play something and he'd explode with frustration, racing across the studio to stop the tape and insist that they try something else. What else? *He didn't know*. There were two major things he now had a problem with: guitars and the sound of his own voice, both of which had previously been rather important to the success of Radiohead.

"I didn't want to use my own voice," he said in a TV interview. "I thought we could still write good songs and not have to rely on this guy singing in this emotional hyperbole all the time. Let's try something else. It can still be good."

He felt like the fixed idea that the world had of Radiohead was starting to become more of a hindrance than a help. "It ends up that you can't be creative anymore," he said. "That identity thing gets in the way." The same fault lines that had emerged around the time of *The Bends* were back with a vengeance. The rest of the band appreciated and understood that Thom had a lot to deal with. They understood that he didn't want to repeat what they'd done with the previous albums but they felt, understandably, that his perfectionism was preventing them from doing anything at all. Even worse, many of their arguments weren't even about music.

"It was just 'fall-out'," Thom said to Nick Kent. "Really sad.

Personally speaking, during that time I was just a total fuckin' mess. No one could say anything to me without me turning round and launching a vicious tirade at them. It got really, really bad."

Nigel Godrich was starting to lose patience with them. Talking to *Mojo*'s Nick Kent, he said they were acting like "a bunch of method actors." Some days his role, according to Thom, was to act like "the adjudicator at a trial."

"My job involves a lot of psychology," Nigel said to *Rolling Stone* in 2006. "The dynamic between people is very complicated. Ed is very much a diplomat. Jonny's brilliant, and what comes out of him comes out very quickly. And with Thom – a lot of the time – I think he's the king of self-sabotage. So I'm just trying to prevent him from destroying things he doesn't realise are valuable."

It was a vicious circle. Without the release of making music, Thom was deeply unhappy and yet that unhappiness was preventing the band from getting anywhere. All they could do was just wait for him. The main problem was that he'd had enough of so-called 'emotional music'. After months on tour, he started to feel like a fake when he sang songs that wore their heart on their sleeve. That's why he was so keen on acts like Autechre or Aphex Twin, musicians who were finding new ways of expressing themselves without what he saw as the saccharine sentimentality of so much rock. This meant that he didn't even like writing lyrics anymore. The words had been the cornerstone of Radiohead's music since the *Drill* EP but not now. Thom was fed up of the scrutiny that his lyrics always went through, as they were strip-searched for clues to his own state of mind. This time he was determined to keep that closely under wraps. "Even now," he said, "most interviews you do, there's a constant subtext: 'Is this you?' By using other voices, I guess it was a way of saying, 'Obviously it isn't me.'"

More seriously there were obsessive fans who had always looked to him for guidance, taking songs like 'Exit Music' and 'The Bends' as mantras to live by. Endlessly regurgitating his own feelings seemed hopelessly indulgent. There were more important things to worry about. He was obsessed with the way the global market-place took works of art and put them on the same level as a can of Coke or a pair of Nikes, as something to be sold. He'd been reading books by liberal and left-wing authors like Noam Chomsky and Naomi Klein. The latter's *No Logo*, a polemic about the ubiquity of advertising, made such a big impression on the band that they even considered naming the record after it.

But music had always been the way Thom dealt with his emotions. Having deliberately excluded himself from doing the same thing this time, he was spiralling downwards. What was music for if it wasn't to express what he was feeling? The rest of the band didn't know what to do with their singer and they weren't sure what they were supposed to be doing in the studio.

"Phil, Colin and I went through some major dilemmas at various stages," Ed said to Nick Kent. "How could we contribute to this new music? We all wondered if it wasn't better to just walk away. It was a very scary thing at first."

After a month in Paris the band gave up and scrapped most of what they'd done. "We soon became gridlocked," Phil said. "Paris was very much a case of tripping ourselves up." They next moved to Medley Studio in Copenhagen but these sessions only lasted for two weeks and were even worse. What did a band with three guitarists do in a studio while making a record with hardly any guitars on it? "Copenhagen was two weeks of us having a pretty horrendous time," said Ed in *Q*. "At the end of it, we had about fifty reels of two-inch tape, and on each of those tapes was fifteen minutes of music. And nothing was finished."

In the past, when Thom brought in a demo they all knew what they had to do. Generally it would consist of him playing the acoustic guitar and singing. They could then build a song around it, adding bass, guitar and drum parts. This time the demos he was bringing in often just consisted of samples, weird noises and scraps of sound. It wasn't clear what exactly they were supposed to do.

In April 1999, they moved to Barsford Park in Gloucestershire, attempting to recapture the success of the early *OK Computer* sessions, but the slow, painful process of trying things out and rejecting the results just continued. Perversely, Thom got a corporate style whiteboard and wrote the titles of all the songs they were working on up there. There were fifty or sixty. Hardly any were finished. Some he hadn't even played them and some were little more than ideas.

Perhaps surprisingly, the member of Radiohead who was most enthusiastic about their new direction was Jonny Greenwood. By 1998 he was acclaimed as one of the most original and exciting guitarists of his generation but he'd started on keyboards and had no desire to be stuck in the rock band rut either. He once said that he often felt that 'Radiohead' itself was a sixth member of the band who, whenever they'd done something once, would shout "bored now", forcing them to do something completely different next time.

There must have been moments when the rest of the band thought that if Thom and Jonny wanted to make an electronic album so badly, then maybe they should just make it on their own. But Thom was adamant that he wanted to make a Radiohead album. He said that he wouldn't have the confidence to go it alone. Things started to move on when he bought a piano. He couldn't write songs on the piano anything like as easily as he could on a guitar but the new way of working helped overcome his block. Similarly, Jonny largely abandoned the guitar in favour of playing a kind of early synthesiser called an Ondes Martenot.

At least this way they knew they couldn't repeat themselves. Slowly things became easier. In June 1999, Ed O'Brien began keeping an online studio diary and the first entry finishes with the, almost defiant, line: "A fucking brilliant rehearsal. It's great to be in our band."

A week later, the optimism has disappeared and things have gone backwards again. "A pretty frustrating day," he says of July 27, "but now we've been doing this for so long, you realise it can't all be like last week."

By then some of the band, Jonny in particular, were starting to think that maybe it was easier when they had a record company deadline. On August 4, they had another "frank" discussion. Once again they realised that all they'd learned during this recording process was how *not* to do things. But how many times can you learn the same lesson? "It's taken us seven years to get this sort of freedom," said Ed, "and it's what we always wanted, but it could be so easy to fuck it all up."

It's not surprising that things were taking so long. It was as if a group of people who'd never played the guitar, bass or drums before suddenly decided to make a rock record. First of all they had to learn how to use their new instruments. "I spent a year just learning how computers work," Colin said.

In September 1999, their new studio in Oxfordshire was finally ready and they were starting to feel much more comfortable. It was a beautiful converted barn in the middle of the countryside, not far from the village hall where they'd had their first rehearsals. It had a high, vaulted ceiling, perfect acoustics and natural reverb. By now, the rest of the band had figured out how they could fit in to the new way of doing things. After scratching around for month after month, things suddenly seemed to click into place. The only worry for any band having their own studio is that the economy and convenience can send the levels of self-indulgence sky-rocketing.

"You set up your own studio and the first thing you think is, 'OK, we're gonna go so far up our own arses now and never come out the other end,' said Thom to *Hot Press*. "And so I think we were quite heavily paranoid about that. It was something that we'd always wanted. But when we got it, we were a bit dumbfounded for ages, about the fact that we could go in and do stuff whenever we wanted and we weren't paying anybody."

But things were moving forward much faster now. It helped that, although there was a great deal of digital manipulation, it was all done live. They didn't record songs in a straightforward fashion and then mess about with them on the computer. When Thom created the weird, disorientating effects on his vocal, he would sing directly into the antiquated, proto-synth devices they were using. It was peculiarly satisfying. It didn't sound like him and that was exactly what he wanted. He was bored of the sound of his own voice and bored of the sound of Radiohead's guitars, but somehow they'd found a way around that.

He also found a way to save the lyrics that, previously, he'd been writing and then furiously screwing into a ball and throwing away. He simply cut them up, put them into a hat and then shuffled them around. "That was really cool," he said in an interview with Dutch TV, "because … I managed to preserve whatever emotions were in the original writing of the words but in a way that it's like I'm not trying to emote."

It's ironic that, during a time when "emoting" was becoming increasingly popular with all the bands who'd drawn inspiration from *The Bends* and *OK Computer*, Thom couldn't think of anything worse. He'd discovered that however real the emotion might have seemed initially, it always started feeling false when it had been through the music industry wringer for a few months. Among other things it was impossible to sing a song onstage night after night and "mean it" just as much every time. It had taken him a long time to get used to that fact. It had also severely dented his confidence but the recording of 'The National Anthem' helped bring that back.

It was based around a riff he'd had since he was sixteen. The band had recorded a version of it in the mid-1990s and decided that it was too good to be a B-side. But they'd never managed to get it quite right. Thom had been listening to a lot of Charles Mingus and he wanted it to have the same kind of aggressive sound as the jazz musician's notorious 1962 *Town Hall Concert*. It was supposed to be a rehearsal for an album Mingus wanted to record but instead it was publicised as a concert. Most members of the audience thought they were there to listen to a new record, instead the poorly rehearsed musicians jammed hysterically over the top of each other as Mingus urged the crowd to ask for their money back. At the time it was considered a disaster but it was exactly the kind of inspired chaos that Thom was looking for.

Unfortunately, he knew that it would be difficult to make the typical session musician understand that. He'd been frustrated in the past by some professional session players who came in, did a day's work and then left. He wanted something different. Jonny was in touch with the Head Of Music at Abingdon School who'd taken over from Terence Gilmore-James and he asked him whether he knew any good brass players. The new head suggested another occasional teacher at the school, Andy Bush, who was also a successful jazz musician.

"I think they'd previously used a fixer in London to book their string players and it hadn't been an altogether happy experience," Andy told this author. "I'm sure they got musically what they wanted but they didn't enjoy the work-to-rule aspect of a lot of mainstream session players. Sometimes you get a situation where people turn up, they're not really that bothered what they're doing, you're there for three hours and then you go away. It's not very personal. They'd had their fingers burnt with people watching the clocks and getting their contracts out. They wanted to find a connection with someone who was more sympathetic to their way of working. And, hopefully, somebody who was interested in their music. Which I was and, accordingly, I booked guys who all really liked Radiohead even before we met them."

Andy put together a group of eight players who were summoned to Oxfordshire to help out. For all of them it was a bizarre but inspiring experience. They arrived and Jonny handed them the sheet music that they were supposed to play but they quickly realised it wasn't really necessary. Saxophonist Steve Hamilton, who played on the sessions, told this author that they were allowed to do pretty much whatever they wanted.

"Jonny Greenwood presented us with parts which were completely dispensed with after about five minutes," he says, "and we just made it up as we went along. There was a core part that they wanted to hear but only very subliminally, I think. We just basically digested that and made up our own thing and made a bit of a noise."

To start with, it didn't quite work. The horn players weren't used to performing together in such a loose, improvised fashion and it was hard to see exactly what Thom and Jonny wanted. It's not entirely clear if they knew themselves.

"It wasn't gelling," says baritone sax player Stan Harrison, who also played. "It wasn't unified. I said to Thom and Jonny Greenwood, 'One way for you to solve this problem would be for you to conduct us. If you want us to play louder then make this type of hand motion, softer this type of hand motion, more frenetic this kind of hand motion. At least then we'll have more of an idea of what the whole thing is supposed to feel like."

They weren't sure. The whole point was that it was supposed to be improvised and both Thom and Jonny felt slightly embarrassed about conducting a group of talented, professional musicians. [With admirable modesty] they were both conscious that their own creativity and imagination often outstripped their technical proficiency. Who were they to 'conduct' anybody? But when they accepted that the session needed some kind of direction, things took a sudden leap forward.

"Thom or Jonny said, 'I've never done anything like that before, I don't know,' says Stan. "But we tried it and within seconds they were jumping up and down and spinning around. I think Thom was on my side and Jonny was on the other side. It was something that I wish had been filmed. It was just so much fun to watch. All of a sudden they were taking these conductor roles when ten seconds before they were so reluctant to do it and then they were going crazy!"

It was a hot day but, once he'd got started, Thom threw himself into the role of conductor with an enthusiasm and energy that startled and inspired the horn players. "It almost felt like he was doing a Jackson Pollock," says Steve. "He was jumping up and down, doing what he does onstage, but he was doing that almost in an exaggerated fashion. It seemed a little bit bizarre. Musicians are typically, by nature, a little bit reserved sometimes but it was actually completely spot-on. He got exactly what he wanted out of us by whatever he was doing. I'm not sure what he was doing! It did actually inspire us to really give it some. He was saturated with sweat just from jumping up and down."

In fact Thom jumped up and down so vigorously that, he said later, he ended up breaking his foot. Nevertheless he was delighted with the result. He wanted them to create the kind of discordant, violent energy that he felt was trapped in a traffic jam and they got it absolutely right. On the finished version, you can almost hear the angry car horns.

"On the day I said to them, 'You know when you've been in a traffic jam for four hours and if someone says the wrong thing to you, you'll just kill 'em, you'll fucking snap and probably throttle them?" he said to *Juice* magazine.

The horn players didn't escape the band's notorious perfectionism. Thom and Jonny were excited and enthusiastic about what they were hearing but they kept thinking that they might be able to get something better. "They kept coming up to us and saying 'This is so good, this is brilliant, that's the take we love,'" says Steve. "And then, 'Can we do another one?' It was the usual thing – 'That's perfect, let's do another one.'"

Meanwhile the rest of the band kept coming in and complimenting them on what they were coming up with. "It was a pleasure working with them," Steve says. "They were so complimentary. They kept saying, 'Oh, it's so good, thank you for coming down and doing this.' It was almost embarrassing how often they said how good it was. Well, actually it isn't that good! We're just mucking around on our instruments."

But they were all impressed by the creative relationship between Thom and Jonny. "Thom didn't communicate that much with us," says Steve. "It was more like he was driving the ship and Jonny was first officer relaying the artistic information to us. I remember it being very intense but I've never done a session where you could really just do whatever you liked within quite a broad framework.

I remember getting in the car with one of the other players afterwards and the typical thing with musicians is that you give them a gig and they moan about it. We said, 'It's really bizarre, there's nothing to moan about.' They were really nice. They cooked us a really nice dinner and the music was good and they were really complimentary!"

With its weirdly catchy bass riff, played on record by Thom, 'The National Anthem' proved that they could make electronic music that had the same bite as rock. Months later, when they played it live for a French TV station, they showed the session musicians how much they'd appreciated their contribution.

"One nice thing they did in Paris, they presented us all with a platinum disc of *Kid A*," says Steve. "Bands very often don't bother to do that sort of thing and they did it personally. I remember being quite chuffed about that. They called us into a room when we were doing [French TV channel] *Canal Plus* and Thom said, 'I'd just like to thank you for all your hard work and present these to you.' It was very sweet. I was quite touched. Bands don't tend to do that anymore."

15

TRAVELLING CIRCUS

By the end of 1999, Radiohead had finished six songs and it seemed like they were all moving in the same direction. Thom was pleasantly surprised to be able to sit back and listen as Jonny took over the demo he'd done for 'How To Disappear Completely', writing a string arrangement, conducting an orchestra and playing the Martenot. This record – to be called *Kid A* – was the album where Thom had dominated proceedings more than any other but it was a relief when he realised that the rest of the band were with him.

"Thom drove the album," said Ed afterwards to *Q*. "It was an eye-opener for me. He has a great art school ethic. He did art at university and he has that kind of drive: OK, I've done that. Now I'm going to move on. I think I can be vaguely objective about this, and I think Thom is in the line of the John Lennons, the David Bowies, part of that heritage. He has an incredible gift."

By now, all of Radiohead were experimenting with sampling, cutting-and-pasting rhythm, as well as finding new roles for themselves within the band. They had one more big bust up, on February 1, but by Spring 2000, all of a sudden, they had thirty songs. Many of these, typically, were tracks that they'd rejected back in Copenhagen and Paris when their confidence was at a low ebb. They listened to songs like 'Morning Bell' and 'Spinning Plates' and suddenly realised how good they were. According to Thom, they listened to them and said, "That's fucking amazing, why the hell did we stop working on that?" Part of the reason why things suddenly accelerated was because many of the songs only needed minor tweaks. Often when they'd got close to finishing something, Thom had veered off to start something else. "I was doing that for about six months," he said to *Hot Press*, "because I really didn't want to finish things and have to put them out to people and have to deal with all that crap that I'd essentially forgotten about."

They'd had weeks and months of doing almost nothing but, eventually, Thom realised that was part of the creative process, too.

It was much easier to deal with in their own studio where there wasn't an accountant hovering in the background worrying about how much it was all going to cost. As with *OK Computer*, though, the hardest part was still to come. They had to choose what songs to put on the album and what order to put them in. It sounds simple but Thom always found it unbearable.

"The track listing is always the hardest part for me," he told *NY Rock*. "It is so difficult and almost painful. I can only use the old metaphor about songs being like children. My songs are my kids and some of them stay with me. Some others I have to send out, out to the war."

This might seem extreme but the rest of the band agreed about how important it was to get the track-listing right, even if they weren't as obsessive about it as Thom. "I can assure you: it's hell," Colin said. "We have meetings that take hours – often from 4p.m. until midnight – only about the order of the songs."

"I don't think you have any idea how vital it is," said Ed, "until you actually fuck it up, which we did big time on the first record." Perhaps he meant the unfortunate segue from 'Creep' to 'How Do You?', but then the second song wouldn't have fitted well anywhere.

The glut of material caused another argument as they tried to decide whether to release a double album. With such a dramatic change of direction, some of the band thought that it would be too much to take. But then again they'd put so much work into the songs that for them not to see the light of day now seemed ridiculous. They'd worked on 'Knives Out', alone, for 373 days despite the fact that it was, as Ed wrote in his studio diary, one of the most straight-ahead songs they'd done in years.

It was as if they weren't sure they were allowed to do anything that simple anymore. For months they'd fiddled around with it, adding things, changing things, before, finally, deciding that it was fine as it was.

Meanwhile, outside the studio, speculation was growing as to what they had been doing exactly all this time. *Melody Maker* even sent their News Reporter to Oxford to see if he could find out what they were up to by interviewing friends and neighbours. The attention bemused Radiohead. They'd never really understood the feverish reaction to *OK Computer* and they weren't ready to deal with the extraordinary anticipation for *Kid A*. It was particularly worrying that the *Melody Maker* article promised that Radiohead were about to "return rock to us". At this point, they still weren't entirely sure how the record was going to sound but they had no intention of doing anything of the sort.

When the record was finally done, the overwhelming feeling was one of relief. Immediately after the sessions were over, Thom was asked to record a duet with Björk for the soundtrack to her film *Dancer In The Dark* and that proved to be a very different experience in the studio. Suddenly the weight was off his shoulders. Björk was somebody who shared Thom's approach to music. They were both perfectionists who approached things very differently to most musicians. But it wasn't easy to blend Björk's exuberant voice with Thom's much softer tones. The result, 'I've Seen It All', is odd but also very haunting. Björk pitches her voice much lower than usual, almost whispering, while Thom murmurs alongside like a ghost. If nothing else it was a reminder that making music didn't need to be the tormented business of so many Radiohead sessions.

The opportunity to go out on tour should have been another relief but Thom wasn't sure he was ready to be a travelling salesman again. Long before *No Logo*, he'd had problems with the sponsorship-festooned tour circuit. But Chris and Bryce suggested that they now had the clout to do things differently. They didn't have to play the usual giant Carling toilets. They could do things their way, hire a massive marquee and play in their own space with the best possible sound and with complete control. Thom still wasn't convinced.

"If ultimately I had been left to it, I wouldn't have done it," he said in a TV interview. "And the others said: Go on, it will be great, you'll like it!' I had real horrors about the tent and everything, I thought we were crazy."

It was a pretty crazy idea. It must have been much more expensive than playing normal shows. It was more expensive, even, than the first shows they played after recording, a series of gigs in extraordinary venues across Europe. The first two dates were supposed to be held at Roman amphitheatres in France. The first one in Arles almost had to be cancelled due to torrential rain but they just about managed to get through it. The second night they weren't so lucky. When they arrived in Vaison La Romaine, a bigger amphitheatre cut into the side of a hill with an amazing view of the

French countryside, the sun was blazing. Then it started raining again. The water was flowing down the roads and flooding the stage, threatening the equipment. A previous year's flood had killed eleven people so they decided that they couldn't risk it. Their crew spent much of the night drying everything out with hairdryers before they headed off to Barcelona.

But as the European shows went on, they were growing in confidence. When they played seven new songs, the reaction from their fans was ecstatic and the early reviews were equally positive. When they headed out in the big tops they sounded even better. Their complete control over the sound meant the dates, in London's Victoria Park and at Warrington then Glasgow, were among the best they'd ever done. And the new stuff was greeted with far more enthusiasm than any other similarly enormous band could expect when unveiling a new direction.

It helped that many of the fans already knew the songs, or versions of them. Things had changed since 1997 and *OK Computer*. Napster was a huge phenomenon and at least fourteen songs from the *Kid A* sessions had been illegally circulating on the internet, some for up to two years. The music industry as a whole was starting to tremble. Chris and Bryce were worried, too.

"It was funny," Thom said in an interview with the *New Yorker*, "because when we were working on *Kid A* … our managers – you know, they occasionally go to the States, and they keep in contact with what's going on – used to come to the studio and hang out and say, 'Things are changing.'"

But it turned out that the changes benefited them. For once they were at the right place at the right time. Fans had been given a chance to get used to the weird new sounds of *Kid A* before they arrived and so they were prepared. Ironically, it was reviewers at many of the music magazines who were caught on the hop. It garnered many good reviews but some hacks were just confused. Even songs like 'The National Anthem', which, with its hugely catchy bass line is now a live favourite, were greeted as weird aberrations. Part of the problem was that, in response to the leaks, EMI had decided not to send out preview copies to journalists. Instead they were invited to listening sessions where they were given one sitting with the album before going home and writing about it. In 2008 this is, sadly, normal practise but at the time it was very new and rather bizarre. "All the reviewers were saying, 'Uh, this isn't Radiohead, we don't recognise it, it might be good later on, but right now I don't get it all,'" said Thom.

Listening to *Kid A* now, it's easy to forget what bewilderment it caused when it first came out. Part of its success was that it redefined what people thought of as Radiohead's sound. On YouTube now, under a performance of 'High And Dry', there's a comment from a confused young fan saying that, although cool, the song doesn't sound much like Radiohead. A whole generation has grown up for whom the band mean adventurous sonic experimentation and nothing else. But *Kid A* wasn't Radiohead's *Metal Machine Music,* Lou Reed's famously unlistenable fuck-you to the music industry. The title track, admittedly, wafts and wanders a little. But 'Everything In Its Right Place', 'The National Anthem', 'Idioteque' and 'Optimistic' are proper pop songs with highly memorable hooks, albeit very different to the kinds of hooks they'd used before.

After the hype following *OK Computer*, it was inevitable that many journalists would be preparing to cut Radiohead down to size again. When the record came out, though, it didn't matter. It went straight in at Number 1 in the UK and many countries in the world, including, incredibly America, the first time a British act had done that for three years. They immediately went out there to play, starting at New York's famous Roseland Ballroom. The response was phenomenal. "The day before we did the gig at the Roseland, people were queuing round the block three times to get tickets," says Andy Bush. "It was like The Beatles. It was colossal."

The response in America for *Kid A* was the same as the response for *OK Computer* in the UK. *OK Computer* didn't do all that well when it was first released in the States. It was adored by other bands but Radiohead didn't get all that much press or airplay. Many DJs and magazines were determined, as British outlets had been after *The Bends*, not to get caught on the hop again. So when Radiohead flew out there for *Kid A*, they were like conquering heroes and they were even invited on to sketch show *Saturday Night Live*.

Saturday Night Live is an American institution. It's been running continuously since the 1970s and it's launched the careers of some of the world's most successful comedians. On the surface it was all fun and glitz but underneath it was ferociously professional and efficient. Thom had been warned by Michael Stipe that it could be a difficult show to play. To make things more tricky, they chose to play 'The National Anthem' with the full eight-piece brass section.

"It was very American," sax player Steve Hamilton remembers. "Very intense from the crew's point of view. You'd have ten minutes here then one minute rest and then another ten minutes, so it was a little bit uptight but I don't think that came across to the band or to us that much. [Actress] Kate Hudson was presenting the show and she was practically naked so I think everyone was happy!"

"I was struck by how self-effacing the Radiohead guys were in the face of a deluge of hysterical enthusiasm, from the audience, from the presenters, from the floor managers, the whole thing," says Andy Bush. "There was a little bit of that lovely dour British thing going on. The Brits can't quite hack the Americans whooping it up. It was funny. The audience were just going ape and as soon as it was over Thom and the guys were just sitting around impassively like nothing had happened."

But although Thom might not have been matching the audience for enthusiasm and joy, it was still a great moment. To come to a place that was so far removed from everything that they were about and to take it over in the way they did was an incredible feeling. It was one of those moments that the kid who, half-sarcastically, half-seriously wished he was "special" had dreamed about. "The highlight of the whole *Kid A* thing was our *Saturday Night Live* performance," Thom said later. "I was so proud of that. I was walking on water for a week after that – I felt so good."

"It was like we were going over there with them on the crest of their wave," says Steve Hamilton. "We turned up and played a gig at the Roseland Ballroom first and they were Number 1. It was a real buzz. Everyone was so happy and delighted about it. You couldn't have been there at a better time with them. You got the feeling that they were really enjoying themselves."

By now, it was as though the horrible, drawn-out arguments of the long recording process had never happened. They were back to enjoying what they were doing and enjoying each other's company. They could look back on the recording sessions like a long war that they'd eventually won. "*Pablo Honey* was done in three weeks," said Ed dryly in a TV interview. "*The Bends* was about sixteen weeks total recording time, *OK Computer* was six months and *Kid A* was … generations."

"Everybody was completely at peace with each other I think," says Steve. "I've never seen any of them shout or argue. They all seemed like good mates. They didn't seem like the kind of people who would have rows, apart from Thom maybe, they seemed very relaxed with each other. They were very complimentary about what we were doing. Which is rare! You shouldn't praise musicians too much or they'll ask for too much money."

The only disappointment was how quickly *Kid A* vanished from the charts. It didn't have the longevity of *OK Computer* or *The Bends*. Few of the tracks were played on the radio and most of their fan base bought it in the first week. It didn't help that they refused to release any singles or make any videos for it. They'd always had an odd, ambivalent attitude towards the art form. Despite the fact that they'd made some of the most memorable videos ever, Thom still referred to them as "commercials". He didn't think they represented the album as a whole.

"Music videos just make me think of [Peter Gabriel's] 'Sledgehammer'," he said to *Jam*, "and that was when it was innovative. It is like tap-dancing, [that's] what I compare it to. It had its day, really ... I think miming is absurd."

He resented the fact that they would spend hundreds of thousands of dollars making videos, as much money as they would spend on the album, just to get it on MTV next to all the other adverts. "The thing that really did my head in was going home and turning on the TV and the ads for fucking banks and cars being more like MTV videos than the MTV videos," he said to *Juice* Magazine. "And it seemed like there was nowhere to go. Whatever the new aesthetic was would be in a fucking car advert a week later."

This was even truer than he thought.

"I do quite a lot of music for commercials," Steve Hamilton says. "And I've had quite a lot of briefs from people saying that they love that track and they want a similar sound. When I tell them that I played on it, 'Wow! That's mad, man!'"

Instead of videos, then, for *Kid A* Thom and Stanley Donwood came up with one minute "blip-verts", video clips featuring excerpts from the album. "Four minutes is too long for a car advert, so it is certainly too long for a record," Thom said.

They put far less conventional effort into promoting *Kid A* than they had *OK Computer*, but Thom was still a bit put out that it didn't do as well commercially. He seemed to forget that their last album was helped on its way by a massive, two-year long tour that almost broke him. "Book me on a nine-month tour and I'll be back home doing a Liam [Gallagher] within a week," Thom warned in a TV interview. Still, there was a part of him that thought people ought to somehow get the music anyway.

"I was a bit disappointed that, in Britain, *Kid A* didn't stick around very long because of the likes of Robbie Williams and all that," he said.

Still, there was always *Kid A: Part II – Amnesiac*.

16

KID B

In retrospect, Radiohead's fifth studio album, *Amnesiac*, wasn't a very good marketing move. It was the first album that Radiohead had done where they hadn't leapt dramatically forward from the one before. Before its release, there were rumours that these were the songs where they'd gone back to the safe, familiar territory of rock guitars. Afterwards the fact that it contained great tracks like 'Pyramid Song' and 'I Might Be Wrong' was rather overlooked in the disappointment that it didn't have another 'Paranoid Android' or 'Fake Plastic Trees'. It was, some said, simply 'Kid B'. This suspicion was bolstered by Colin's description of the selection process, which was widely misinterpreted.

"I'm not sure they are two records," he said to *JAM*. "We had that group of songs to make one record, and the other ones are left over. We had, say, 23 songs and we wanted to have around 47 minutes of music, so we chose the best combination out of that number (for *Kid A*), and the rest are waiting on the bench, waiting to be picked for the next team line-up."

This, perhaps inadvertently, makes the likes of 'Pyramid Song' and 'Knives Out' sound like the little kid with glasses who's the last to get picked for the football team. The alternative version of events that Thom and Jonny offered was more flattering – these were simply songs that wouldn't fit alongside the ones from *Kid A*.

"*Kid A* pulled itself together very easily and really obviously. But *Amnesiac* didn't," Thom said. Even on *Amnesiac*, there were great songs that didn't make the cut. Ed's online diary had tantalised fans with repeated mentions of a track called 'Cuttooth' which, he kept promising, was almost finished. It was mentioned more times than any other song and it sounded like it was going to be the centrepiece of the record. The original version was over eight minutes long. In the end, it was cut down to just over five minutes and relegated to a B-side. Listening to it now, it's an interesting glimpse of a different kind of album that Radiohead could have made. It sounds more like *Xtrmntr*-era Primal Scream than anything they put on *Kid A* or *Amnesiac*. It's got a rumbling, aggressive, industrial quality. The song was partly cannibalised for 'Myxomatosis' on the later *Hail To The Thief* album, with Thom borrowing a couple of lines of lyrics.

There was only one song that they added to the *Kid A* sessions for *Amnesiac* and that was the extraordinary, disconcerting 'Life In A Glasshouse'. It was a seemingly autobiographical tale of somebody who feels that they're always being watched by the press and, more specifically, the effect it has on that person's partner. There were obvious parallels with Thom's own life. The song was written during the period captured in *Meeting People Is Easy* and director Grant Gee thinks his continuous scrutiny might have, consciously or unconsciously, helped inspire it.

"Originally it had the line, 'little cameras in every room/they're watching me', he says, "which was us because we used to go in and rig little tiny, £49 pinhole cameras in their dressing rooms whenever we could. And just record them in there so we wouldn't have to be in the room. That was one of our innovations to overcome this problem of, 'Hello! I'm just filming you! Pretend I'm not here.' So we'd stick cameras with gaffa tape to the corners of the rooms."

Thom has said that it was inspired by an interview he read with the wife of a celebrity. Her house was staked out by the press and she cut up the papers with her picture on them and pasted them over the windows so the photographers were looking in at the images they'd already taken.

When 'Life In A Glass House' was demoed, Jonny said that, "it could sound like a bad Cure song, it could be brilliant." In reality, at this point in their career, there was no chance that it was going to sound like any kind of Cure song. They decided that, just like 'The National Anthem', it needed a jazz element but this time they went for a very different sound, enlisting the help of a pillar of the British jazz scene, Humphrey Lyttelton. Colin had once booked him to play at Cambridge University when he was Entertainments Officer, but by the year 2000 he was in his seventies. He was Eton educated, BBC through-and-through and best known for being the chairman of the whimsical Radio 4 panel show, 'I'm Sorry I Haven't A Clue'.

Despite this he did have a lot in common with them. There had always been a Radio 4 element to their aesthetic and, like them, he combined indisputable poshness with an anarchic streak. In 1941 he fought in southern Italy and supposedly arrived at the battle of Salerno with a pistol in one hand and a trumpet in the other. His only hit, 1956's 'Bad Penny Blues', was recorded with the maverick pop producer Joe Meek. When Radiohead contacted him to ask if he'd work with them, he listened to one of his grandchildren's copies of *OK Computer* and agreed straight away. When he turned up to the recording sessions, the band were shocked to find that one of his band had only been released from hospital the day before after having open heart surgery.

Saxophonist Steve Hamilton met Humphrey when he joined Radiohead for a performance of 'Life In A Glass House' on *Later With Jools Holland* and he told this author that while the collaboration might have seemed incongruous to start with, it ultimately made perfect sense. "I knew Humphrey before and we were chatting in the canteen and it did seem a bit odd that he was doing this thing with Radiohead," he says. "And it looked a bit odd as well, but it all came together and they were just making music together. I think he thought it was a bit of an adventure. It was at the BBC so he was on his own turf. He probably felt more comfortable there than anybody else. I think he thoroughly enjoyed it. You couldn't fail to get stuck in and enjoy that sort of thing because it was very laid-back. He was at the BBC and playing with his quartet, playing his own style of music. It just happened to be with a really cutting-edge band. He seemed completely unfazed by it."

"It was a pretty inspired idea from Radiohead to put that New Orleans funeral cortege thing in their music," says Andy Bush. "That's what they were after and what better guys to get, I think Humphrey really liked it. Whether guys of that generation are into that genre I don't know, but they all respected them for having really fertile ideas. I think they were genuinely happy to be there. It's unusual for somebody to write a script, musically, that incorporates all those disparate elements and it really, really works."

Seven years later, when Humphrey died, Jonny wrote on the Radiohead website: "We were all sorry to hear of Humphrey Lyttelton's death – he was an inspiring person to record with, and without his direction, we'd never have recorded/released 'Life In A Glasshouse'. So go and find 'Bad Penny Blues', and celebrate his life with some hot jazz."

'Life In A Glass House' confused people a little when it first came out but, like so many Radiohead songs, it's an experiment that paid off and one that gets better with every listen. The fact that Thom was happy to put out a song with a coherent narrative, a story that may or may not have been semi-autobiographical, also suggested that he was starting to recover from the fear of self-revelation that had struck him prior to *Kid A*.

He'd been surprised when he read Radiohead's early press to see how much was read into his lyrics. Ever since then he'd retreated from the direct approach of, say, 'Creep', towards increasingly oblique messages. On 'High And Dry', when he wanted to write about bands losing the plot, or his own relationship, he transferred the story to Evel Knievel. On *OK Computer*, most of the tracks are observational, stories about the things he'd seen in the previous few years. By the time of *Kid A* and *Amnesiac*, even that seemed like too much self-exposure. Most of the lyrics are deliberately obscure.

"We had this whole thing about *Amnesiac* being like getting into someone's attic, opening the chest and finding their notes from a journey that they'd been on," Thom told Nick Kent. "There's a story but no literal plot, so you have to keep picking out fragments. You know something really important has happened to this person that's ended up completely changing them, but you're never told exactly what it is."

This is best represented visually by the video they made for 'I Might Be Wrong', the first American single release. "They wanted it to look like it'd been buried for years and then dug up," director Sophie Muller says, "like it had been there for thirty or forty years and it had been attacked by worms and rotted."

The video is deliberately obscure, filmed in black and white with dark, blurred images of Thom and Jonny reeling about in front of the camera in a massive, empty room. It was made to look as uninviting as possible, the antithesis of the typical music video. "The suggestion I made was that we use a pinhole camera and make it look very unpolished," says Sophie. "If you use a pinhole camera, there's no lens, it's just a sheet of paper with a pinhole in it, so the image comes through the pinhole and reflects on the back of the camera and that's it. You need a lot of light for there to be any image. So we had to use a very powerful light and they'd be very near it. We tried a lot of things, like slowing the song down four times and getting them to sing. I couldn't even recognise the song. It just meant that the lens would be open longer for each frame. Thom really got into that. He found it quite exciting because he finds it quite boring doing normal playback."

Thom liked it because, unlike so many of their other videos, it wasn't a big, 'showy' statement. If it said anything, it was that they were desperate to go back underground. The title of the album referred to Thom's feeling that, like a goldfish, he was just going round and round in circles and doing the same thing over and over again. Never learning from his mistakes.

"Most of the stuff on *Amnesiac* is about being trapped in one particular lock in your heart or your head," Thom said in a TV interview. It was a feeling he'd had a lot during the period after *OK Computer*, constantly thinking the same things over and over. *Amnesiac* then, also represented a desire to forget. It was a theme he'd go back to with his later solo album *The Eraser*.

"The song ['I Might Be Wrong'] really comes as much from what my long-term partner Rachel was saying to me, like she does all the time, 'Be proud of what you've done. Don't look back and just carry on like nothing's happened. Just let the bad stuff go,'" he said to Nick Kent. "When someone's constantly trying to help you out and you're trying to express something really awful, you're desperately trying to sort yourself out and you can't – you just can't. And then one day you finally hear them – you finally understand, after months and months of utter fucking torment: that's what that song is about."

This sense of agitation and fear is one of the things that comes across most strongly in both *Kid A* and *Amnesiac*, but the latter album is a little softer and slower. Outside America, the first single to be released was 'Pyramid Song' and this might have surprised many people who'd read the reviews and assumed that Radiohead were now an unlistenable art rock band. It was a gentle, almost lush song with one of Thom's most poignant vocals. It was written after a day spent looking at Egyptian figurines in a museum and it has an exotic, dream-like feel.

"The Egyptians have these rowboats that when they die they go through the Milky Way in," he said in an interview with *Yahoo*. "It was based on that and a fusion of experiences that I had dreamed … I was reading the *Tibetan Book Of The Dead* too; that is guaranteed to fuck you up."

Despite very little airplay, 'Pyramid Song' was Radiohead's biggest hit in the UK since 'Paranoid Android', peaking at Number 5. It was a vindication of Thom's belief that it was the "best thing they'd ever put on tape". Further vindication came when they played their only UK gig of the year, back in their hometown of Oxford. It was an outdoor festival at South Park on the edge of the city with support from Humphrey Lyttelton's band, extraordinary Icelandic newcomers Sigur Rós, Beck, and fellow locals Supergrass. In some respects it was similar to their Glastonbury performance four years previously. Inevitably it rained. It always seemed to rain for them at big festivals. And, despite the fact that it was their own show, they had the same problems with equipment meltdown that they'd had in 1997. "The only UK gig – no pressure," Thom quipped as his keyboard failed completely.

But, from the opening bass line of 'The National Anthem', they comprehensively proved how good the songs on *Kid A* and *Amnesiac* were. The idea that they were oddball experiments or deliberately inaccessible was washed away with the rain. They also proved that they'd finally accepted their past with a remarkable, communal sing-a-long performance of 'Creep'. Even for a band who'd always insisted that Oxford was no more than the place they happened to live, it must have been an emotional moment. It was the climax of three incredible years when, for the second time, they'd almost lost it and come back even stronger.

The second single to be released from *Amnesiac*, 'Knives Out', received more airplay than anything else they'd done for a long time. It was a little more conventional, with a jangly guitar sound that was reminiscent of The Smiths. It wasn't one of their best songs but, helped by a brilliant, bizarre video from French director Michel Gondry, it too went Top Twenty in the UK.

Still, the long slog of recording had worn them all out. The next time they made an album, they swore once again, they would do it quickly and not over-think things. *Amnesiac* is dedicated to "Noah and Jamie", the first children of Thom Yorke and Phil Selway and, inevitably, they were now the priority. The arrival of his first son was also the moment that Thom's political campaigning took on a new seriousness and a new urgency. Even when he was a student he'd been socially concerned but he was starting to feel like many of the issues he cared about most were now a matter of life and death.

17

ELECTIONEERING

On June 18, 1999, Thom's commitment to political change took a far more concrete expression than it had ever done before. It was the G8 meeting in Cologne, Germany and he was there, with a delegation including Bono, Bob Geldof, Youssou N'Dour and Perry Farrell of Jane's Addiction. The idea had been to have a photo call in front of the conference building and then hand a petition over to the German Chancellor, Gerhard Schröeder, calling for the West to cancel Third World debt by the year 2000.

But, as they were hustled down a narrow street by the German police, far away from the conference hall, Thom wondered why he'd come. "There were seventeen million signatures on that petition," he wrote in an article for Jubilee 2000 (the international coalition seeking the eradication of such debt). "There were 50,000 people in a human chain around Cologne and yet we were patronised, trivialised and bullied by both the G8 and the media."

Throughout the day, the authorities changed the route of the march, causing increasing frustration. Eventually they were searched for weapons and then allowed to meet the Chancellor on the steps of a museum well away from where the G8 meeting was being held. It was, Thom thought, a kind of game. The politicians were trying to give them as little as possible while making it look like they agreed with every word they said. He'd always been highly dubious about whether there was any point to this kind of PR politics and his experiences in Germany confirmed his belief that he was right.

"Thom Yorke has zero tolerance for politicians," Bono wrote in an online diary of the protests. "That video where he looks like Johnny Rotten in a shopping basket ('Fake Plastic Trees') is closer to his personality than the choir of street angels that haunts your ear. He was bristling with nervous energy and I wonder if that was a rocket launcher in his bag."

"Politicians nod and say 'yes', but that's what's dangerous about this particular moment in time," Thom said to the *BBC*, "because what's predicted at the end of the G8 summit this weekend, after we've handed in the petition, is they'll announce that they've come up with a package which is basically what we asked for, which is actually not true at all – it's a complete fabrication."

Before getting to Cologne, he'd spent hours poring over facts and figures about debt, ready for any question that was put to him. Instead he found that journalists were confusing the Jubilee 2000 Campaign with the Reclaim The Streets riots back in London. There was little interest in the substance behind the protests. He saw how skilful the politicians were at taking credit for the movement towards dropping the debt, without actually promising to do anything. Tony Blair, in particular, was a target for Thom's ire.

"You have Blair standing there smiling saying, 'It'll all be fine, we'll cancel all these debts now,' he said to Ireland's *Hot Press*. "He was scoring all these celebrity points with Bono and Bob Geldof, and Alastair Campbell running around, you know, making sure he got the coverage he wanted, even though they actually hadn't delivered anything at all. And, you know, I kinda saw the light in a certain way, but in another way it was incredibly disillusioning."

But then he came from the generation that had seen Bono at Live Aid and seen that charity on its own wasn't enough, so it wasn't as if he was an innocent before Jubilee 2000. It seemed like every other month since then there had been another charity concert, they even played one, 'Free Tibet' in 1997, and yet the root causes of the problems remained. Since Live Aid, the West had taken vastly more money from the developing world in interest payments on debt than it had given back with charity. Thom likened the West to a loan shark and called the approach "basically extortion".

Thom had been willing to try the new approach to politics of Bono and Bob Geldof in the late 1990s. It involved, essentially, treating politicians as compassionate people who were open to persuasion. Instead of spitting at world leaders from the outside, they were now trying to change things from the inside. But when it didn't seem to work, Thom was angrier than ever. This came across in the songs like 'You And Whose Army?' on *Amnesiac*, which was none-too-subtly aimed at Blair and his supposed 'cronies'. If he thought things were bad in 1999, though, they took a distinct turn for the worst in 2000 with the election of George W Bush in America. As a highly prescient headline in satirical newspaper *The Onion* said about America that year, 'Our Long National Nightmare Of Peace And Prosperity Is Finally Over'.

That year, Thom had a sense of hopelessness that was only occasionally blasted away by righteous indignation. He could easily have given up on politicking but there was another issue that seemed even more important than Jubilee 2000. The special edition of *Kid A* included what, at the time, seemed a bit of a curio, a chart giving details of the melt-rates of glaciers around the world. Even then there were still many people who disagreed with the science of man-made global warming but, as it became harder to deny that it was happening, Thom couldn't understand why nothing was being done.

"Like many of my friends and anyone who has kids, it's a difficult thing," he said later, in an interview to promote Friends Of The Earth. "You wake up in the middle of the night thinking about it. You look into the eyes of your children and hope that they don't grow up in a future that has riots for fuel or constant floods and infrastructure collapse."

Part of his despair between *OK Computer* and *Kid A* came from a feeling of helplessness. Every new scientific study was producing more evidence to suggest that global warming was a massive threat to the state of the planet and yet it didn't seem like there was anything he or anybody else could do. It would be several years before he would feel that there was any possibility of change. Despite this, he'd always gone through cycles of despair and enthusiasm. Even at university he was heavily involved in politics.

"He's always had a real conscience and been involved in politics, campaigning and standing up for his beliefs," Exeter University student Eileen Doran told the author for this book. "A lot of us got involved in that. It was the time of fighting against student loans and all that. He's always been somebody who cares about what's happening in the world. Pretty much how he is now really. He's not really all that different now as far as I can tell."

Thom's politics have only rarely touched directly on his music. The cynicism of 'Electioneering' and the menace of 'You And Whose Army?' were exceptions but generally he liked things to be more oblique. An example was a new track that appeared at the end of 2001 on the *I Might Be Wrong: Live Recordings* album. 'True Love Waits' was a treat for fans who wished the band would abandon all the electronic stuff and go back to something more 'traditional'. It was a delicate, acoustic track partly inspired by a story Thom read about a child who was left behind by his parents when they went on holiday, living on a diet of lollipops and crisps. That was Thom's territory. With the next album, though, they would choose a title that put politics right back at the centre of their stage.

18

HAIL TO THE THIEF

"When we finished *Kid A* and *Amnesiac*, we were thinking, *So, what kind of lurch in another direction are we gonna take now?*" Thom said to *The Daily Telegraph* after the release of the band's sixth album, *Hail To The Thief*. He knew by now that some kind of a "lurch" was exactly what the public and the press were expecting. It was a new and bizarre form of pressure. The pressure to do absolutely anything they wanted, as long as it was completely different to anything they'd done before. He spent six months doing nothing except being a father until, he says, Rachel suggested: "'Why don't you just do a record where you let it happen? No agenda, nothing.' And that sort of made things click." Ed O'Brien said, "The whole thing was to do it quickly and not think about it too much, which was new for us, obviously." They'd vaguely thought about knocking out an album quickly before, but this time they meant it. They couldn't take another three years like the ones leading up to the release of *Kid A* and *Amnesiac*. They went back into their rehearsal space and tried out the new songs for three months as they had prior to *OK Computer*, recording the results every day and listening to the tapes every evening. But this time Thom refused to obsess over them as he had before. Instead, he let Jonny scrutinise the details. He wanted this record to be done without the endless over-analysis of previous albums. When word started filtering out about these sessions, it provided further encouragement for fans of their early stuff.

"It's all loud and it's all guitars," Jonny said. "It's exciting to make loud music again. It's sounding good and fresh." He even said in one interview that they'd been covering Neil Young's 'Cinnamon Girl', rediscovering the joys of guitar chords. "In two days of rehearsal, we've played it between ten and fifteen times," he enthused. "Loud minor chords. Distortion. Fantastic!"

Then, as they had so many times before, they took the new songs out on the road, playing them during a tour of Portugal and Spain.

Thom wrote and rewrote them as they went, never quite sure whether what they would play on any given night would be the finished version or not.

"We booked this little tour where we actually didn't decide what we were going to play," he said to *Launch*, "because that was the only way that we were able to get it together fast enough. Certainly with me, I was writing stuff that I wouldn't normally write lyrically, 'cause I really didn't have time to think about it. Whatever I had, that was it, too late, tough." Then, when they had the songs ready, they prepared to go back into the studio in, of all places, LA, the home of the vampires who'd populated 'Paranoid Android'. It was the home of Hollywood, plastic surgery, cock-rock and hair metal. Not a very Radiohead place at all, then. Nevertheless, Thom was perfectly happy. Nigel Godrich had suggested that they record in the famous Ocean Way studio in Hollywood. It was where Brian Wilson had driven himself half-mad trying to finish The Beach Boys' 'Good Vibrations', so it was very suited to Radiohead's similarly painstaking approach. Although Thom had often spoken about his distaste for professional studios, the chance to go and record somewhere like that couldn't be passed up. Also, they had bad memories of the decision to start the previous records in Copenhagen in the middle of winter. The Californian sunshine seemed more appealing. They were family men now and it simply wasn't feasible for them to take years making another record. After a long time out of the studio, Thom was itching to get back in.

"When I go to the studio now," he said to *Launch*, "whether it's our own studio or somewhere else, it's something I've been looking forward to for months. So I don't resent it in any way. I'm like, 'Yes, yes, at last!'" They even took a little dip into the celebrity pool, going to a film premier and the party afterwards. "We went to LA for the sunshine and the glamour," Thom joked.

Unlike for most bands, however, LA didn't provide a lot of distraction. Essentially they treated it almost like a day job. They went to the studio for two weeks and recorded a song a day. It was that simple. It was, in fact, much like various other periods of recording they'd had on previous albums. The difference was that it was neither preceded by months of anguish nor followed by months of painfully picking the songs they'd recorded apart. They didn't give themselves the chance.

There was no agenda and no rules about what instruments they could and could not use. If they felt a song needed a guitar, they would use a guitar and if it needed something generated on the computer, they would use that. The only agenda they had was that everything needed to be done quickly, without the over-analysis of the last three albums. Thom wanted the songs to be shorter, too. Out with any prog-rock comparisons.

"After doing a take, I'd run into the control room and go to the sound engineer [Darrell Thorpe], 'How long is that Darrell?'" he said in a TV interview, "and he'd go, 'Five minutes thirty', and I'd go, 'OK, let's cut two minutes off.'

It struck Thom that The Beatles had managed to make experimental tunes in multi-parts, like 'Happiness Is A Warm Gun', that came in under three-and-a-half minutes, so why couldn't Radiohead? To him, six-minute songs seemed rather self-indulgent at this point.

The result wasn't quite the guitar-fest that they'd promised or the *OK Computer II* that some people had hoped for. On *Hail To The Thief*, Thom's piano was much in evidence again while the guitars mostly provided texture and roughage. There were tracks like 'Where I End And You Begin' that indisputably rocked, or 'Go To Sleep' which was almost blues, but there was also plenty of the uneasy electronica that had marked *Kid A* and *Amnesiac*. Contrary to almost everybody else who heard it, though, Thom thought that it was their big, shiny pop album.

"I think," he said in an interview with *Blender* magazine, "that if you managed to persuade the record company to put any of the tracks on the radio, it would sound like pop. But everyone thinks of us as an 'album band' and listens to the record all in one go. People scrutinise it so closely. I have so had enough of this! No one gives that much of a shit."

This is an extraordinary thing for the front man of supposedly the most "serious" rock band in the world to say, 'Stop listening to my records so closely!' But he had a point. *Hail To The Thief* is not an easy album to listen to in one gulp. It's rough and edgy; most of the songs are packed tight with sonic glitch. But listen to them in isolation and they have an energy that's very different to the songs on other, more polished, albums. Tracks like 'There There', 'The Gloaming', 'Myxomatosis' and 'A Wolf At The Door' were every bit as good as anything they'd done in the past. The latter, particularly, is brilliant. It's a bleary-eyed fairytale, menacing and hilarious at the same time. Thom's vocal is fantastically deadpan. To start with, he sounds like he's reading the vocals off an autocue and getting increasingly freaked out by the words he's being forced to say. This effect is enhanced by a chorus that, perhaps because it's surrounded by so much clatter and angst, is gloriously 'chocolate boxy', like something out of a Disney film. It's the last track on the album and it stands alongside 'Street Spirit' as one of the best album closers Radiohead have ever recorded.

One review in *The Guardian* newspaper criticised *Hail To The Thief* for its tone of vague anxiousness. It was, Thom might have responded, exactly how he was feeling after the birth of his son. He even wrote a song for Noah – 'Sail To The Moon' – one of the most personal things he'd ever written, although the lyrics were dream-like, woozy and hard to make out. You couldn't call any of Radiohead's records direct exactly, but this one was particularly oblique. It was odd then, that they took the decision to call it *Hail To The Thief*, seemingly a direct comment on the controversial election of George W Bush in America.

"The reason we called it *Hail To The Thief*", he said in a German TV interview, "is stating the bleeding obvious. The most powerful country in the world is run by someone who stole an election. Now that's bad. That's bad for everybody. Especially as he was bought the election by extremely powerful companies with lots of money."

Yet in other interviews Thom always desperately shied away from this, the most obvious interpretation of the name. It was partly because the idea of making anything as glib and one-dimensional as a 'protest record' appalled him. More seriously, he was also worried about his own safety and that of his family.

"I was unhappy," he said, "about the potential consequences of calling it *Hail To The Thief*. Personal attacks, threats … people can get quite upset. So I wasn't wild about that." He much preferred a more surreal explanation. In another TV interview he claimed that the title referred to thieves of souls. "There is an idea Dante had," he explained. "Certain people have done things that are so bad that they're still here but their souls have gone. I don't know about you but I've met people like that. It's much more about that than the Bush thing."

It seemed like he'd had second thoughts about the album title pretty much as soon as they'd thought of it. "It will annoy me if people say it's a direct protest," he said, "because I feel really strongly that we didn't write a protest record." At the time this sounded slightly ridiculous. The phrase 'Hail To The Thief' originally came from a jibe at 19th Century US President John Quincy Adams, who was widely believed to have stolen an election. It was a play on words on the song 'Hail To The Chief', played at Presidential inaugurations. When George W Bush won the election in 2001, many protesters sang 'Hail To The Thief' in response. It was perhaps perverse to borrow the phrase for an album and then get annoyed that people assumed it might have something to do with Bush. It seems like Thom wanted people to take its topicality on board in a subliminal way, without thinking that Radiohead were making a direct statement. "Someone has given us money to stick the phrase 'hail to the thief' on walls all around the world," he said to *Blender*. "That made me chuckle for ages."

The alternative title was *The Gloaming* but Thom hadn't been sure about that either. He thought it sounded much too dark to represent the whole album. "The record definitely enters a dark place in the middle," he said, "but it isn't the whole thing."

At that point, Thom could look back and say that the anxiety and fear he'd expressed with *OK Computer* and *Kid A* had been pretty justified. The events of September 11 and the subsequent war in Afghanistan and build-up to conflict in Iraq had destroyed the optimism and complacency of the 1990s. Rather than the vague *fin de siécle* unease that songs like 'Lucky' had expressed, he was now being inspired by real events in the world, even if he still wasn't writing about them directly.

"When we were doing *Kid A* and *Amnesiac*, I had this thing that we were entering a very dark phase," he said to Andrew Mueller. "But it did strike me that things were going to kick off one way or another."

But, for Radiohead, *Hail To The Thief* represented a kind of full-stop. It was the last record of the six-album deal that they'd signed with Parlophone back in 1991. Unlike the vast majority of other bands, they'd completed the deal without having to stick out a filler album or a *Greatest Hits* and they'd easily paid back their advance and come out in profit. *Hail To The Thief* would be their farewell to the traditional record label 'business model'. Yet, perhaps surprisingly, not before they reversed all the decisions they'd made about promotion on the last two albums. They made videos for the three singles 'There There', 'Go To Sleep' and '2+2=5' including a particularly excellent one for 'There There', which featured a cartoon-like Thom in a dark fairytale wood. They even went back on the publicity trail with apparent enthusiasm. This reached its bizarre apogee when they laughed and joked on the show *Friday Night With Jonathan Ross*, while the BBC interviewer struggled to suppress his astonishment that they'd agreed to come on his programme at all. It seemed like a calculated attempt to turn around the popular perception that they were gloom-rockers. Thom even agreed to Ross's suggestion that they should write Britain's next Eurovision entry. "We were trying to persuade the record company that to promote *Kid A*, we're not going to do any TV, but we'll do Eurovision," he joked.

Thom said to *Pitchfork* afterwards that *Hail To The Thief* had been an attempt to "engage with the monster again" (the music industry as a whole, not Jonathan Ross) and that "it wasn't very pleasant." True to form, they regretted the decisions they'd made around *Hail To The Thief* and as always they vowed never to do things the same again. They thought they'd recorded it too quickly. Thom wished he could go back and fix the songs. He didn't feel it was their best work and he didn't feel like they'd moved forward in the same way that they'd done on their previous records. This was true but *Hail To The Thief* nevertheless, was another great album. It might be somewhat overshadowed by *Kid A* and the later *In Rainbows* but it has songs that are every bit as good. The problem was that Thom and Radiohead had, for the first time, started repeating themselves. The jerky, cut-up electronica, which had been so startling on *Kid A* and *Amnesiac* was now, as they said themselves, just another tool that they used like a guitar.

"What was great about *Kid A* was that it heralded a new period and it meant we went off in some cool new places," Ed O'Brien said to *Associated Press* writer Jake Coyle afterwards. "But the downside was that in the whole period up until the end of *Hail to the Thief*, we picked up some nasty habits."

"We were going along in a certain trajectory and then suddenly with *Hail to the Thief*, it was: we can't carry along in that way anymore," Thom added. "To me, the hardest thing was finding a reason to carry on."

Thom mocked the idea that they were supposed to "lurch" in another direction with each record but it seems like, more than anybody else, he felt that they needed to do something new every time. The truth was that he still hadn't recovered from the three years of making *Kid A* and *Amnesiac*. When the time came to make a new record, he wasn't able to face taking that long again and so they chose, as a legitimate experiment, to do things quickly. It worked but he soon realised that he wasn't happy to send his songs out into the world like that, without making them absolutely perfect. He was caught in a trap. If he wasn't prepared to put in the kind of effort that he felt Radiohead albums needed, then what was the point of the band? At least they'd got through the recording sessions without wanting to kill each other, but *Hail To The Thief* didn't seem essential in the way that the other albums had. Were they just going through the motions? For roughly the hundredth time since they'd started the band, Radiohead had another crisis of confidence but, as always, it took them completely by surprise. "One of the biggest things, not just for me but for everybody, was that at the end of the *Hail To The Thief* thing, we completely lost our confidence," Thom said in a TV interview. "It was a weird feeling and deeply unpleasant."

After the release of the album, Radiohead went on tour, finishing with a performance at the Coachella Festival in the US in May 2004. They flew "round the world the wrong way" Thom said afterwards – east to west – so the whole three weeks was a battle with jetlag. Just as on previous tours, Thom struggled to sleep. It was a painful reminder of why they'd moved away from this kind of thing after *OK Computer*. They felt like they were on autopilot again. The plan was that afterwards they would go back to their rehearsal rooms and start working on new material. But somehow there was nothing there. They tried things out for a few weeks before deciding that there was no point. They might as well go home. In 2004, Thom became a parent for the second time, when Rachel gave birth to their daughter, Agnes, and, once again, he was hit by the thought that there was more to life than Radiohead. In September 2004, Thom joined a protest at Fylingdales in North Yorkshire against Tony Blair's decision to let the US use the UK in their 'Star Wars' anti-missile programme without consultation. It was the start of another period when he would vigorously re-engage with politics. It was also, although he didn't know it yet, the start of a new feeling of optimism that maybe one day change would come.

19

THE BIG ASK

The period when Radiohead recorded and released *Hail To The Thief* was dominated by the build up to war in Iraq and the eventual invasion. The death of Ministry of Defence weapons inspector David Kelly particularly shocked Thom. At the same time the evidence that humanity was causing global warming was becoming incontrovertible. At one point, he told the *LA Times*, he was worrying about it so much that it almost caused him to "flip my lid". As his son Noah got a little older, he wondered what kind of world they were leaving to him. "My son really loves wildlife and draws polar bears," he said, "and every time he draws a polar bear, I want to tell him they probably won't be there by the time he's my age."

The science that he was reading was so alarming that the situation almost seemed hopeless. In 2003, after the UN report on climate change was released, he was approached by environmental organisation Friends Of The Earth about supporting their 'Big Ask' campaign. By then, governments around the world had accepted the reality of global warming and the need to cut carbon emissions but there was no actual progress. The British government had even committed to a significant reduction in emissions by 2020. However, environmental organisations feared that, unless this pledge was made more concrete, nothing would be done. In 2020, whichever administration was in power would simply blame their predecessors for the lack of progress. 'The Big Ask' was for a cut in carbon emissions of 3% each year, every year.

Its simplicity and reasonableness might not have impressed Thom a few years previously. After his experiences with Jubilee 2000, he was deeply cynical about attempts to change the world through existing structures and democracy. However, by 2005 the situation seemed so desperate that anything was better than nothing. "There's no longer a sense of powerlessness, which is what I had for so long about it all," he said. "It seemed to be the first sane, reasoned way out of what is an international emergency."

Nevertheless, he was still reluctant to be the face of the campaign in the way that Friends Of The Earth wanted. He was very aware of the fact that, as the singer in a touring rock band, his carbon footprint was far larger than that of the average person, even in the energy-hungry West. They persuaded him that it didn't matter. A certain amount of hypocrisy was unavoidable but it wasn't an excuse for doing nothing.

"Stop pointing fingers," he said in a TV news interview later. "I'm a hypocrite. We're all hypocrites because we've all been born into a carbon life. This is what we do. The structure of our existence is based on expanding energy use. We're all hypocrites."

Still, for all his bravado, he did sometimes wonder whether the environmental cost of Radiohead tours could be justified. A study by an organisation called the Edinburgh Centre for Carbon Management (ECCM) calculated that the 545,000 fans who saw Radiohead on the *Hail To The Thief* tour generated 5,335 tonnes of CO_2 during their journey to the gigs. The five band members own flights added another five tonnes.

"Some of our best ever shows have been in the US," Thom said to *The Guardian*, "but there's 80,000 people there and they've all been sitting in traffic jams for five or six hours with their engines running to get there, which is bollocks."

In a way, his ambivalence made him a better spokesperson for Friends Of The Earth. The fact that he owned up to the essential problem with his position made it easier to deal with the inevitable accusations of hypocrisy. In one interview with *Channel 4 News* presenter Jon Snow, he was asked what he was doing to help. "Not enough," he replied.

"You're not supposed to say that," he said to *The Guardian*. "You're supposed to say, 'I'm doing this and this and this. I'm planting trees, somewhere, probably.' I'm not! I'm not doing enough! None of us are."

The ECCM calculated that 50,000 trees would need to be planted and maintained for 100 years in order to offset the amount of CO_2 produced by the *Hail to the Thief* tour. In any case, Thom was highly dubious about "carbon off-setting" as a way of dealing with carbon emissions. The only useful tool that he did have was celebrity. He'd long had an instinctive antipathy to the idea that celebrities were on a higher plane than everybody else, able to tell people how to live; at the same time, he'd seen the disproportionate power celebrity could have.

"You're not in any way qualified to do it," he said of the phenomenon of celebrity-as-spokesperson, "but I was so sick of hearing so many unqualified people say that global warming doesn't exist, I thought, 'Well, I'm no less qualified than they are', so I can deal with doing it."

Between 2003 and 2006 he was heavily involved in the Big Ask campaign. His website bore the message: "If you are concerned about climate change, if it scares you speechless and wakes you in the night, if you are bothered about the flooding you keep seeing, or those high winds, or that there is something not quite right about the fact you're still walking round in a T-shirt in October, please find out about the Big Ask campaign."

But, despite trying to take the sting out of the accusations of hypocrisy by being the first to confess, Radiohead were still criticised. Blur singer Damon Albarn supposedly told *The Sun* newspaper: "Radiohead – I'm not gonna get into anyone, but bands who care about certain things and then go on one-and-a-half year stadium tours are just total hypocrites ... In one sense you've got this developing humanist thing ... Then you're creating these massive impersonal events where you're set up as the subject of thousands of people's adoration. Where is the humanity in that? That's just idolatry."

Thom's response to that was a sarcastic. "You're right Damon, I should probably just give up." But perhaps there was a part of him that evidently wondered if maybe he should. "We always go into a tour saying, 'This time, we're not going to spend the money. This time we're going to do it stripped down," he said in a joint interview with David Byrne of Talking Heads in *Wired* magazine. "And then it's, 'Oh, but we do need this keyboard. And these lights.' But at the moment we make money principally from touring. Which is hard for me to reconcile because I don't like all the energy consumption, the travel. It's an ecological disaster, travelling, touring."

Not that he particularly wanted to tour at that point anyway. In 2005 Radiohead had very little to do with each other and they genuinely weren't even sure if they'd ever make another album. The summer of 2005 was the twentieth anniversary of Live Aid and, in response, Bob Geldof and others organised a sequel – Live 8. A few years previously, Thom would have been first on the list to participate. It was a bigger version of Jubilee 2000, a cause he'd once been heavily involved with. But he was more cynical now. Also it wasn't clear that Radiohead were actually a functioning band at that point. "We couldn't work out whether we should be carrying on or not," he admitted. "We couldn't really get it together."

He was also highly dubious about whether Live 8 was the best answer to global poverty. "It was a form of distraction," he said to Craig McLean in *The Observer*. "Holding a big rock concert and reducing the issues to bare essential levels, I think, ultimately, was to the detriment of the ['Make Poverty History'] campaign."

Despite his willingness to get involved in the democratic process, he was still extremely wary about being co-opted by politicians. In 2006 he was asked to meet Tony Blair to discuss environmental issues. It was an awkward moment. It was the kind of access that Friends Of The Earth worked hard to get but he wasn't sure if there was any point.

"i have no intention of being used by spider spin doctors to make it look like we make progress when it is just words," he posted on the Radiohead website. "i dont have powers of persuasion, i just have temper and an acid tongue."

It was the kind of situation where he knew he'd feel guilty if he did meet the Prime Minister and guilty if he didn't. He also knew he'd be criticised if he did meet him and criticised if he didn't. In the end he refused. He didn't want to be Bono.

"The difference between me and Bono," he told Brian Draper of *The Third Way* magazine, "is that he's quite happy to go and flatter people to get what he wants and he's very good at it, but I just can't do it. I'd probably end up punching them in the face rather than shaking their hand, so it's best that I stay out of their way."

Tony Blair's people were equally wary of Thom. They wanted to meet him but only on their terms. "They wanted to know that I was on-side," he said to Craig McLean. "Also, I was being manoeuvred into a position where if I said the wrong thing post-the-meeting, Friends Of The Earth would lose their access. Which normally would be called blackmail."

In 2006, he and Jonny performed an acoustic set at a benefit for The Big Ask at London's Koko venue. It was a gig that attracted a lot of attention. By then, Radiohead hadn't released a record for three years and there was speculation as to what their new songs would sound like. In his role as an ambassador for Friends Of The Earth, Thom wrote to the leaders of all three main political parties asking them if they wanted to attend. Except he didn't invite Tony Blair, he invited chancellor Gordon Brown instead.

Gordon didn't turn up, he sent young minister David Miliband, but new Tory leader David Cameron did. At the time he was eagerly espousing his green credentials not to mention his youthful indie credentials as a fan of The Smiths and a lover of 'Fake Plastic Trees'.

"I sent this rather sad letter saying I'd love to come to the concert, thank you for asking,' Cameron told Sue Lawley on *Desert Island Discs* four weeks after The Big Ask Live. 'PS: please play this, my favourite song, and he did.'

After the gig, Thom met the politicians and had the disconcerting realisation that they were not much older than he was. They'd grown up listening to similar music and the wives of both David Miliband and David Cameron claimed to be fans of Radiohead. It was all too easy to see how the likes of Bono could find themselves getting sucked into that circle, holding their tongue where necessary, in the interests of having more influence in the long run.

But Thom wasn't like that. He didn't think there was any mileage in cosying up to the people whom he regarded as the problem. After George W Bush got back into power in 2004, his response was that it was no bad thing, it would radicalise people and force them to get involved.

And, if there was any doubt, his next album – the debut solo work, *The Eraser* – made it very clear that his views hadn't mellowed at all.

20

ERASERHEAD

"There are no budding solo artists in this band," Jonny Greenwood said emphatically in 1997. Although Thom had always been the driving force of the band, they were very much a *collective*. They took his ideas and gave them a shape. When he was asked in 2000 if he'd have tried to make *Kid A* as a solo record if the rest of them had wanted no part in it he said, "No, I wouldn't have had the confidence."

However, in 2005, the confidence that Radiohead had given him was gone. Instead he had a pile of songs that didn't seem to call for any contribution from Jonny, Phil, Colin or Ed at all. "There was no point in going to the others and saying, 'Phil, do you want to try a beat on this?' Or, 'Colin, do you want to play some bass?' Because the sounds and ideas were not from that sort of vibe," he said to *Rolling Stone*.

It was time to live out his dream of having complete control in the way that the Aphex Twin or Squarepusher did. The hardest thing was having to tell the band that. It was the most concrete expression of what they all felt, that Radiohead had been running on empty for a while. "I formally asked everyone if it was cool, not really expecting it to go anywhere," he said in a TV interview. "I just wanted to know what it felt like to take responsibility for the music. Also, we'd just had enough of being Radiohead. To this day I'm not really sure why. None of us were in the right head space."

By then, they'd been Radiohead as a professional concern for fourteen years. They'd known each other and made music together much longer than that. It's no surprise that they needed a break. "We stopped about two and a half years ago, the band that I'm in, Radiohead," he said in a TV interview to promote *The Eraser*, "Why did we stop? It just got a bit weird and boring and self-perpetuating. It felt like everyone was under [an] obligation to do it rather than because we wanted to do it."

When he talked to the rest of the band they were only too pleased to let him go off and do his own thing for a bit. It seemed like the best way, in the long run, of keeping Radiohead together. Having been in the band for so long and done so much together, going it alone was his last real challenge. He knew that he could write great songs without them. He'd written many Radiohead demos on his own. But he'd never finished them off. He'd always been able to rely on the band to put his ideas into some kind of framework and tell him when the song was finally finished. Not having that safety net gave him the same kind of excitement that he'd rediscovered during *Kid A* when he put his guitar away for a while. He found it impossible to work when things were too easy.

"I wanted to work on my own," he said to David Fricke of *Rolling Stone*. "It wasn't casting aspersions on anybody. I just wanted to see what it would be like. Luckily, I happen to be in a band where nobody has a problem with that. In fact, I think there was some sense of relief that finally I was going to do it. Rather than saying it and chickening out."

Initially he wasn't even sure that it was an album he was making. He went into Radiohead's studio in Oxfordshire with Nigel Godrich to try out a few songs and, slowly, through further sessions at Thom's second home by the sea and at Nigel's Covent Garden studio, it began to emerge as a whole. Initially all he had was a collection of breaks and beats, broken rhythms that he would play with on his laptop every time he got a spare moment on tour or at home. In the studio he listened to them again, forced, for the first time, to make his own decisions about what worked and what didn't.

One track 'Black Swan', had a sample of Ed and Phil playing in the studio in 2000, another 'The Eraser' included piano chords played by Jonny that Thom had recorded on his Dictaphone. By the time Thom had finished with them, though, they were unrecognisable. The tunes were even more jittery, skittish and hyperactive than on the last Radiohead albums. One difference, though, was that Nigel Godrich saw an opportunity to make Thom put his voice high up in the mix for the first time since *OK Computer*, without hiding it behind effects or distortion.

"I kept begging Nigel to put more reverb on it," he said to David Fricke. "'No, I'm not doing reverb on this record.' 'Please hide my voice'. 'No!'"

THOM YORKE

Curiously, for all its hyper-modern, electronic sound, in some ways *The Eraser* harked back to Thom's earliest recordings, alone with a four-track. The technology might have moved on since 'Rattlesnake' but the impetus hadn't. One track, 'Analyse', seemed to go back even further. It was written after he came home to his central Oxford house and found that there had been a power-cut. The street was dark, with candles in the windows, just as it would have been when the houses were built in early Victorian times. Or as perhaps they might be in a post-fossil fuels future. Either way, it's a beautiful image in a song that was otherwise as restless and nervous as everything else on the album.

Another track, 'Atoms For Peace', saw him, once again, battling with his own lack of confidence. "Being a rock star, you're supposed to have super-über-confidence all the time," he said to David Fricke. "It was my missus telling me to get it together basically."

As the recording process went on, Thom increased in confidence. When he'd got the bass riff for 'And It Rained All Night', he phoned up a friend, excitedly saying, "Listen to this!" There were moments when he wondered whether *The Eraser* should be a Radiohead album after all. "It made me realise how incredibly sketchy I am," he said in a TV interview, "and that it's usually the band who pick up the pieces and put them into a coherent form ... there were weird periods when I was making the record when I thought, *Maybe I should stop this and ring everybody up and say, 'maybe you should come down and have a listen to this and maybe we could do something.'*"

But these were only fleeting thoughts. It's debatable whether they would have come back at that point anyway. Everybody knew that it was something he needed to get out of his system. Most of *The Eraser* does sound much more sketchy than anything on a Radiohead album. It's the direct product of Thom's brain. It crackles with his nervous energy. However, tracks like 'And It Rained All Night' and 'Analyse' have their own jittery power. And the single, 'Harrowdown Hill', was one of the most powerful songs Thom had ever recorded.

He wrote it about the death of government weapons' inspector David Kelly and, harrowingly, it seems to be sung partly from his perspective as he goes into the woods to die. When he spoke about it later, Thom seemed surprised how quickly people picked up on the song's theme but, in contrast to many of his songs, it's almost painfully direct. 'Harrowdown Hill' is the place in Oxfordshire where David Kelly's body was found. He'd apparently taken painkillers and then slashed his wrists.

In the immediate aftermath there were numerous conspiracy theories. Some people said that there wasn't enough blood by his body for it to be plausible that he'd bled to death. Thom references this in the lyrics but his real anger doesn't just depend on the far-fetched idea that Kelly was killed by the British secret services. It's more pertinent that he was left to be a scapegoat for the government. Kelly had supposedly told a journalist, Andrew Gilligan, that the government's claim that Iraq could attack with chemical weapons in "fifteen minutes" was false. This was later denied but Thom felt that Kelly had been hung out to dry and that the Government knew what kind of pressure he'd be under. "It made me very sad and upset that the Ministry Of Defence, or rather the Government, thought that it was OK to use this poor man as a scapegoat for the misgivings of an entire country," he said in a TV interview.

It's not surprising that Thom didn't feel he could put a song like that out under the Radiohead banner. Not everybody in the band shared his political views. It's painfully explicit and if the song had become a conventional chart hit, Thom might have even had qualms about the effects on Kelly's family. Nevertheless, it is undoubtedly a beautiful work of art and it's clearly not intended to be exploitative. Just as he'd done with 'Sulk' years before, Thom couldn't help but be influenced by what was going on around him. This ultra-sensitive radar was part of what made him such a great songwriter.

When he'd finished the record, Thom kept it secret from all but those who were closest to him. He played it to the rest of Radiohead and then wondered vaguely what he should do with it. There was no chance that he would give it to EMI. Nor did he want its release to inspire a wave of articles proclaiming the break-up of Radiohead. In the end, he just sat on it for a while. By the time it was finished, he'd got his hunger back. He went straight from recording *The Eraser* to working on the next album with the band. *The Eraser* could wait until the re-emergence of Radiohead made it perfectly clear to everybody that they were still together.

It took a while for the right moment to release the solo record but, in May 2006, he issued a characteristically grumpy/shy message on his website about the new album (www.theeraser.net): *"I want no crap about me being a traitor or whatever splitting up blah blah... this was all done with their blessing, and I don't wanna hear that word solo. It doesn't sound right,"* he said.

Just as when he'd tried to tell people that *Hail To The Thief* wasn't about George W Bush, this was slightly odd. If it wasn't a solo album, what was it? Even he didn't know. He toyed with the idea of calling it a "side project" but that didn't work either. It made it sound like it was something he'd knocked off in his spare time, rather than the concentrated piece of work that it was.

He tried to justify the initial post by claiming that, "if it was a solo album, it would demand that I've walked away from Radiohead, which I obviously haven't."

In some ways, it was just a continuation of what he'd been doing with the band. The title, *The Eraser*, went back to the same themes of memory that he'd been dealing with on *Amnesiac*. One (never entirely serious) alternative title for *Hail To The Thief* had been, *Little Man Being Erased*.

"There's a certain element that runs through the record of trying to forget about things," he said, "trying to put things out of your mind and not being able to."

Fortunately most people understood that *The Eraser* didn't mean the end of Radiohead. When it was released in July 2006, it received positive reviews. Critics in both *The Guardian* and *The Times* welcomed it primarily as a sign that Thom was back making music. "Historically, solo albums have tended to grow out of cracks in dried-up bands," said Pete Paphides in *The Times*. "In the case of Radiohead though, *The Eraser* might just constitute a lifeline."

Alexis Petridis in *The Guardian* was less impressed by the record as a whole but he agreed that it offered encouragement for fans of Radiohead. *"The Eraser* may well be the occasionally diverting sound of Thom Yorke clearing his pipes in preparation for something remarkable," he said.

This impression was enhanced by the way that the record was allowed to slip out with relatively little fanfare. Instead of a single, it was preceded by the appearance of 'Analyse' over the credits of Richard Linklater's animated film *A Scanner Darkly*. And instead of stepping back into the promotional machine of EMI, it was released through independent label XL. "It didn't feel right to do it with EMI," he told Craig McLean in *The Observer*. "It was done in a different context so it felt like it should be put out in a different context."

Nevertheless it's a sign of the cachet his name still had, within or without Radiohead, that on release it went straight in at Number 2 in the *Billboard* chart and Number 3 in the British charts. He'd reached the enviable point where enough people were paying attention to Radiohead's vast internet presence, their own website and the many unofficial sites, that it scarcely mattered if the mainstream ignored what he was doing. People would still hear about it directly from him.

It helped that when he released 'Harrowdown Hill', he commissioned an equally extraordinary video to go with it from American stop-motion animator Chel White. Thom had seen a film of Chel's called *Passage* and he was struck by the way it juxtaposed dream-like images of people underwater alongside images of war and atrocities. This was what he wanted for 'Harrowdown Hill' – something that captured the song's mixture of rage, grief and strange beauty. As always, though, he gave the director a completely free reign to create something that was a work of art in its own right.

"It was a relief to write a treatment for a song that I really liked," Chel told the author for this book. "It's hard when you hear a song and it doesn't give you any images and then you have to struggle to find them. With this one I didn't have that problem at all. I maybe had the opposite problem that there were too many images. I talked with [commissioning editor] Dilly about doing a collage technique that was very frenetic with many images flashing but I realised, I think we both realised, that that wasn't the way to go."

Instead the video starts with a silhouette of an eagle flying over a landscape, which initially is the beautiful English countryside. Then, as silhouetted hands grab at the eagle's wings, it flies along a motorway and over an industrial city before scenes from the Poll Tax Riot of 1990 are spliced in. It culminates with a scene of Thom, wearing a shirt and tie, sinking through the water of a black pool. The way it mixes politics and something much more surreal fitted the song perfectly.

"As soon as I heard the song, I knew it couldn't be directly about the David Kelly case," says Chel. "We'd have to work with images that would indirectly relate to it, rather than refer to it directly. It's looking at the larger subject of secrecy and government control in the wake of the invasion of Iraq and everything else. To me, the video is more of a call to consciousness than a call to arms. I don't like to hit people over the head with metaphors but the eagle is partly a metaphor for David Kelly."

For the underwater scenes Thom flew to Los Angeles. It must have been an uncomfortable reminder of his experiences with the 'No Surprises' shoot eight years previously. He was weighted down and dropped into a deep pool that was painted black. "It was about twenty feet deep and the last thing they'd done in there was drop a Hummer in and shoot it from underneath," says Chel. "Which was probably about as far away from what we were doing as possible."

For somebody with slight claustrophobia, it was a daunting prospect but, although it proved easier than 'No Surprises', Thom still found it difficult. The pool was painted black, as normal swimming pools never are, and so it was very easy to become disorientated underwater.

"I did get a sense that he was pushing himself and he did get a little frustrated," says Chel. "I think he was rather tentative about the whole idea of jumping in, but it was about him addressing that fear. I didn't really know to what degree he was comfortable or uncomfortable with the concept of being weighted down and dropped into a very deep pool. I think it was something that, at first, he wasn't all that comfortable with. I think we did eighteen takes and the last three were just gold. Over the course of it he got more and more comfortable and I think by the end of it he could have been a pearl diver! He was very much a *perfectionist*. When he got to the point when he was comfortable with it, he'd look at the takes and say, 'OK, I'll try it differently this time.'"

One very underrated skill that Thom has had throughout his career, from his time in Headless Chickens to the present day, is the ability to step back and let talented people get on with what they're good at. He admitted that he didn't have the eye for video direction but, along with trusted commissioning editor Dilly Gent, he seemed to be able to find people whose vision matched his. Chel White says that he was given all the freedom he needed to make the video for 'Harrowdown Hill'.

"It was ideal in most ways," he says. "He liked my ideas, we talked about it a little bit and we met up, and we went about doing it. There wasn't very much editorial control on his part. Which was wonderful. I think what he was looking for was an artist to see it through. It was a very satisfying project for me because there was so much of my vision in it."

The 'Harrowdown Hill' video was the only part of the campaign for *The Eraser* which had any of the hallmarks of old Radiohead album campaigns. XL would probably have liked him to play a few shows to promote it but, by then, he was back on the road with Radiohead, road-testing the songs that would appear on their next album, *In Rainbows*.

21

IN RAINBOWS

In August 2005, using his characteristic unpunctuated style, Thom Yorke wrote on the Radiohead website that, "there are giant waves of self doubt crashing over me and if i could alleviate this with a simple pill ... i think i would."

One such pill, it turned out, was *The Eraser* album but, for a long time, it wasn't clear whether that would be enough. "There was a lot of me trying to pick myself up off the floor," he told the *New York Times* afterwards. "Because I really sort of dropped – what's the word? Sunk ... dropped down and went into this big lull and couldn't do anything. There's a lot of internal monologue stuff going on."

Even after he'd got the agitated beats of *The Eraser* out of his system it wasn't easy to go back to the frequently torturous working methods of Radiohead. In an interview with Julian Marshall of *NME* that they did at the start of the recording process for the next band album, Thom went back to a very familiar theme, that Radiohead itself had a kind of personality. Sometimes it was a friend and sometimes it wasn't. By that point he was describing it, rather bitterly, as a monster.

"Personally, one of the things I find hardest is being part of the whole Radiohead thing," he said, "and I'm not really interested in that anymore. I'm trying to work out what exactly it is that keeps me wanting to do it. None of us really want to be part of that band, like that anymore, just because it's a particular monster. And you don't want to be in this situation where you're just feeding the monster. It should be the other way around, whatever that means!"

However, doing nothing wasn't an option either. He'd spent a while outside of the Radiohead loop and found that he didn't exactly know how to do anything else. The band had been in his life since he before was twenty years old. The only solution was to go back in the studio but this time, as Thom saw it, to do things properly. *Finally*. If their last album, *Hail To The Thief*, had been an experiment in just cranking out a record as quickly as possible, this one would herald a return to their meticulous perfectionism.

So, in February 2005, it was the same old story. The band returned to their rehearsal rooms with the usual simple agenda: *to do things completely differently to the previous album.* For the first few months, they were essentially just deciding what they wanted to do. There was no real progress. Then, on August 17, they went into a studio for the first time since 2004. On day four they finally reported progress, but it would be their last burst of optimism for some time.

Thom was distracted by numerous other things. There was his work for Friends Of The Earth, the request to meet Tony Blair, the recording of *The Eraser* and, more importantly, two small children. Later on, Jonny Greenwood would note that, between them, they'd had six children since they were last Radiohead. Still, by September 30 they did at least have one, semi-ironic sign of progress – a school-style blackboard covered in song titles. Just as during the *Kid A* sessions they had dozens of ideas, but they weren't sure what to do with them.

In October 2005, Colin reported on their website blog *Dead Air Space* that, during a week-long recording session, they'd been recording a song a day. At the end of the month, Ed added that he thought they'd got 'Bodysnatchers' and Thom said that some of the recording blitz had been "great fun."

They also had an actual, proper song out there and available for fans to buy. It was their latest contribution to the 'War Child' charity and a follow-up to 1996's 'Lucky'. A beautiful, piano-led ballad called 'I Want None Of This', the track offered few clues to what would come next but it didn't in any way suggest that this was a band on the verge of falling apart. It was very slow and simple, with backing vocals cooing gently over Thom's unadorned vocal, like a Welsh voice choir.

However, when Thom listened to the rest of the tracks they'd recorded, he had severe doubts about the direction they were heading in. In January 2006, he decided that they needed to get serious. They'd spent the best part of a year getting nowhere. Nigel Godrich was away producing Beck so they brought in the services of producer Mark 'Spike' Stent and he immediately took them to task for their lack of focus. Initially it seemed like just what they needed, "to stop answering the phones and thinking of excuses to leave the building, instead get on with it," as Thom wrote on *Dead Air Space*. They felt that they'd perhaps become too comfortable with Nigel Godrich. It was too easy for them to repeat themselves because they knew exactly what worked and what didn't. Stent was best known as one of the most successful mixers in the business but he'd also produced big albums for Björk and Massive Attack among many others.

When he came to Radiohead's studio, the new producer was surprised to see that there was, in Thom's words, "shit all over the place". There were broken instruments on the floor and everything was completely disorganised and random. He immediately set about sorting everything out until Thom said it, "now looks like NASA". He made them realise how lucky they were to have such an array of equipment available. They had everything they possibly needed, not to mention all the time in the world. But that was part of the problem. Without a record label, without an A&R, they had so much freedom that they were paralysed. Thom compared it to the situation of Roadrunner in the cartoon – running over the edge of the cliff and suddenly looking down.

Again he was finding himself slightly scared of his instruments as he had been before *Kid A*. They had too much time to think. There was nobody checking up on them and no definite release date for whatever they might finally produce. They didn't even know what they would do with the album when it was finished.

"I think it's a nutty situation to be in to have no definite release system," admitted Thom to *NME*. "It's really liberating not to feel part of the record company structure. It should be an extremely positive place to be in, but it's also an extremely strange situation to be in. One of the things you discover really quickly when you discover you're not committed to anything is that you need some level of commitment because otherwise you just start fucking about, which is what we did for ages."

In the first quarter of 2006, they had to reluctantly accept that they still weren't ready. The studio reports in February and March were full of gloom. The best they could come up with after one unspecified crisis was that they were "shaky but intact". But by March things hadn't got much better. Things were as bad as they'd been at the worst moments of *The Bends* and the early days of the *Kid A* sessions.

They reluctantly told Mark Stent that it wasn't working. They were so used to Nigel Godrich now that they found it difficult to cope with Spike's different working methods. "What we need is someone who is what I'd call a tutor – who is a guy you're answerable to," Thom said to *NME*.

It was ironic that that man was apparently Nigel. The reason they'd worked with him in the first case was that he was more like a peer than the traditional producer as school master. But he was one of the few people that they trusted to tell them whether something was good or bad. They had a desperate craving for good advice, combined with a stubborn refusal to accept it from anybody outside their close circle.

"Working with Spike Stent felt a bit too much like there was an adult present," said Jonny to *The Word* magazine. "With Nigel we can reminisce about old ZX Spectrum games. He's our generation. It feels more like we're in it together."

"We need an A&R man," contradicted Colin Greenwood, "for the first time in our career we don't have a record contract and we need an A&R man. We don't want a record deal, but we want their A&R."

With no release date lined up, they booked another tour, just as they had done halfway through recording so many times before. It was a deadline of sorts. And instead of playing in the studio, it meant they could just go back to their rehearsal studio and practise without having to worry about recording the results.

"Rather than it being a nightmare," Thom said to the *New York Times*, "it was really, really good fun, because suddenly everyone is being spontaneous and no one's self-conscious because you're not in the studio. So it was really good just hanging out and working for about four or five hours a day. It felt like being sixteen again."

"The key thing in actually propelling it forward was Nigel coming back into the process," said Phil Selway. "The reality when we got in there was it still wasn't good enough. We really had to raise our standards quite a lot."

Some of the songs, such as 'Nude', they'd had for years. It was the same old problem. They often couldn't finish ideas. It was too much pressure to say, 'OK, that's it, that one's done'. Thom always preferred to work on something fresh. The new ideas and the new songs were always more exciting than painstakingly putting the finishing touches to something in the studio.

Fortunately the reaction to the songs when they played them live gave them another boost. Sold-out crowds around the world were almost as enthusiastic about the new stuff as they were about the old. The first show was Thom and Jonny's Friends Of The Earth benefit at Koko in London. It was a relatively small venue for them and tickets were soon going on eBay for ridiculous amounts until Thom was moved to request that anyone selling their ticket give 30% of the proceeds to the charity. The shows that followed were some of the biggest, or at least the longest, that they'd done. At the Bonnaroo Festival in Tennessee, USA, they played 28 songs from all sections of their career.

At another show in America they were bemused to discover that one of President Bush's daughters was in attendance, complete with retinue of bodyguards. As they came to the last song, they saw a commotion at the back of the hall and only later did they discover that it was fans taking exception to her security guards attempt to push past everybody to leave.

There were more smiles on tour than there had been for a long time. They played thirteen new songs on the road and the process simultaneously sharpened them and gave the band confidence that what they were doing was worthwhile. Inevitably, the thirteen songs were soon available for free all over the internet. But Thom didn't mind.

"The first time we ever did 'All I Need,' Boom! It was up on YouTube," he said to the *New York Times*. "I think it's fantastic. The instant you finish something, you're really excited about it, you're really proud of it, you hope someone's heard it, and then, by God, they have. It's OK because it's on a phone or a video recorder. It's a bogus recording, but the spirit of the song is there, and that's good. At that stage that's all you need to worry about."

Radiohead were still humble enough to be flattered that people wanted to bootleg their songs and they appreciated the fact that people were able to listen to them before they came to the shows. And the songs were evolving every time they played them so the bootlegs captured a sound that would never be heard again. The only downside was that these versions of the songs weren't quite what the band intended the world to hear. "There's a compliment there," Thom said to *Rolling Stone's* Mark Binelli, "the fact that people want to get a hold of what you've done. But it's not the definitive version, if the ends are chopped off, if you haven't made the choice to do it yourself."

After the tour, in October 2006, they accepted the inevitable and brought Nigel Godrich back to finally capture the magic of the live shows. But initially they found that they'd played the songs so often that they were bored with them. They seemed stale. "We played them eighty times live or so, and we'd rehearsed them to death," said Ed O'Brien. "It just didn't happen when we got back into the studio initially." It was a galling reminder of Brian Eno's old adage: "Whatever worked last time, never do it again."

Nevertheless Nigel suggested that they try another old trick, recording out of the traditional studio environment. This time it was to be Tottenham Court House in Marlborough, Wiltshire. Tottenham Court House wasn't the lavishly appointed estate of Jane Seymour. It was a decrepit, crumbling mansion built in the 1830s. They couldn't even live there. They hired camper vans and lived in the grounds, recording in the library and playing cover versions at night to get back the joy of playing together. And, just as there had been on previous albums, there was one moment when everything suddenly clicked into place. They had a meeting in the library and began a ritual that they'd had since Abingdon, everybody playing percussion to try and loosen up. The result was the delicate, inspired clatter of 'Reckoner'. It was a song they'd first played live in 2001 but it had never sounded like this. Thom described it later as a "first-thing-in-the-morning" song and he gave it one of his most beautiful vocal performances, a falsetto which rises way above the background noise. Like 'My Iron Lung' on *The Bends* this was the song where they at last started to feel they were getting somewhere again.

But there was one similarity with St Catherine's Court. Thom claimed that both houses were haunted. This inspired another song that they finished there, 'Bodysnatchers'. It came out in a period of what he described as "hyperactive mania" and it has a suitably manic feel, ending in a brilliant 1950s sci-fi horror rant from Thom. As well as Victorian ghost stories, Thom said later that it was inspired by the film *The Stepford Wives* and the feeling of being unable to connect with anybody else.

After a few weeks, Thom reported that the album was coming together. Songs that they'd written years ago were falling into place.

'Nude', which they played for the first time on the *OK Computer* tour, was finished at last.

After Tottenham Court House, they moved to another mansion, Halswell House in Taunton, then Nigel's studios in Covent Garden and then their own studio in Oxfordshire. It was the end of another incredibly disjointed recording process but the result – to be called *In Rainbows* – was probably their most coherent album since *OK Computer*. Although songs like the gentle, ethereal 'Nude' and the jagged, raging 'Bodysnatchers' seemed to have little in common, there was a sense of dislocation and alienation in virtually every track.

This came across in numerous different ways. 'House Of Cards' seems to be about wife-swapping, loneliness and, in passing, the end of civilisation. Thom said to the *New York Times* that much of the album was inspired by "a sudden realisation of the day-to-day, tenuous nature of life. Most of the time I was really, really trying not to judge anything that was happening. I was trying to just, not exactly knock it out, but not trying to be clever. That's all."

Some of the lyrics he wrote were pretty extraordinary. 'Videotape', for example, was about filming happy moments in the knowledge that they'll be watched after the person in the film is dead. It's a very subtle, almost minimalist song and, as was so often the case with Radiohead's simple songs, it took them months to capture on tape.

After all their work, they finally had a record that sounded like them. It gave no indication of its long gestation period. Despite some characteristically dark lyrics, it sounded more confident and less troubled than any of the previous four albums, including *The Eraser*. There was a huge amount of pressure on them during the recording process but for the first time the pressure only came from them. There was no record company waiting. There were, however, numerous record companies interested, including EMI.

The length of time *In Rainbows* had taken meant Chris Hufford and Bryce Edge had had plenty of time to try and think about how they should put it out. They had meetings with EMI, now taken over by a venture capital company run by a businessman called Guy Hands, but it wasn't productive. Chris and Bryce suggested that if EMI wanted to sign them again, they needed to give them more control over Radiohead's back-catalogue. EMI later put out a statement claiming that this was a demand for millions of dollars.

"It fucking pissed me off," Thom said to Andrew Collins in *The Word* magazine. "The idea that we were after so much money was stretching the truth to breaking point … and I'll tell you what, it fucking ruined my Christmas."

The fact that their next record deal was with independent XL suggests that money was never the deciding factor. They just wanted to be in control of their own music again. And EMI was never the band's favourite option. "I like the people at our record company," Thom said to *Time* magazine in 2005, "but the time is at hand when you have to ask why anyone needs one. And, yes, it probably would give us some perverse pleasure to say, 'Fuck you' to this decaying business model."

They'd always had an ambivalent relationship with EMI. On the one hand, they had a lot of respect for many people who worked there. They understood that without the support EMI had given them, paying for them to tour the world for two years before they became successful, they might never have left Oxford.

Despite this, there was still some bitterness about some of the things they were made to do and the decisions that were made for them. In their early days, they trusted the record label and there was a certain amount of disillusionment when they realised that EMI didn't always know what they were doing. There was also the knowledge that if things hadn't worked out with 'Creep', they potentially could have been dropped. That was certainly the feeling they had on some of their early support tours. "In the way they've treated the record business recently, I see them as gaining revenge for the pressure they were put under," Ash of early tour-mates the Frank and Walters says.

Record labels in 2007 weren't the same as they'd been in 1991. "The shareholders are greedy," Thom said. "The companies themselves are poisoned and fucked up. If they go down, bye bye, good riddance." Jonny wondered aloud whether Radiohead would have ever got anywhere under the current system. "They're starting to rely on radio play and videos [instead of touring]. That's horrific to us, the way that radio's going, that they're in charge of who breaks bands. We would never have left Oxford without funding."

There are countless examples of bands and musicians who have fought with their record label, from Prince to George Michael, but they've very rarely got anywhere. Often the music has suffered as the artist starts to think that they don't need help anymore. But Radiohead were different. In their polite, but fiercely determined way, they fought the music industry … and won.

22

TEARING DOWN THE WALLS

Radiohead's first idea for escaping the clutches of the record industry was simply to stop making records in the traditional sense. After *Kid A*, they told everybody that they'd had enough of the pressure to make the 'greatest album of all-time'. They were going to release singles, or EPs, or somehow 'serialise' their music on the net.

"We'd really like to have more regular communications with people," said Colin Greenwood, "as opposed to just having this massive dump every two-and-a-half years, and fanfares and clarion calls." But for reasons that have never fully been explained, the "massive dumps", as he rather unflatteringly called some of the best albums ever, have continued. Virtually every time they went into the studio they would emerge, sometimes years later, with an album. "The worst-case scenario," Thom said to the *New York Times,* "would have been: sign another deal, take a load of money, and then have the machinery waiting semi-patiently for you to deliver your product, which they can add to the list of products that make up the myth, la-la-la-la." Even the money wasn't that attractive anymore. He felt like it would just paralyse them, that they would find new ways to spend it rather than producing anything.

The impetus for their eventual revolutionary decision to put *In Rainbows* out online on a 'pay-what-you-like' basis came from a discussion that Chris and Bryce had. Radiohead had given them a lot of time to think during the protracted recording sessions. One night, during a philosophical conversation about the value of music, they came up with the idea of trying to find out exactly what it was worth.

The fact that they didn't need a record company and the fact that Radiohead's internet connections had supplanted traditional marketing meant that they had far fewer expenses than in the past. They also had direct links with the thousands of fans who regularly accessed their website. Initially Thom took some convincing.

"We all thought he [Chris Hufford] was barmy," he said to David

Byrne in *Wired*. "As we were putting up the site, we were still saying, 'Are you sure about this?' But it was really good. It released us from something. It wasn't nihilistic, implying that the music's not worth anything at all. It was the total opposite. And people took it as it was meant. Maybe that's just people having a little faith in what we're doing."

It did seem barmy. In 2007, the idea that people should have to pay for music was under threat. A whole generation of music fans had emerged who had rarely, if ever, bought a CD. They were used to downloading music as soon as it was available, often illegally and for free. For them, there was no such thing as a release date and no such thing as music as a physical product. It was an attitude that Thom had a lot of sympathy for but, at the same time, he was aware that to provide the server and the bandwidth for people to get *In Rainbows* would, itself, cost them money. They couldn't be in a position where they were actually paying for people to get their music. Nevertheless, money wasn't an issue. As a music fan, he always appreciated the fact that most illegal bootleggers were just obsessive fans who wanted to listen to his tunes.

"I think the reason people circulate music on the net is because they can't get access to it anywhere else because radio is bullshit," he said in a TV interview. "I find it quite amusing that the record industry chooses to blame the internet for its demise, whereas everyone knows damn well that it's because they're not flogging things that people want to buy."

In the past, bands and labels had been able to get away with putting 'filler' tracks on albums but the internet was making that harder. "All those records that had two good songs and ten rubbish ones, maybe those days are over," said Jonny in the same interview. It probably didn't escape Radiohead's attention, then, that had the internet existed in 1993, they would maybe never have sold two million copies of *Pablo Honey*. It didn't fit the template of, "two good songs and ten rubbish ones" but it certainly had some filler on it, as everybody involved subsequently admitted.

With *In Rainbows* there was no filler. It was an album that Thom was still proud of even when it was about to come out, a new experience for him. He was even quoted as saying that it was their *Transformer*, *Revolver*, or *Hunky Dory*. This was slightly taken out of context. He meant that it was a concise, cohesive record like the classics by Lou Reed, The Beatles and David Bowie, not that it was in any other way comparable with them.

Thanks to the number of different versions of their tracks circulating on the internet fans were already aware that *In Rainbows* could be something special but would they actually be prepared to pay for it? It helped that the innovative release of the album was, inadvertently or not, the biggest marketing stunt Radiohead had ever done. The announcement was typically simple and downbeat:

"Hello everyone. Well, the new album is finished, and it's coming out in 10 days; we've called it In Rainbows. Love from us all. Jonny." But, with those 24 words, they were front-page news for the first time since *Kid A*. There were articles about them in the business press as well as the music press.

In practice, the way it worked was very simple: buyers were able to download *In Rainbows* from Radiohead's own server for nothing (apart from a small admin fee) or, if they wanted, they could pay up to £99.99. Nevertheless, it was a brave experiment, one that Chris Hufford described as "virtual busking."

Initially Chris and Bryce had wanted to put the album out digitally without having a physical version at all. But they were overruled by Thom and the rest of the band. They were aware that that they still had a large fan base that preferred something more solid. Not least in parts of the world where broadband internet connections were not yet ubiquitous. So they settled on a compromise. The record would come out digitally first and then as a plush box-set and then as a normal CD.

One of the best things from Radiohead's point of view was that, as soon as the record was finished, they were able to put it out. There weren't the long lead times that were inevitable when you're producing a physical product. Some people might have wondered whether anybody would bother to buy an album that they could get for nothing but Thom pointed out that this had been the case for the last few years anyway. *Kid A*, *Amnesiac*, *Hail To The Thief* and *The Eraser* had all been leaked online before they were officially available. All they were doing was 'leaking' it themselves.

They can't have been prepared for the reaction. Their American label described it as a giant "listening party" in the hope, presumably, that people would take the hint and buy the record when it came out in physical form. But it was also like a giant scientific or sociological experiment. What did people think Radiohead's music was worth? The difference between this and normal busking, of course, was that people had to decide what they were going to pay before they heard the tunes. Some people proudly boasted that, despite making the effort to download the album, they didn't like Radiohead and so had paid nothing. Others did careful calculations to try and decide what was a reasonable amount to pay for a record that hadn't gone through the hands of a retailer or a manufacturer.

Radiohead's management never released figures as to how much people paid and there were wildly varying estimates. Online survey company comScore suggested that around three fifths of downloaders took it for free and the rest paid an average of $6. This made the average price per download $2.26. This was much better than they would have got on a normal fifteen-percent royalty deal. If these figures were correct, they made more money on the digital sales of *In Rainbows* than they had on the digital sales of all their other records put together. The band refused to confirm the exact figures but the experiment was clearly a success – so far. "People made their choice to actually pay money," Chris Hufford said. "It's people saying, 'We want to be part of this thing.' If it's good enough, people will put a penny in the pot." The only real problem was that they condemned themselves to years of people in shops saying, 'Why don't you just pay what you think it's worth! Hahaha!' It was probably funny the first time. They still had the physical release of the record to come. Nobody had a clue whether people would go out and buy an album that they'd already had the opportunity to download for free. "The record company doesn't know," Colin Greenwood said. "They called our office and said, 'We've made this amount of records, is it enough?' And our manager's office said, 'I don't know.'"

They released *In Rainbows* in physical form on January 1, 2007. It wasn't a time of year that many big records came out and it went straight in at Number 1. People had been able to listen to it and they'd decided that they liked it enough to want the finished article with the artwork and everything else. It was the most unexpected triumph of Radiohead's career. They'd never set out to be businessmen. It was just that Thom had, from his earliest days, found the process of getting his songs into the marketplace almost intolerable. He didn't understand it; he didn't think it was very efficient or effective, even by its own terms.

The singles that emerged from *In Rainbows* demonstrated a further willingness to do things differently. They produced videos that were very different to anything they'd done before. The first two, 'Jigsaw Falling Into Place' and 'Nude', were defiantly DIY. The first was filmed on "helmet cams" that they all wore as they played the song and the second featured shots of the whole band moving in slow motion. The third, 'House Of Cards', bizarrely, used a scanner rather than a camera to capture a 3-D image of Thom's face, a party and other scenes. For the fourth, 'Reckoner', they simply announced a competition and declared that winner Clement Picon's beautiful animation was the official video.

Interestingly they also made the "stems" of 'Reckoner', the component instrument tracks, available for anybody who wanted to remix it. They had accepted that it was now impossible to control music once it was released. They knew that people could do whatever they wanted with it and they were happy to encourage that. The old "model" of releasing music was finished. Over.

In Rainbows was just the latest step in a long journey that Radiohead had been on since they first started to appreciate the potential of the internet. Around the time *Kid A* came out, session musician Steve Hamilton was struck by the amount of time Thom spent online. "He's quite an internet freak," he told the author, "and he was busy answering messages on their website a lot. That was all quite new for them and he was going on and probably delighting people by answering messages personally."

At first it just seemed like a way that they could bypass the conventional media. Traditionally, if bands had something to say, they would talk to a press officer, who would write a press release, which would be picked up and re-written by a journalist. "By the time the person who likes you reads something about you, it has gone through five people," said Jonny.

With their own site, *Dead Air Space*, they reached the point where they barely needed to give interviews. Their infrequent musings were the answer to slow news days at music magazines and websites all over the world. Thom *deliberately* wrote in an ungrammatical, poorly punctuated and badly spelt manner, in part, probably, to prevent too much being read into what he was saying; but it didn't work. Whatever they wrote would immediately be examined by the world's music press in the same way that Western diplomats used to scrutinise the cryptic messages of the Kremlin.

Eventually they weren't just bypassing the media. They were bypassing everything. The internet was a way of getting their music from their studio to the fans within days of it being completed. They made the music industry look completely irrelevant. It was a triumph and one that they, for once, seemed able to enjoy. Mark Cope of The Candyskins knew them well at the beginning of their career and he says that, on meeting them in autumn 2008, he was struck by how much they've changed. "Thom's *great*. I saw him last week and he's a lot happier now. The whole stress of being in a band has stopped, really. I think they've actually started to enjoy it. I think they're enjoying each other's company now. I heard stories that it was very tense. A lot of the road crew had been with them from the beginning and they said, 'One day it can be really good and one day it can not.' But Thom realises it is only a band. It's not life and death. It's just a question of growing up. I think at one point he took himself a bit too seriously. They've all got kids now and nice houses and they're proud of what they've done and the fact that they haven't compromised at all. But they probably look back on it and think, *We could have had a bit more of a laugh*. They're renowned for having the worst backstage parties in the world! [However] the last ones have been really good! There used to be one bottle of beer there. They were so un-rock 'n' roll but I think they're starting to enjoy it now a bit more!"

When they began rehearsing for the tour at the end of 2007, Radiohead started by trying out a series of covers. It wasn't that they planned to play any cover versions. By now they had far too many great songs to fit into a normal set anyway. Most gigs would immediately be followed by comments on websites saying, 'They were amazing but why didn't they play ...' It was just that they were having fun for a change. They knew they would never have to do the kind of touring that they did after *Pablo Honey*, *The Bends* and *OK Computer* again. For Thom, being part of Radiohead had always been "heaven and hell" and, in 2007 and 2008, it was, for a change, closer to the former.

"I think they enjoy making music together now," says Mark. "I don't think that's going to change. I think Thom doing his own stuff got that out of his system. What I heard from the road crew [on the recent tour] was that every gig was really, really good and they all had a really great time. They haven't got to prove themselves anymore. I think they've proved themselves. They reached the end of their contract with their record company and came out in profit, which not a lot of bands do, really. They reached the end of their contract without needing to do a *Greatest Hits*. That doesn't happen very often at all."

Also, for someone who agonised so often and so lyrically that success was changing him and his friends, Thom has managed to cling on to his sanity. Maybe it helped that he was so well prepared for what would happen. When he wrote songs like 'The Bends' and 'Fake Plastic Trees' he already seemed, in his late teens and early twenties, to have a better understanding of the vacuity of stardom than most people who've lived through it. He'd thought about what it was like to be a rock star for years. He drew pictures of what a band would look like when he was at school. He'd been thinking about it constantly since he was seven, remember. He may have been the least likely person to want to be a rock star, or to become a rock star, but he was also the best prepared.

Of course, every time he went into the studio, all that preparation seemed to count for nothing. At the time of writing, Radiohead are back in the studio working on their eighth album and, no doubt, the process is pretty painful. "It's always awful," as Colin Greenwood sighed to Grant Gee at the start of the *In Rainbows* sessions. Their refusal to do the same things that have worked so brilliantly in the past means that at the start of every recording session they've had to spend weeks just sitting around figuring out what to do next. And because they have periods when they don't often see each other apart from when they're recording and touring, the first few weeks are mostly just about hanging out as they've done since they were at school. "It made me realise that [recording with Radiohead] was as much for the craic, as we say, than anything else," Thom said to *Pitchfork*. "It's an excuse to hang out."

If being in Radiohead hasn't always seemed like much fun, that's because *the bad times created the best songs*. As many people said of *Meeting People Is Easy*, if they'd wanted to paint a picture of a band having a laugh on the beach, they could have done. But that would've been boring. Few other songwriters have taken on the subjects that Thom Yorke has made his own – dislocation, confusion and anxiety – and made them so powerful, beautiful and triumphant.

The stereotype of Thom as a gloom-sodden misery-guts can only really be held by somebody who's never seen him perform. The energy that he's always put into Radiohead's live shows, the unabashed enjoyment of performing, is not what you'd expect from the miserabilist of legend. After Radiohead's greatest moments, live or in the studio, he should have thought back to the seven-year-old who had such confidence and ambition. It might not have worked out quite as he expected, but Thom Yorke did become a rock star. He also did what few other rock stars have ever done. He changed what it meant to be a star, what it meant to be in a band and even what it meant to release records. After more than fifteen years, it's perhaps too much to expect that he'll do it once more but, then again, nobody should bet against him.

RADIOHEAD & THOM YORKE UK DISCOGRAPHY

RADIOHEAD

STUDIO ALBUMS
Pablo Honey: *You / Creep / How Do You? / Stop Whispering / Thinking About You / Anyone Can Play Guitar / Ripcord / Vegetable / Prove Yourself / I Can't / Lurgee / Blow Out*
Parlophone 1993

The Bends: *Planet Telex / The Bends / High and Dry / Fake Plastic Trees / Bones / Nice Dream / Just / My Iron Lung / Bulletproof... I Wish I Was / Black Star / Sulk / Street Spirit (fade out)*
Parlophone 1995

OK Computer: *Airbag / Paranoid Android / Subterranean Homesick Alien / Exit Music (for a film) / Let Down / Karma Police / Fitter Happier / Electioneering / Climbing Up the Walls / No Surprises / Lucky / The Tourist*
Parlophone 1997

Kid A: *Everything In Its Right Place / Kid A / The National Anthem / How to Disappear Completely / Treefingers / Optimistic / In Limbo / Idioteque / Morning Bell / Motion Picture Soundtrack*
Parlophone 2000

Amnesiac: *Packt Like Sardines in a Crushed Tin Box / Pyramid Song / Pull/Pulk Revolving Doors / You and Whose Army? / I Might Be Wrong / Knives Out / Amnesiac/Morning Bell / Dollars and Cents / Hunting Bears / Like Spinning Plates /
Life in a Glass House*
Parlophone 2001

Hail To The Thief: *2+2=5 / Sit Down, Stand Up / Sail To The Moon / Backdrifts / Go To Sleep / Where I End And You Begin / We Suck Young Blood / The Gloaming / There There / I Will / A Punch-Up At The Wedding / Myxomatosis / Scatterbrain / A Wolf At The Door*
Parlophone 2003

In Rainbows: *15 Step / Bodysnatchers / Nude / Weird Fishes/Arpeggi / All I Need / Faust Arp / Reckoner / House Of Cards / Jigsaw Falling Into Place / Videotape*
Self-released 2007 / XL 2008

COMPILATION ALBUMS
I Might Be Wrong - Live Recordings: *The National Anthem (live from Vaison la Romaine 05/28/01) / I Might Be Wrong (live from Oxford 07/07/01) / Morning Bell (live from Oxford 07/07/01) / Like Spinning Plates (live from Cleveland 08/08/01) / Idioteque (live from Oxford 07/07/01) / Everything In Its Right Place (live from Vaison la Romaine 05/28/01) / Dollars And Cents (live from Oxford 07/07/01 / True Love Waits (live from Los Angeles 08/20/01)*
Parlophone 2001

The Best Of: *Just / Paranoid Android / Karma Police / Creep / No Surprises / High And Dry / My Iron Lung / There There / Lucky / Fake Plastic Trees / Idioteque / 2 + 2 = 5 / The Bends / Pyramid Song / Street Spirit (Fade Out) / Everything In Its Right Place*
Bonus disc: *Airbag (Edit) / I Might Be Wrong / Go To Sleep / Let Down / Planet Telex / Exit Music (For A Film) / The National Anthem / Knives Out / Talk Show Host / You / Anyone Can Play Guitar / How to Disappear Completely / True Love Waits*
Parlophone 2007

SINGLES
Creep: *Creep / Lurgee / Inside My Head / Million Dollar Question*
Parlophone 1992
Anyone Can Play Guitar: *Anyone Can Play Guitar / Faithless The Wonder Boy / Coke Babies*
Parlophone 1993
Pop is Dead: *Pop Is Dead / Banana Co. (Acoustic) / Creep (Live) / Ripcord (Live)*
Parlophone 1993
Creep: *(reissue CD): Creep (Album Version) / Yes I Am / Blow Out (Remix) / Inside My Head (Live)*
Parlophone 1993
Creep: *(reissue 12") Creep (Acoustic), You (Live), Vegetable (Live), Killer Cars, (Live)*
Parlophone 1993
Stop Whispering: *Stop Whispering (US version) / Creep (Acoustic) / Pop*

Is Dead / Inside My Head
Parlophone 1993
My Iron Lung: (CD1) *My Iron Lung / The Trickster / Punchdrunk Lovesick Singalong / Lozenge of Love*
Parlophone: 1994
My Iron Lung: (CD2) *My Iron Lung / Lewis (Mistreated) / Permanent Daylight / You Never Wash Up After Yourself*
Parlophone 1994
High And Dry: (CD1) *High and Dry / Planet Telex / Maquiladora / Planet Telex (remix)*
High And Dry: (CD2) *Planet Telex / High And Dry / Killer Cars / Planet Telex (remix)*
(Parlophone 1995)
Fake Plastic Trees: (CD1) *Fake Plastic Trees / India Rubber / How Can You Be Sure?*
Fake Plastic Trees: (CD2) *Fake Plastic Trees / Fake Plastic Trees (acoustic) / Bullet Proof..I Wish I Was (acoustic) / Street Spirit (Fade Out) (acoustic)*
(Parlophone 1995)
Just: (CD1) *Just / Planet Telex (Karma Sunra mix) / Killer Cars (Mogadon version)*
Just: (CD2) *Just / Bones (live at The Forum) / Planet Telex (live at The Forum) / Anyone Can Play Guitar (Live)*
(Parlophone 1995)
Street Spirit (Fade Out): (CD1) *Street Spirit (Fade Out) / Talk Show Host / Bishop's Robes*
Street Spirit (Fade Out): (CD2) *Street Spirit (Fade Out) / Banana Co. / Molasses*
(Parlophone 1996)
Paranoid Android: (CD1) *Paranoid Android / Polyethylene Parts 1 & 2 / Pearly*
Paranoid Android: (CD2) *Paranoid Android / A Reminder / Melatonin*
(Parlophone 1997)
Karma Police: (CD1) *Karma Police / Meeting in the Aisle / Lull*
Karma Police: (CD2) *Karma Police / Climbing Up the Walls (Zero 7 Mix) / Climbing Up the Walls (Fila Brazillia Mix)*
(Parlophone 1997)
No Surprises: (CD1) *No Surprises / Palo Alto / How I Made My Millions*
No Surprises: (CD2) *No Surprises / Airbag (Live in Berlin) / Lucky (Live in Florence)*
(Parlophone 1998)
Pyramid Song: (CD1) *Pyramid Song / The Amazing Sounds of Orgy / Trans-Atlantic Drawl*

Pyramid Song: (CD2) *Pyramid Song / Fast-track / Kinetic*
(Parlophone 2001)
Knives Out: (CD1) *Knives Out / Cuttooth / Life in a Glasshouse (Full length version)*
Knives Out: (CD2) *Knives Out / Worrywort / Fog*
Knives Out: (CD3) *Knives Out / Worrywort / Fog / Life in a Glasshouse (Full length version)*
(Parlophone 2001)
There There: *There There / Paperbag Writer / Where Bluebirds Fly*
(Parlophone 2003)
Go To Sleep: (CD1) *Go to Sleep / I Am Citizen Insane / Fog (Again) (Live)*
Go To Sleep: (CD2) *Go to Sleep / Gagging Order / I Am a Wicked Child*
(Parlophone 2003)
2+2=5: (CD1) *2 + 2 = 5 / Remyxomatosis (Christian Vogel RMX) / There There (first demo)*
2+2=5: (CD2) *2 + 2 = 5 / Skttrbrain (Four Tet remix) / I Will (Los Angeles version)*
(Parlophone 2003)
Jigsaw Falling Into Place: *Jigsaw Falling into Place / Down Is the New Up (Live From The Basement) / Last Flowers (Live From The Basement)*
(XL 2008)
Nude: *Nude / Down Is the New Up / 4 Minute Warning*
(XL 2008)
House Of Cards: / *Bodysnatchers: House Of Cards (radio edit) / Bodysnatchers*
(XL 2008)
Reckoner: (digital release only)
(XL 2008)

EPS

Drill: *Prove Yourself / Stupid Car / You / Thinking About You*
Parlophone 1992
My Iron Lung EP (full-length, 8-track version originally only available in Australia): *My Iron Lung / The Trickster / Lewis (mistreated) / Punchdrunk Lovesick Singalong / Permanent Daylight / Lozenge Of Love / You Never Wash Up After Yourself / Creep (acoustic)*

VIDEOS/DVDS

Live At The Astoria: *You / Bones / Ripcord / Black Star / Creep / The Bends / My Iron Lung / Prove Yourself / Maquiladora / Vegetable / Fake Plastic Trees / Just / Stop Whispering / Anyone Can Play Guitar / Street*

Spirit (Fade Out) / Pop Is Dead / Blow Out
Parlophone 1995
7 Television Commercials: *Paranoid Android / Street Spirit (Fade Out) / No Surprises / Just / High and Dry (US version) / Karma Police / Fake Plastic Trees*
Parlophone 1998 (DVD 2003)
Meeting People Is Easy (Documentary)
Parlophone 1998
The Most Gigantic Lying Mouth of All Time (sketches, animation, live performances and interviews)
Self-released 2004
In Rainbows – From the Basement: (live performances): *Weird Fishes/Arpeggi / 15 Step / Bodysnatchers / House of Cards / Bangers + Mash / Reckoner / Go Slowly / All I Need / Videotape / Nude*
(Xurbia Xendless Limited 2008)

THOM YORKE

STUDIO ALBUMS
The Eraser: *The Eraser / Analyse / The Clock / Black Swan / Skip Divided / Atoms For Peace / And It Rained All Night / Harrowdown Hill / Cymbal Rush*
XL 2006

SINGLES
Harrowdown Hill: *Harrowdown Hill / The Drunkk Machine / Harrowdown Hill (extended mix)*
XL 2006

Analyse: (limited edition 12") *Analyse / A Rat's Nest / Iluvya*
XL 2006